D1116312

PRESENTS

SATURDAY SHRINES

COLLEGE FOOTBALL'S MOST HALLOWED GROUNDS

FOREWORD BY KEITH JACKSON

CREDITS

Book design: Chad Painter. **Cover design**: Chad Painter. **Photo editor**: Albert Dickson.

Contributing writers: Tom Dienhart, Michael Bradley, Matt Hayes, Shawn Reid, Joe Hoppel, Dale Bye. **Copy editors**: Corrie Anderson, Jessica Daues, Kathy Sheldon. **Research**: Kelly Dillon, Sarah Gietschier, David Robb. **Page design and production**: Chad Painter, Bob Parajon, Michael Behrens, Bill Wilson, Angie Pillman, Jack Kruyne, Russ Carr, Kristin Bressert. **Photo research**: Jim Meier. **Prepress specialists**: Steve Romer, Vern Kasal, Pamela Speh.

Editors of the SPORTING NEWS thank the sports information staffs of the universities covered in this book for their assistance.

PHOTO CREDITS

T — top, B — bottom, L — left, R — right, M — middle

Bob Leverone/Sporting News — 14, 17,18(2), 19T, 20-21, 23B, 26B, 29BR, 39M, 46, 47T, 47M, 49(2), 58, 59, 60L, 61, 78, 79(3), 80, 82, 83(3), 84, 85(2), 104TR, 107T, 107B, 108(3), 109R, 134, 135(3), 136(2), 137R, 150, 151(2), 152, 153(2), 155R, 156BL, 156BR, 157(2), 170, 171, 172(3), 173, 175(3), 176M, 202, 203, 205

Robert Seale/Sporting News — 16M, 21TR, 28L, 54, 55(2), 56(2), 67(2), 73R, 74, 76R, 77TL, 119T, 127BL, 128TL, 148R, 158, 159(3), 160(3), 161(2), 162, 163TR, 165, 168R, 177(2)

Jay Drowns/Sporting News — 9R, 10, 15T, 30, 32R, 39B, 47B, 48L, 95, 96BR, 96BL, 104BL, 104BR, 111(2), 112B, 120B, 122, 123T, 163BL, 164BR, 183L, 184TR, 184BR, 185BR

Albert Dickson/Sporting News — 2-3, 5, 16B, 22-23, 24L, 26-27, 29TR, 41, 48T, 48B, 62, 70, 71(3), 72, 102, 103(2), 104TL, 106, 107M, 110, 112T, 113, 115(2), 123(3), 124(4), 125B, 126, 127TL, 130, 155L, 168-169, 182, 198

Paul Nisely/Sporting News — 9L, 19R, 90, 91, 92, 117, 142, 143, 144(2)

Michael McNamara/Sporting News — 19B, 200

TSN Archives — 15R, 17R(DV), 21B(DV), 23T, 31R, 33R, 37T, 38(DV), 39T(DV), 39R(DV), 40(DV), 45TL, 57(DV), 73B, 76B, 81, 87, 88(3), 93, 97, 105T, 114, 115R, 116(3), 120T, 121, 129, 137TL, 145, 163(2), 164L, 169, 176R, 183R, 184BL, 185L

John Cordes — 6-7, 28M, 34, 35(2), 36(2), 131, 132-133, 146, 147(2), 148BL, 168L, 168M

Cliff Grassmick — 16L, 28R, 63(2), 64

Ida Mae Astute/ABC Photo Archive — 8

University of Tennessee — 9M

Michael and Susan Bennett/Lighthouse Imaging — 11, 12-13(3)

Patrick Murphy-Racey — 14, 15, 22T, 154

University of Pennsylvania Sports Information — 16T

Eric Evans — 20L, 132L

Boise State Sports Information — 23M

Wide World Photos — 24-25, 33L, 37B, 53, 66, 69, 99, 100(2), 101, 105B, 109L, 125T, 133, 141, 149, 194, 53

Jeff Jacobson/KUAC — 25B

Jay Sailors — 31(3), 32L

Frank DiBrango — 42, 43(3), 44(4)

Jeffrey Foltice — 45B

Mark Philbrick/BYU — 50

Jaren Wilkey/BYU — 51(2), 52TL, 52R

Steve Walters/BYU — 52BL

Carolina Sports of Camden, S.C. — 60

Susan Sigmon/UT Photo Services — 67T

Chris Carson/UT Photo Services — 68(2)

Todd Anderson — 75R, 77B

Ryals Lee/Florida State University Photo Services — 75L(2), 76TL

Harvard Athletic Communications — 86, 88MB, 89(2)

University of Iowa Sports Information — 94

Preston Mack — 96T

Bernard Troncale — 98

Brian Spurlock — 118

David Durochik — 119BL

Ross Dettman — 119R

Peter Newcomb — 127R, 128 BR, 128TR

Ed Mahan — 138, 139L

University of Pennsylvania Sports Information — 139R 140(2)

Brian Wagner — 156T

Darren Carroll — 164TR

University of Washington Sports Information — 174, 176BL

Jon SooHoo — 166-167

M.G Ellis — West Virginia Photo Services — 178

Dan Friend — West Virginia Photo Services — 179TR, 180

Bob Beverly — West Virginia Photo Services — 181TL

West Virginia Photo Services — 179BR, 181B

Stephen Fritzer — Yale Sports Publicity — 186, 187T

Thomas Balch — 187BL, 187R, 188T

Ron Waite — 188B

Yale Sports Publicity — 189

Air Force Academy Athletics Dept. — 191

Boise State Sports Information — 192

Justin Kase Conder — 193

Jeff Jacobson/KUAC Staff Photographer — 195

Steve Hebert — 196

Doug Kapustin — 197

Dave Darnell — 199

Phil Hoffman/NAAA — 201

Syracuse University Athletics — 204, 206, 208

Miami (Ohio) Sports Information — 209BL(2)

Tulane Sports Information — 209TR

Minnesota Intercollegiate Athletics — 210

Will Babin/Image Point Pittsburgh — 210, 211

Princeton Sports Information — 211

Front cover photos by SPORTING NEWS staff photographers and hired freelancers

Steve Franz/LSU — Back cover

Copyright ©2005 by THE SPORTING NEWS, a division of Vulcan Sports Media, 10176 Corporate Square Drive, Suite 200, St. Louis, MO 63132. All rights reserved.

No part of *Saturday Shrines* may be reproduced or transmitted in any form or by any means, electronic or mechanical, including photocopy, recording or any information storage and retrieval system now known or to be invented, without permission in writing from the publisher, except by a reviewer who wishes to quote brief passages in connection with a review written for inclusion in a magazine, newspaper or broadcast.

THE SPORTING NEWS is a federally registered trademark of Vulcan Sports Media, Inc. Visit our website at www.sportingnews.com

This book was produced with 17 cover versions—ISBN 10: 0-89204-795-X, ISBN 13: 978-0-8920-4795-6 (SEC/ACC cover); ISBN 10: 0-89204-804-2, ISBN 13: 978-0-8920-4804-5 (Big Ten cover); ISBN 10: 0-89204-805-0, ISBN 13: 978-0-8920-4805-2 (Big 12 cover); ISBN 10: 0-89204-806-9, ISBN 13: 978-0-8920-4806-9 (Pac-10 cover); ISBN 10: 0-89204-834-4, ISBN 13: 978-0-8920-4834-2 (Alabama cover); ISBN 10: 0-89204-831-X, ISBN 13: 978-0-8920-4831-1 (Arkansas cover); ISBN 10: 0-89204-832-8, ISBN 13: 978-0-8920-4832-8 (Florida cover); ISBN 10: 0-89204-837-9, ISBN 13: 978-0-8920-4837-3 (Georgia cover); ISBN 10: 0-89204-833-6, ISBN 13: 978-0-8920-4833-5 (Iowa cover); ISBN 10: 0-89204-839-5, ISBN 13: 978-0-8920-4839-7 (LSU cover); ISBN 10: 0-89204-842-5, ISBN 13: 978-0-8920-4842-7 (Michigan cover); ISBN 10: 0-89204-840-9, ISBN 13: 978-0-8920-4840-3 (Nebraska cover); ISBN 10: 0-89204-835-2, ISBN 13: 978-0-8920-4835-9 (Ohio State cover); ISBN 10: 0-89204-841-7, ISBN 13: 978-0-8920-4841-0 (Oklahoma cover); ISBN 10: 0-89204-838-7, ISBN 13: 978-0-8920-4838-0 (Tennessee cover); ISBN 10: 0-89204-830-1, ISBN 13: 978-0-8920-4830-4 (Texas cover); ISBN 10: 0-89204-836-0, ISBN 13: 978-0-8920-4836-0 (Texas A&M cover).

10 9 8 7 6 5 4 3 2

SATURDAY SHRINES
COLLEGE FOOTBALL'S MOST HALLOWED GROUNDS

CONTENTS

FOREWORD BY
KEITH JACKSON

I t is common, of course, to write books about people or events. But "where" things happen has considerable meaning, too.

In that vein, the SPORTING NEWS—within the following pages—offers unusual insight and more than a few particulars about the great college football stadiums across the country.

John Rawlings, Senior Vice President/Editorial Director of the SPORTING NEWS, asked for my input in *Saturday Shrines*, guessing that in 52 years of broadcasting college football games (39 of them for ABC Television) I would have some strong feelings about these structures.

Well, I've been lost in most of them at one time or another. And I can assure you that the worst possible news on game day is to hear that

the elevator is not working. "Oh, my Lord, if you'll help me one more time, I won't bother you for 30 days."

Some years ago, before Penn State University became a city, the stadium used to sit out there on the hill, all by itself, looking at Mount Nittany. There was a sign in the slowest-moving elevator in college football that read: IF THERE IS TROUBLE WITH THE ELEVATOR, PLEASE RING BELL. You could have ruptured both thumbs and nobody would hear that bell after 5 o'clock.

Used to go to Knoxville on the third Saturday in October for Alabama-Tennessee. Sat in the booth and gazed up the Tennessee River into the colors of the Great Smoky Mountains. Usually saw a great football game. I enjoyed the Tennessee walking horse

There was a sign in the slowest-moving elevator in college football that read: **IF THERE IS TROUBLE WITH THE ELEVATOR, PLEASE RING BELL.** You could have ruptured both thumbs and nobody would hear that bell after 5 o'clock.

strutting around Neyland Stadium, and always remember General Neyland reminding his warriors, "Touchdowns follow good blocking just as surely as night follows day."

Now, since they decided a hundred thousand seats-plus were necessary, you see a lot of concrete and people.

The Rose Bowl … what ambience! Zin and shorts have replaced the chardonnay and crinoline, but it is still as close to the perfect place to watch a college football game as anyplace I know.

The L.A. Coliseum has been the site of two

Summer Olympics and some of the greatest college football games ever played by some of the best-ever players.

And then there's the Big House, Michigan Stadium. The feel there is much like the Rose Bowl.

When Lloyd Carr was named the Michigan head coach, I mentioned that if he wanted something different for his team sometime, he might try stopping at the stadium 'bout 9 p.m. on a Friday, go inside and sit down and just listen. Just listen.

If you know any of the history—if you've fol-

lowed the Wolverines, if you love college football—and you know how to listen, that Big Ol' House will leave an impression.

Carr did what I suggested, and he nodded his head the next time I saw him.

Memorable things have happened at all of the stadiums covered here—things that have grown beyond being just stories and into legends. And legends are entitled to have a proper home.

Enjoy the book!

SATURDAY
SHRINES

When a
stadium
comes
Alive

The panorama below makes it happen for one fan

BY JOE HOPPEL

What makes a college football stadium come alive? It's a stirring mix of game-week rituals and pageantry capped by the moment when the hated and clearly clueless visitors tee it up and send the ball sailing into the arms of our vaunted return man, an All-American kid in both talent and character who just might take it ALL THE WAY. All rise, please.

As exciting as the long-awaited kickoff might be, it is merely one in a series of orchestrated campus events that make college football so special. To suggest that the fun takes place on Saturday alone is, of course, understating the buildup to the big game. At most universities, logo-festooned RVs begin maneuvering their way into stadium parking lots 24 to 48 hours before game day, the gas-guzzling monstrosities filled with enough provisions to feed a small army of fans—or a small army period.

The grilling and hobnobbing—often done with libation in hand—continue into Saturday, when other long-standing pursuits take place. Exactly what unfolds depends on the traditions of the university and its supporters, but the camaraderie is virtually the same everywhere on a crisp autumn afternoon.

OK, I'll happily admit it. A first-time visit to a stadium rates way up there on my fun-to-do list. It can be a spine-tingling experience—and attending a football game in South Bend, Ind., is as goosebumpy as it gets. After seeing my first college football game 49 years earlier as a seventh-grader, and visiting countless campuses across America in the next five decades, I finally made it to Notre Dame Stadium for a game in 2003. Oh, I had seen a game at Notre Dame in 1978—a *basketball* game, which in terms of priorities seems curious, almost blasphemous.

With football-weekend motel rooms reserved months, if not years, in advance in many college towns, I realized that my early-summer decision to absolutely, positively take in a game at Notre Dame three months later would pose logistical challenges. After repeated inquiries, I finally found accommodations—in Michigan City, Ind., about 40 miles from the Golden Dome.

On Saturday, I left Michigan City around 8 a.m. to allow plenty of time for parking and indulging in the game-day experience. As I drove along the Indiana Toll Road, I thought of Notre Dame lore—of Knute Rockne, the Four Horsemen, Frank Leahy, George Connor, Terry Brennan, Alan Page, Joe Montana, Joe Theismann, Tony Rice and, yes, Rudy; about winning one for the Gipper, the 0-0 tie with Army, all the national titles and the miracle comeback in the Cotton Bowl. In true game-day mode, I was pumped as I took exit 77 and headed toward the campus. By 9:15, I was safely ensconced in a pricey parking lot about four long blocks from the House That

The best mood-setter that day was the festive atmosphere inside the bookstore. It was so crowded that not even Rocket Ismail could have found daylight.

Knute Built. Game time was still more than 4 hours away.

I eagerly set out on a tour of the campus, soaking in the sights and sounds. I gawked at campus landmarks, with Touchdown Jesus, No. 1 Moses and Fair Catch Corby heading my must-see list. I paused to reflect—but not to pray—at the Grotto, although it did occur to me to ask for a little guidance for the visiting Washington State team, should the breaks be beating the boys from Pullman later in the day. (You don't have to be a Notre Dame football fan to admire what goes on in this exquisite setting.)

I was moved by the Notre Dame band's spirited march to the stadium and the appearance of the Irish Guard, but the best mood-setter that day was the festive atmosphere inside the bookstore. It was so crowded that not even

Rocket Ismail could have found daylight, fans clogging every aisle and buying every conceivable article of clothing or knickknack with the Notre Dame logo affixed to it. (It seemed that the revenue taken in that morning could fund most athletic departments for the foreseeable future.)

Fans were upbeat, loud and excited. This was, after all, the season opener of Year 2 of the Tyrone Willingham Era. Coach Ty had returned ND to football glory in 2002, and his image was everywhere—on shirts, hats, badges, posters, book covers, trinkets. Canonization was not out of the question. Not in September 2003, anyway.

Watching Irish fans revel in the here and now was great fun—and so was seeing an old hero and a hero wannabe take a step back in time with those fans. In the entryway of the massive bookstore, there sat Notre Dame

With campus landmarks offering a special backdrop (Touchdown Jesus looms in the background, right), Saturdays in South Bend are as goosebumpy as it gets. On September 6, 2003, fans who made the pilgrimage to Notre Dame Stadium to see the Fighting Irish play Washington State (game action, top right) got bonus excitement—a pulsating overtime game. The Fighting Irish, trailing 19-0 in the second quarter, rallied for a 29-26 victory.

Notre Dame Stadium had been transformed from an almost mythical place into a real, vibrant setting—one in which I connected with the past and savored the present.

coaching legend Ara Parseghian, holding forth with the doting and wide-eyed faithful in a book-signing session. At a nearby table, autographing perhaps fewer books but still heavily engaged with enthusiastic passers-by, was the less-legendary Gerry Faust.

Quite a scene, all of it, but it was soon time to move on to what brought me here: taking in the game, and seeing it in a storied stadium.

If, for the majority of fans, the stadium experience reaches a high point with a convergence of game-day frivolities and the start of the game itself, that's easy to understand. The pomp creates unmistakable autumn splendor, to be sure, but the defining moment for me comes when I plop down in my seat and gaze out at the greensward below. My eyes scan the playing field, the scoreboard, the press box and the rest of the seating areas ... and I begin to visualize things that unfolded here that I have seen only in the mind's eye or on television, or heard on the radio, or read about long ago.

It is then that the stadium comes alive for me.

At Notre Dame Stadium, I pictured Knute Rockne strolling the sideline within these confines; squinting hard,

I saw the great late-1940s Fighting Irish teams crushing one outmanned opponent after another, and the Irish coming onto the field in green jerseys against USC in 1977 after wearing blue in pregame warmups; straining a little more, I sneaked a glimpse of Heisman Trophy winners Angelo Bertelli, Johnny Lujack, Leon Hart, John Lattner, Paul Hornung, John Huarte and Tim Brown working their magic on this turf; I envisioned nine national championship teams playing in this very facility, renovated and expanded and spruced up but the same place nonetheless; and on it went.

A great Notre Dame team was not playing on this day—the 2003 squad needed the luck of the Irish to beat Washington State's Cougars in overtime. No matter. Notre Dame Stadium had been transformed from an almost mythical place into a real, vibrant setting—one in which I connected with the past and savored the present.

Similar emotions—and some not related to football—have played out over the years during first-time trips to other venues. At Tiger Stadium in Baton Rouge, I got caught up in an LSU-Arkansas game, but not until I had replayed—over and over—Billy Cannon's 89-yard punt return against Ole Miss on that field more than three decades earlier; at West Point, I imagined Glenn Davis, Doc Blanchard and Pete Dawkins and powerful Army teams performing wondrous deeds on the Michie Stadium landscape before watching a lesser version of the Cadets play Rice to a tie, all the while thinking of the brilliant military leaders who have come out of the academy; at the Los Angeles Memorial Coliseum, I emerged from a portal and was immediately overwhelmed by the expanse of the stadium and thoughts of USC, UCLA and the NFL Rams, among other teams, playing here, and of the Olympic Games and even major league baseball being contested in the shadow of the striking peristyle; at Vaught-Hemingway in Oxford, Miss., I thought of Archie and Eli and Chucky ... and a campus that convulsed when a black man first enrolled, but one that has come to terms with its past; at Cambridge, Mass., I watched old Harvard and Yale grads gather and reminisce in Harvard Square coffee shops before The Game at Harvard Stadium, where Crimson teams have played since 1903 and where any self-respecting college football fan can't help but reflect on what unfolded in the old place in 1968 (Harvard, down by 16 points with 42 seconds to play, tied Yale in an epic battle of unbeaten archrivals); at Illinois' Memorial Stadium, it's a grainy image of Red Grange outrunning people and a vivid snapshot of Dick Butkus putting a big hurt on people.

It's all heady stuff, and *next time* can't come soon enough. After all, wherever the setting and whatever the flashbacks, there is nothing quite like the exhilaration that a college football fan experiences when a stadium comes alive on a Saturday afternoon.

101

THE FANS, THE MASCOTS, THE TRADITIONS, THE COLLEGE FOOTBALL EXPERIENCE.

1. CHECKERED PAST

You instantly know you're watching a Tennessee game at Neyland Stadium when you see those orange-and-white checkerboard end zones.

2. MAGIC TOUCH

Long ago, a fan brought a chunk of rock from Death Valley, Calif., and gave it to revered Clemson coach Frank Howard. Makes sense, considering the Tigers' stadium also is known as Death Valley. Howard wanted to pitch it, but eventually the rock was mounted on a pedestal. The tradition of Howard's Rock—the players rub it for its mystical powers—officially began in 1967.

HOWARD'S ROCK

things
that make a
Stadium
special
By Tom Dienhart

3. THE WAR CHANT

Don't be surprised if you leave a Florida State game at Doak Campbell Stadium with your head pounding after hearing the band play the war chant over and over and over and over.

4. NOSE-Y TURTLE

His name is Testudo, and the Maryland players can't keep their hands off the statue. The 300-pound terrapin, which is a replica of a similar one on campus, sits adjacent to the locker room. As the players exit for the field, they rub his nose.

5. ROCK ON!

Just call Southern Mississippi's M.M. Roberts Stadium "The Rock." Forget grass drills. Back in 1938, several players helped build the Golden Eagles' digs by hauling in cement.

6. TWO'S BETTER THAN ONE

If having one band is good, two must be better. At least that's what they think at Virginia Tech. Fans can see the traditional band, the Marching Virginians, before the game and also be entertained by the Highty-Tighties, the regimental band of the Corps of Cadets.

7. HOME ON THE PLAINS

Soak up a large serving of Auburn football history by strolling around Jordan-Hare Stadium before kickoff. There are 10 11x29 murals celebrating the likes of Heisman Trophy winners Bo Jackson and Pat Sullivan.

8. PALOUSE PRIDE

When you're sitting in Washington State's Martin Stadium, take a look around. You're in Palouse territory. What's the "Pah-loose"? It's an area between the moist forest of the Rocky Mountains and the dry Scablands of Washington.

9. LET'S HAVE A TOAST

No one knows how to toast better than Penn students, who literally throw toast while singing a song at the end of the third quarter.

10. SIGNATURE SONG

You'll endure more head pounding following a USC game at the Los Angeles Coliseum, where the Spirit of Troy blares "Conquest" every 30 seconds—or so it seems.

11. CHEAP SEATS

Best place to see a game for free? Climb up Tightwad Hill, which overlooks Cal's Memorial Stadium and offers breathtaking views of the San Francisco Bay.

12. SWAY TO THE MUSIC

If you're at Florida Field at the end of the third quarter, you'd better get up and be ready to sing. That's when everyone belts out "We Are the Boys of Old Florida," with arms interlocked, swaying back and forth.

13. GANGWAY, HERE COMES RALPHIE!

14. PINK AND PASSIVE

You have to hand it to Hayden Fry. The guy knew how to play head games. To soften Iowa opponents, he had the visiting locker room in Kinnick Stadium painted pink. It was hoped the passive color would take the fire from teams' bellies. The locker room remains pink.

15. BANNER BLUES

It looms about 10 feet over the field, pulled taut by Wolverines supporters. It's Michigan's "Go Blue" banner. As the players enter the field from a tunnel tucked into one side of the stands, they leap like schoolchildren to touch the big blue banner.

16. PARTY'S ON!

Jacksonville's Alltel Stadium plays host to only one Division I-A regular-season game a year, but it's a doozy: the World's Largest Outdoor Cocktail Party, a gathering of 80,000-plus Georgia Bulldogs and Florida Gators fans for one of the most heated rivalries in the nation.

17. WORKING OVERTIME

It's always a non-stop party at Wisconsin, even after the game has ended. Badgers fans and band members party on during the Fifth Quarter, when the band conducts a wild concert highlighted by the Budweiser jingle that ends with a twist: "When you've said Wisconsin, you've said it all!"

18. ALL FOR ONE

They're dressed in black and gold, and they're swarming. It's the Iowa football team, which collectively holds hands as it slowly jogs on and off the field.

19. BIG, BAD DRUM

The guys in the silver helmets at Purdue's Ross-Ade Stadium push what's billed as the "world's largest bass drum." But wait, Texas claims it is carting around the world's largest drum, Big Bertha. Let's get out the tape measure and settle this.

4. NOSE-Y TURTLE

CHEVY CHASE BANK

CONFERENCE CHAMPIO

NCAA

SUPPORT

20. VALLEYS OF DEATH

Take a walk through the valleys of death at Clemson and LSU. Scary—and loud—isn't it?

21. 'WAR-R-R-R EAGLE!'

It's a majestic sight before Auburn games, when high above the stadium soars War Eagle, an eagle that's a symbol of school spirit that helps promote wildlife conservation.

22. THE 12TH MAN

It shouts out from an overhang at Texas A&M's Kyle Field—HOME OF THE 12TH MAN. The story goes like this. E. King Gill had played football during the 1921 season but left the team at the end of the year to focus on basketball, where he was more of a factor. Even though he had left the team, Gill attended the Aggies' Dixie Classic bowl game. When injuries started to pile up, Gill was summoned to the field. He went under the stands and put on one of the injured player's uniforms. Though he didn't get into the game, his willingness never has been forgotten. In homage to Gill's readiness, the Texas A&M students stand for the entire game, showing symbolically they are ready to enter the game if needed—just like Gill.

23. RIDE 'EM, COWBOY

When Wyoming scores, make sure your child checks out Cowboy Joe, a pony that trots around War Memorial Stadium after the Pokes score a touchdown. That's also when the band—Western Thunder—strikes up the fight song, "Ragtime Cowboy Joe."

24. FEEL THE ROAR

Whenever Penn State makes a first down, the P.A. system at Beaver Stadium blares the screech of a Lion.

25. REMEMBERING FREDDIE

They tap little Freddie Steinmark's picture. It's the least the Longhorns can do as they leave the dressing room and head to the Memorial Stadium field. Steinmark was a gutsy safety who started for Texas from 1968-69, when the Longhorns won a national championship, two league titles and 20 of 22 games. He also was a nifty punt returner. But Steinmark was stricken with bone cancer and missed his senior year in 1970. He battled the disease, even enduring a leg amputation, before dying in 1971 at age 22.

26. A FEW GOOD MEN

While the football at West Point might not be up to old-time standards these days, the setting is. It begins with Michie Stadium, which sits on the banks of the Hudson River. And the stadium buzzes when skydivers deliver the game ball from the clouds.

27. HURRICANE WARNING

The plumes of smoke start to billow from the southwest corner tunnel of the venerable Orange Bowl. That's the cue: Bring on the Canes! Miami's mascot, Ibis, leads the Hurricanes' smoky charge onto the field. It's a tradition that began in the 1950s, when university transportation director Bob Nalette developed the idea of using fire extinguishers to replicate the smoke effect. In fact, the pipe that Nalette welded together still is in use. It's an entrance that even Elvis could appreciate.

28. BREATHTAKING

Talk about views. Fans in the north upper deck of Husky Stadium are treated to a panoramic view of Mount Rainier, the Olympic Mountain Range and downtown Seattle.

29. THE FLATS

Wanna talk history? A great place to start is Georgia Tech's Bobby Dodd Stadium. This is where, in 1916, the Yellow Jackets thumped Cumberland College, 222-0, in the most lopsided game ever.

27. HURRICANE WARNING

21. 'WAR-R-R-R EAGLE!'

30. CABOOSE OF A DIFFERENT FEATHER

How many stadiums can claim their own railroad? South Carolina can. Well, it's not really a railroad. The Cockaboose Railroad is a series of hopped-up cabooses that sit adjacent to Williams-Brice Stadium. Most feature overstuffed chairs, fine wood walls, fancy cheese trays and bottles of bourbon.

31. SHRUB HUBBUB

Is there shrubbery anywhere to match the hedges at Georgia's Sanford Stadium?

32. WORDS TO LIVE BY

The orders came from Gen. George C. Marshall, chief of staff for the U.S. Army during World War II: "I want an officer for a secret and dangerous mission. I want a West Point football player." The words inspire today from a plaque on the southeast corner of Army's Michie Stadium.

33. PAINTED WHITE

Missouri rocks. Well, at least its north end zone does. That's where you'll find a series of whitewashed rocks that form the letter "M." Credit the Class of 1927 for carving the stones, which in 1957 were rearranged by pranksters to form an "N" the night before the Missouri-Nebraska game. The handy work quickly was undone.

34. HAIL TO THE CHIEF

Many fans get to their seats early at an Illinois game to see the school's Chief Illiniwek do an authentic pregame dance.

35. DUCK ON A HOG

No, you aren't hearing things at Oregon's Autzen Stadium. That's the rumble of a Harley-Davidson that's decked out in Oregon colors. The big bike leads the Ducks onto the field before every game.

36. THUNDER IN MANHATTAN

Speaking of motorcycles, Kansas State has been playing host to Harley Days since 1997. It has become one of the most anticipated events of the year in Manhattan, with hundreds of bikes on hand.

37. FSU PRIDE

The Florida State crowd reaches a fever pitch before the game starts. That's when Chief Osceola, riding atop his horse, trots to midfield and plunges a flaming spear into a Seminoles logo.

38. GRAND ENTRANCE

Warning: South Carolina's pregame entrance might make your ears bleed. With the strains of "2001—A Space Odyssey" screaming through the P.A. system at Williams-Brice Stadium, the Gamecocks assemble in a tunnel. At just the right time in the song, the players burst onto the field. It's pandemonium.

39. LOUD & CLEAR I

Heard in the stands at Alabama: "Rama Jama Yellow Hammer Give 'em Hell Alabama!"

40. LOUD & CLEAR II

Heard in the stands at Arkansas: "Woooooooo, Pig! Sooie!"

41. LOUD & CLEAR III

Heard in the stands at Virginia: "Wah-hoo-wah!"

38. GRAND ENTRANCE

35. DUCK ON A HOG

40. "WOOOOOOOOO, PIG! SOOIE!"

CALIFORNIA

42. LOUD & CLEAR IV
Heard in the stands at Cal: "Go Bears!"

43. EAR SHOT
Consider yourself warned: If you go to a game at Toledo's Glass Bowl, bring earplugs. Yeah, the fans can get loud. But the real head-ringer is a Civil War-era cannon that is shot off at the beginning of games, at the end of quarters and after Toledo touchdowns.

44. THANKS, FELLAS
Talk about respect. When the opponent leaves the field after games at Nebraska's Memorial Stadium, the fans applaud.

45. LETTER PERFECT
There's the "Y" at BYU, the "A" at Arizona State, the "A" at Colorado State and the "C" at Cal, all beacons of pride, and all tempting to the paint brushes of vandals.

46. BILL THE GOAT
Yes, that's a goat on the sideline of Navy games, a tradition that started in 1893 and has continued uninterrupted since 1904. His name is—what else?—Bill.

47. RAM TOUGH
It might just be a statue, but North Carolina claims to have the "world's largest ram," which sits near Kenan Stadium in front of the football center.

48. FINISHING TOUCH
It's arguably the most famous band formation in America: the script Ohio, which is punctuated by someone—usually an Ohio State tuba player—dotting the "i."

49. PACK YOUR WALKIN' SHOES

Pregame strolls to the game. Tennessee has the Vol Walk. Other places have ...

50. TIGER WALK DOWN VICTORY HILL (LSU)

51. YELLOW JACKET ALLEY

52. DAWG WALK

53. ILLINI WALK

54. TIGER WALK (AUBURN)

55. OLE MISS' WALK OF CHAMPIONS

56. BLACK KNIGHT WALK

57. AND A ONE, AND A TWO ...
Come on, join in and sing the Tennessee anthem: "Rocky Top, you'll always be home sweet home to me, good ol' Rocky Top, Rocky Top Tennessee!"

58. DON'T CALL THEM SKIRTS
You can't help but notice them when the Notre Dame band takes the field. They are the skilled marchers of the Irish Guard. Clad in kilts and donning bearskin shakos atop their noggins, they embody the Notre Dame spirit.

59. H-EEE-RR-E COMES NEBRASKA!
Nebraska is famed for its pregame Tunnel Walk. With the Alan Parsons Project song "Sirius" playing on the P.A. system, the Huskers hit the field at just the right moment in the song—much to the delight of the red-clad denizens.

60. LAID TO REST
Not all of the action is lively in and around these Saturday afternoon shrines. Coach Frank Howard is buried in a cemetery on the south side of Clemson's Memorial Stadium. Bob Zuppke, George Huff and Ray Eliot are buried east of Illinois' Memorial Stadium in Mount Hope Cemetery. In fact, they say Zuppke's grave is even with the 50-yard line at the stadium. Georgia has entombed past Ugas adjacent to Sanford Stadium. And former Reveilles—Texas A&M's collie mascots— have been laid to rest just outside Kyle Field. R.I.P., all.

61. THE PLACE TO BE

Meet you at the Quad. It's a popular place near Bryant-Denny Stadium for Alabama fans to congregate before games, with Denny Chimes serving as the backdrop.

62. BODY LANGUAGE

It's a sea of arms making a chopping motion, and the accompanying war chant is deafening. This is Florida State's Doak Campbell Stadium. But if it's a chomp, done with both arms extended and moving up and down, then you know you're at Florida Field.

63. DING!

Clang, clang, clang! There's nothing like the ringing of a cowbell at Mississippi State's Scott Field—be it legal or not.

64. DING!

There's also ringing at Georgia, where the school's Chapel Bell is pulled following victories.

65. DING!

Can't get that ringing out of your ears? That's because Arizona State has a victory bell just outside Sun Devil Stadium that fans themselves can rock 'n' roll.

66. BIG HOUSE

Think of it as a football stadium on steroids—Michigan Stadium is the nation's biggest venue with a seating capacity of 107,501.

67. SMALL POTATOES

In contrast, the smallest I-A stadium is Idaho's Kibbie Dome, which seats just 16,000.

68. HAVE BOAT, WILL TRAVEL

Have a boat? It's a mode of transportation at these places:

- **Tennessee, which is famous for its Vol Navy.**
- Washington, where fans cruise to Husky Stadium on Lake Washington and are shuttled ashore by members of the university's crew team.
- Army, where some fans travel up the Hudson River to Michie Stadium.

69. SUPER STADIUMS

While there's nothing better than deciding bragging rights for a year on a sun-splashed Saturday in mid-October, some college venues also have played host to the biggest sporting event in the world: the Super Bowl.

- L.A. Coliseum, USC (Super Bowls 1, 7)
- Metrodome, Minnesota (26)
- Orange Bowl, Miami (2, 3, 5, 10 and 13)
- Rice Stadium (8)
- Rose Bowl, UCLA (11, 14, 17, 21, 27)
- **Qualcomm Stadium, San Diego State (22, 32, 37)**
- Stanford Stadium (19)
- Sun Devil Stadium, Arizona State (30)
- Superdome, Tulane (12, 15, 20, 24, 31, 36)

Note: Tulane's old stadium played host to Super Bowls 4, 6 and 9.

70. ATTENTION!

It's three hours before kickoff at West Point on a cool October morning. There, out on "the Plain," is a parade of cadets in full dress gear. It's a spectacular sight at a spectacular venue.

71. WAVE ON

It started innocently enough on October 31, 1981, at Washington's Husky Stadium. A cheerleader exhorted fans to stand and make a human wave. And stadiums haven't been the same since.

72. HIGHBROW TAILGATING

It's tailgating at its finest, with crystal wine glasses, checkered blankets spread out and cheese balls stabbed with spreading knives. It's the Grove at Ole Miss, where men are in slacks and button-downs and women are in dresses, heels and hats.

78. GIDDYUP!

73. FUNKY MUSIC
It's a rollicking, frolicking experience to see the Marching 100 of Florida A&M raise the roof on another hair-raising and backside-shaking halftime show.

74. FINGERS DO THE TALKING
Fans in the stands can do more than yell to support their teams. They also can use hand signals. There's Texas' Hook 'em Horns, N.C. State's Sign of the Wolf, Baylor's Bear Claw and Texas Tech's Guns Up.

75. SMELL THE SMOKE
From the grills ...
- Wisconsin brats
- LSU gumbo
- Arkansas pulled pork
- Texas brisket
- Mississippi catfish
- Ohio State hamburgers and hot dogs
- And for an after-game snack, grab a bag of boiled peanuts at Clemson.

76. GIVE ME SHELTER
Leave your jacket at home when checking out games at these schools, the only I-A indoor venues:
- Idaho's Kibbie Dome
- Minnesota's Metrodome
- Syracuse's Carrier Dome
- Tulane's Superdome

77. FOOTBALL AND CORN DOGS
The Texas-Oklahoma matchup in Dallas isn't the only game associated with a state fair. N.C. State's Carter-Finley Stadium sits on the North Carolina fairgrounds, and the state fair takes place each fall, meaning more than 150,000 folks jam the area when a Wolfpack game and the fair overlap.

78. GIDDYUP!
There's a place for horses on the sidelines, with the two ponies that tow the Sooner Schooner, Texas Tech's Masked Rider, Florida State's Osceola, Oklahoma State's Bullet, Virginia's Sabre and USC's Traveler.

79. LIGHTS!
LSU's Tiger Stadium has a Hollywood connection. Some football scenes for *Everybody's All-American* were shot during halftime of the 1987 Alabama-LSU game. Studio execs wanted to continue shooting after the game, encouraging fans to hang around. Alas, Bama won in an upset and the crowd dispersed.

80. CAMERA!
During halftime of the 1992 Tennessee-South Carolina game at Columbia, scenes for the movie *The Program* were filmed.

81. ACTION!
And Notre Dame got in on the act, too. At halftime of the 1992 Boston College-Fighting Irish game, footage for *Rudy* was shot.

82. BLOWIN' IN THE WIND
They call it the waving of the wheat at Kansas. That's when fans extend their arms up and sway them back and forth. Remember, wheat is king in this state.

83. VARSITY BLUES
Don't adjust your TV set. That *is* blue turf at Boise State's Bronco Stadium.

84. HEAVEN SENT
Look, up in the sky. It's a bird, it's a plane, it's the Wings of Blue, the Air Force Academy's elite parachute team that descends into Falcon Stadium before each game.

85. TACKLING HUNGER
After Georgia Tech fans feed their football hunger at Bobby Dodd Stadium, they can walk over Interstates 75/85 to The Varsity. They need to make sure they know what they want, because the counter help immediately will ask: "What'll ya have?" Try the chili cheese dog, onion rings and frosted orange.

86. ROSE BOWL EAST

Pearl Harbor had just been bombed, so large crowds were forbidden on the West Coast when it came time to play the Rose Bowl after the 1941 season. Duke, matched against Oregon State in the big game, offered to play host, making this the only time the Grand Daddy of Them All was played outside Pasadena, Calif. The home-field advantage didn't help the Blue Devils, who lost to the Beavers, 20-16.

87. PLAY ON

One of the most stirring pregame moments takes place at Georgia when a solo trumpeter wails out the notes to the school fight song, "Glory, Glory to Old Georgia," from a corner of the upper deck of Sanford Stadium.

88. HEAR HIM ROAR

It can be an unnerving sight (and sound) for opponents when LSU parks the cage of mascot Mike the Tiger in front of the visitors' locker room. The big fella is then paraded around the field, with the cheerleaders riding on top. It's said LSU will score as many touchdowns as the number of times Mike roars.

89. FOOTBALL AND ETHNIC FOOD

Looking for some good Cuban food? Head down to Calle Ocho (Eighth Street) near the Orange Bowl in Miami, and take a step back in time to Little Havana before catching the game.

90. FERTILE GROUND

To get a sense of Ohio State's history, take a stroll through Buckeye Grove outside venerable Ohio Stadium. The school has planted a buckeye tree for each Ohio State All-American.

91. UCLA SPIRIT

It's called the UCLA Eight Clap Cheer, and it goes like this: "One, two, three, four, five, six, seven, eight ... U ... rah, rah, rah ... C ... rah, rah, rah ... L ... rah, rah, rah ... A ... rah, rah, rah ... U-C-L-A, fight, fight, fight!"

90. FERTILE GROUND

98. LIONS' ROAR

92. BRING YOUR LIGHTER
Heavy metal fans out there, check out the entrance by Virginia Tech. With Metallica's "Enter Sandman" blowing out the speakers, fans in the stands begin jumping up and down. At just the right point in the song, the Hokies burst onto the field amid ear-ringing cheers.

93. TAKE ME HOME
It's pure West Virginia, a moment fans live for. As the band plays "Simple Gifts," it marches inward and forms a snug circle while playing softer and softer. Then, the Pride of West Virginia spins and begins marching outward, getting louder and louder.

94. GETTING READY
It's a simple question fans are asked before kickoff at Ole Miss: "Are you ready?" And the fans answer: "Hell, yes!" That begins a classic college cheer: "Hotty Totty! Gosh a Mighty! Who the Hell are We? Flim Flam, Bim Bam, Ole Miss, By Damn!" That's the team's cue to hit the field.

95. FILL 'ER UP
A converted gas station that's a short walk from Memorial Stadium, the Esso Club is where Clemson fans gather to fuel up on beer, food and fun.

96. NO BELCHING PERMITTED
The birthplace of tailgating? Many claim it's Yale, where the trunks of Volvo, Saab and Mercedes-Benz owners are packed with brie, pate and fine wine. And don't forget the linen tablecloth and candelabra.

97. I HAD THE RED SCHWINN
Feel like riding your bike to the game at Oregon's Autzen Stadium? Go ahead. This is the only stadium in the nation that offers valet bike parking.

98. LIONS' ROAR
It's a cheer that seemingly reverberates off nearby Mount Nittany. One side of the Penn State crowd yells: "We are!" The other answers: "Penn State!"

99. IT'S IN THE CARDS
It's a visually stunning sight to behold: the Cal card stunts. Berkeley is where the colorful displays first took place, dating to a rugby game against Stanford in 1910.

100. ONLY AT HARVARD
After wins at Harvard, the Crimson team sings the school fight song, "10,000 Men of Harvard." But singing it in English isn't enough; they also belt it out in Latin. Only at Harvard.

101. PLAY IT AGAIN, AND AGAIN, AND AGAIN ...
Go to any Michigan game—heck, watch any Michigan game on TV—and you're bound to find yourself humming "The Victors" for the next several days. It's played that often at Wolverines games and is that great of a song.

the 40

ALABAMA · ARIZONA STATE · ARKANSAS · ARMY · AUBURN · BYU · CALIFORNIA · CLEMSON · COL... · ... COTTON BOWL · FLORIDA

best

STATE · GEORGIA · GEORGIA TECH · HARVARD · ILLINOIS · IOWA · LEGION FIELD · LOUISIANA STATE · MIAMI · MIC

SATURDAY SHRINES

SATURDAY SHRINES

ALABAMA

These are the sidelines that legendary Paul "Bear" Bryant and his famous houndstooth-check hat prowled from 1958 to 1982, as he led the Tide to six national titles. A stirring pregame video montage of great Alabama moments keeps fans in their seats.

Listen closely to hear a low, gruff growl by coach Bryant. And calls of "Roooolllll Tide!" erupt often before, during and after games. The 2004 campaign marked the 75th anniversary of Bryant-Denny Stadium, which also is named for Dr. George Denny, the university's president in the early 20th century.

SETTING The environment around the stadium, a place locals call T-Town, could be described as bucolic, and it creates a classic Saturday-afternoon college scene. Revelers enjoy strolling University Boulevard for food and drink. RV owners who have bought off-campus parking spots begin showing up as early as Wednesday. RV owners with spots on campus begin arriving on Friday, cuing up for miles on Hackberry Lane and Paul Bryant Drive.

STRUCTURE Bryant-Denny Stadium is an intimidating structure that juts high into the sky. Spiral walkways dot the four corners of the stadium and give it a distinctive look. A north end zone expansion is planned, and it will feature premium seating that will push capacity to about 91,000. The lower bowl is brick, and the rest of the facility is concrete. During the east side upper deck and entrance tower additions (the most recent renovations), an A-Club room for former lettermen and a scholarship room were added.

FANS This is as passionate a group as you'll find anywhere in the nation. Many fans congregate at the Kickoff on the Quad three hours before game time, for Alabama's "official" tailgate party. The Quad is grassy area in the center of campus that features Denny Chimes, a bell tower named in honor of Dr. George Denny. On most game days, there are about 25,000 people on the Quad, milling about in anticipation of kickoff, and many line up to join the Million Dollar Band on the Elephant Stomp to the stadium. The band marches down University Boulevard, turns and enters the north entrance of the stadium. During games, the band plays the fight song "Yea, Alabama," and if the Tide wins, the band blares "Rama Jama Yellow Hammer Give 'em Hell Alabama."

MAJOR RENOVATIONS In 1961, the stadium underwent a 12,000-seat renovation, and a new press box and elevator also were added. The other big changes occurred in 1988, when a west side upper deck was added, and

Bear Bryant coached the Crimson Tide to six national titles. One crown came in 1964, when Joe Namath was at quarterback.

ALABAMA

in 1998, when an east side upper deck and two levels of skyboxes were constructed.

MILESTONE MOMENTS

• In 1973, the Tide beat Virginia Tech, 77-6, and ran for 748 yards en route to totaling a school single-game record 833 yards of offense.
• The first game in Denny Stadium was played September 28, 1929, as the Tide posted a 55-0 win over Mississippi College.
• Alabama and Auburn played in Tuscaloosa in 1901 and then didn't meet again on Alabama's campus until November 18, 2000, because for years, the schools met annually in Birmingham in the Iron Bowl.

FAST FACTS

• Located near the stadium is the Bryant Museum, which pays homage to Bear Bryant through various displays and artifacts.
• When fans return to campus, they eat at Dreamland, a world-renowned barbecue restaurant. The locals will tell you to order the ribs and white bread.
• Alabama is associated with elephants, thanks to a sportswriter in the 1930s who dubbed a group of large Tide offensive linemen the "Red Elephants." The red referred to the color of the team's jerseys.

CAPACITY THROUGH THE YEARS

1929: 12,000

1946: 31,000

1961: 43,000

1966: 60,000

1988: 70,123

1998: 83,818

This is as passionate a group as you'll find anywhere in the nation.

X MAGIC MOMENTS

in the history of Bryant-Denny Stadium

I. BUSTING THE GENERAL, *October 18, 1930.* From 1927 through 1932, Gen. Robert Neyland's Tennessee Volunteers lose only one game, an 18-6 decision to an Alabama team led by Albert Elmore and John Henry Suther. Entering the game, Tennessee had boasted a 33-game unbeaten streak—and the Vols wouldn't lose in their next 28 games, either.

II. FLYING FOOTBALLS, *October 1, 1994.* Bama's Jay Barker hooks up with Georgia's Eric Zeier in an aerial circus, with Barker throwing for a stadium-record 396 yards in a 29-28 victory. Michael Proctor, whose first-half field goal ricocheted off the goal post and through, wins it with a 32-yard kick with 1:12 remaining.

III. STUFFING THE LIONS, *October 13, 1984.* No. 11 Penn State takes on a 1-4 Bama team that steps up to the challenge defensively and shuts down the Nittany Lions in a 6-0 Tide win. Van Tiffin kicks 53- and 23-yard field goals. In the season finale that year, Tiffin's field goal helped beat Auburn.

IV. THE FIRST ONE, *October 11, 1958.* Alabama stumbles out of the blocks with a loss and a tie in Bear Bryant's first season, but a 29-6 triumph over Furman becomes Bryant's first victory as Tide coach.

V. GRAND REOPENING, *September 5, 1998.* Shaun Alexander rushes for 115 yards and five touchdowns, including two in the fourth quarter to break a 24-24 tie, in Alabama's 38-31 win over BYU. The game is the first in refurbished Bryant-Denny, which has 13,000 new seats and skyboxes.

VI. FUMBLING TOWARD VICTORY, *October 31, 1981.* Despite 11 fumbles—and turning the ball over on seven of them—Alabama slips past Mississippi State, 13-10, when the Tide's Tommy Wilcox intercepts a tipped pass at the Bama 1-yard line with 19 seconds left.

VII. DIVISION TITLE BOUND, *November 13, 1999.* Despite No. 8 Mississippi State's stout defense, Bama gets two field goals from Ryan Pflugner and a late TD pass from Andrew Zow to Shamari Buchanan in a 19-7 win that keeps Alabama on track for the SEC West crown.

VIII. GROUND EXPLOSION, *October 27, 1973.* Virginia Tech is crushed by Alabama's ground attack in a 77-6 Tide rout. Alabama runs for a then-NCAA record 748 yards and has 833 yards of total offense.

IX. STORIED MATCHUP, *September 6, 2003.* The nation watches intently as Oklahoma and Alabama, two of college football's most tradition-bound programs, hook up in Tuscaloosa. A third-quarter fake punt is the key play in a 20-13 Oklahoma victory.

X. THE FULL 100, *October 7, 1949.* Duquesne doesn't put up much of a struggle in a 48-8 Alabama romp, a game that features the Tide's first 100-yard kickoff return for a touchdown—by Jim Burkett.

VII. DIVISION TITLE BOUND Linebacker Victor Ellis and the rest of the Tide defense came up big against Mississippi State in 1999.

SIMPLY UNFORGETTABLE

Bear Bryant's coaching tenure. For two-plus decades, a sighting of the houndstooth-check hat that sat upon Paul "Bear" Bryant's head signaled that Alabama was in town and ready to do some damage. Few—if any—coaches in college history were as recognizable and as revered as Bryant.

From the moment he came back to his alma mater in 1958, Bryant was a beloved icon. Sure, he had success at his three other head-coaching stops, Maryland, Kentucky and Texas A&M, but his 25 years in Tuscaloosa defined him.

Bryant played for legendary Tide coach Frank Thomas on two SEC title teams and the 1934 national champions. He spent four years as an Alabama assistant, also under Thomas, before turning Kentucky and Texas A&M into powers as head coach. Then the call came from Bama.

Bryant's record in Tuscaloosa brought about almost sustained jubilation. Crimson Tide teams won 14 SEC crowns during his tenure and six national titles. Alabama was particularly dominant in the 1970s, when it captured eight SEC championships and was the scourge of the South. Bryant's teams won 72 of the 74 games they played in Bryant-Denny.

SUN DEVIL STADIUM

ARIZONA STATE

Despite a nickname that suggests otherwise, the Sun Devils like to come out at night. In fact, Sun Devil Stadium is synonymous with night football. Have you ever been to Tempe in September? Or October, for that matter? Average highs are near 100 degrees. The stadium is tucked in the Phoenix suburb of Tempe, which is full of colorful sunsets and sweeping vistas dotted with sugaro cactus.

Not only does the stadium offer great sightlines, but the nearby Mill Avenue offers a collection of eclectic shops and eateries. There also are block parties that bring the area to life. To the north is a new development called Rio Salado, an oasis that features boating, shopping and apartments, among other things.

SETTING The stadium was constructed between two mountain buttes, which help make Sun Devil Stadium one of the best football settings in the nation. One butte, located on the west side of the stadium, is known as A Mountain. Throughout the year, the A is painted many different colors. Before the Arizona game each November, ASU students protect the A from Wildcat painters who try to change the A to their own school colors. For the most part, the A is to remain gold.

STRUCTURE The stadium has aged gracefully. In fact, many are surprised to hear Sun Devil Stadium was opened in 1958. The facility began as a single-level structure, and during the first round of renovations in 1977, an upper level was added. The field was named for leg-

endary Arizona State coach Frank Kush on September 21, 1996, a night the Sun Devils stunned two-time defending national champion and top-ranked Nebraska, 19-0. Players enter the field running through Tillman Tunnel, a tribute to former Sun Devil Pat Tillman, who was killed in Afghanistan in 2004. Inside the tunnel, the Sun Devils have posted a quote from Tillman. It was the last thing he said before running onto the field for the famous Nebraska game: "Give 'em hell Devils." Tillman's No. 42 was retired and is now displayed on the facade of the press box.

FANS The Sun Devils faithful can get vocal, but they can't be described as rabid. Fans get to their seats in time to watch the band spell out "Go Devils," and when Arizona State scores, fireworks are shot off from one of the nearby buttes and mascot Sparky does pushups while students count along. After wins, fans can ring the Victory Bell, which sits outside the south end of the stadium next to a statue of Kush. Any fan can ring the bell after a victory. Often during Dirk Koetter's postgame radio show, the bell can be heard clanging.

MAJOR RENOVATIONS
The first major additions

'Give 'em hell Devils.' — *Pat Tillman*

ARIZONA STATE

came in 1976 and 1977 and boosted the capacity from 30,000 to 57,722. The NFL's Cardinals arrived in 1988, when Sun Devil Stadium received a new press box, increased seating and the south end structure that is now the Nadine and Ed Carson Student Athlete Center. And before Super Bowl XXX was played in the facility after the 1995 season, the lights and parking lots were upgraded. The most significant upgrade came in 1977, when an upper deck was added.

MILESTONE MOMENTS

• Arizona State christened Sun Devil Stadium with a 16-13 win over West Texas State on October 4, 1958.
• The Sun Devils' first stadium was Normal Field, from 1897-1926. ASU also has played at Irish Field (1927-35) and Goodwin Stadium (1936-1958).
• ASU clinched each of its two Rose Bowl bids with home wins over Cal in 1986 and 1996.

FAST FACTS

• Sun Devil Stadium was filled for a visit from Pope John Paul II in 1987.
• Soccer legend Pele played an exhibition game with the New York Cosmos in Sun Devil Stadium in 1976.
• Four national titles have been decided in Sun Devil Stadium, which has played host to the Fiesta Bowl since 1971. (The Fiesta will switch to the NFL Cardinals' new stadium, effective with the 2006 season.)

CAPACITY THROUGH THE YEARS

1958: 30,000	1977: 70,491
1976: 57,722	1988: 73,379

X MAGIC MOMENTS

in the history of Sun Devil Stadium

I. STREAK IS OVER, *September 21, 1996.* No. 1 Nebraska comes to Tempe riding a 26-game winning streak and two consecutive national titles but gets shut down and shut out, 19-0, by the 17th-ranked Sun Devils.

II. THE CATCH, *November 29, 1975.* John Jefferson's amazing, flat-out diving catch in the end zone with 30 seconds left in the first half is the key play in ASU's 24-21 win over Arizona in the final game of the Devils' 11-0 regular season.

III. PASADENA BOUND, *November 8, 1986.* John Cooper's Sun Devils throttle California, 49-0, to clinch ASU's first-ever Pac-10 championship and secure the school's first Rose Bowl bid.

IV. HUSKING NEBRASKA, *December 26, 1975.* Co-Big Eight champion Nebraska comes to Tempe for the Fiesta Bowl and has the Sun Devils down, 14-6, entering the fourth quarter, but the WAC champion Devils stop the mighty Cornhuskers, 17-14, completing a 12-0 season.

V. FIRST FIESTA, *December 27, 1971.* The Sun Devils outgun Florida State, 45-38, to win the inaugural Fiesta Bowl and complete an 11-1 season.

VI. OVERTIME SPECIAL, *October 19, 1996.* Arizona State stops Pac-10 favorite USC in two overtimes, 48-35. The Sun Devils trailed, 14-0, just 4½ minutes into the game but fought back and sealed the victory with an interception return for a touchdown on the Trojans' final play.

VII. SUPER 'BOYS, *January 28, 1996.* Dallas gets two interceptions from Larry Brown and stops Neil O'Donnell and Pittsburgh, 27-17, in Super Bowl XXX.

VIII. BUCKEYE MAGIC, *January 3, 2003.* In the Fiesta Bowl, Ohio State upsets heavily favored Miami, 31-24, in double overtime, snapping the Hurricanes' 34-game winning streak and capturing the Buckeyes' first national championship since 1968.

IX. CHAMPS AGAIN, *January 2, 1989.* Notre Dame and quarterback Tony Rice roll past third-ranked West Virginia, 34-21, in the Fiesta Bowl to win the national championship—the Irish's first in 11 years—in Lou Holtz's third season at ND.

X. PAPAL AUDIENCE, *September 14, 1987.* Pope John Paul II celebrates mass for more than 70,000 people during his U.S. visit.

VII. SUPER 'BOYS

SIMPLY UNFORGETTABLE

Frank Kush. It's impossible to deny Kush's impact on the ASU program. It's also tough to look past what he and his teams did for the university.

From 1958, when Kush took over in Tempe, until he left in 1979, Arizona State's enrollment more than tripled, from 10,000 to 37,122. Certainly that wasn't all due to Kush, but his teams' successes brought considerable media attention and national recognition to the school. Kush also was a major factor in the Pac-10's decision to admit Arizona State in 1978.

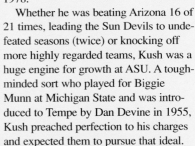

Whether he was beating Arizona 16 of 21 times, leading the Sun Devils to undefeated seasons (twice) or knocking off more highly regarded teams, Kush was a huge engine for growth at ASU. A tough-minded sort who played for Biggie Munn at Michigan State and was introduced to Tempe by Dan Devine in 1955, Kush preached perfection to his charges and expected them to pursue that ideal.

In 1970, Kush led the Sun Devils to an 11-0 record that included a 48-26 rout of North Carolina in the Peach Bowl, ASU's first bowl berth in 20 years. The Devils hit the double-figure win total each of the next three years and were 12-0 in 1975, when they defeated co-Big Eight champ Nebraska in the Fiesta Bowl. By the time Kush left, he had established Arizona State among the top Division I programs, won eight conference championships, had a 6-1 bowl record and posted a .764 (176-54-1) winning percentage. They had football at Arizona State before and after Frank Kush, but there was nothing like the 21 years he was in charge.

RAZORBACK STADIUM

SATURDAY SHRINES

ARKANSAS

38

The passion runs deep in Fayetteville, a city of 60,000-plus tucked in the northwest corner of Arkansas. Football is celebrated like a high holy day for a fandom that's not afraid to show its pride by wearing hog hats. And there's no more

renowned rallying cry than the calling of the hogs: "Woooooooooo, Pig! Sooie!" There are a lot of loyal fans, many of whom never attended the school. With no major competition from a pro team or other major college, the Razorbacks command a statewide fan base, which is why the school still plays a few games in Little Rock.

SETTING The Hogs play in Ozark country, so the terrain around Fayetteville is hilly. From the south end zone, the Boston Mountains are visible. There are good tailgating areas north of the stadium, and fans also like to mingle in Hog Trough, the school's "official" tailgating party, where food venders cater to the masses. A few hours before kickoff, the team is dropped off and walks through the Hog Trough to the stadium. And there are few more classic entrances than when the Hogs run onto the field through a giant block A formed by the band.

STRUCTURE Reynolds Razorback Stadium is a state-of-the-art facility that features some of the best premium seating in the nation. The concrete and steel foundation is enclosed in a brick and glass facade. Fans like to sit in the Red Zone, which is in south end zone. From there, they have a great view of the game on a big screen in the north end zone while also being close to the action. Fans can get a sense for Arkansas' football heritage by walking through the concourse of

the stadium before the game. On display are tributes to the school's best teams and players in areas called "Championship Alley," "All-American Alley" and "Bowl Alley."

FANS The Razorback fans are a vocal bunch that gets into every game. When the team gets a first down, the P.A. announcer will say: "That's another Arkansas Razorback … " And the crowd will finish: "First down!" The crowd also calls the hogs before kickoff, and as the kicker approaches the ball, the fans yell "Woo!," and as the ball is in the air, they say, "Pig! Sooie! Razorbacks!" Before games, cheerleaders parade Big Red, a live Razorback, around the field in a cage. As the finale to the halftime show, the crowd shouts out each letter of "Go Hogs" until the band has spelled it out on the field.

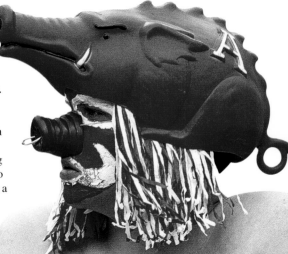

ARKANSAS

MAJOR RENOVATIONS One of the most significant renovations was a $110 million project that was finished before the 2001 season. The additions brought the capacity from 51,000 to 72,000. Additionally, many luxury seats were added, giving the facility the look and feel of an NFL stadium. Razorback Stadium also underwent two makeovers in the 1950s that added more than 10,000 seats.

MAJOR RENOVATIONS

• Arkansas' first game in Razorback Stadium was September 24, 1938, a 27-7 win over Oklahoma A&M.
• The first game on artificial turf was September 27, 1969, a 55-0 victory over Tulsa.
• In a contest billed as the "Game of the Century," No. 1 Texas beat No. 2 Arkansas, 15-14, on December 6, 1969. The game was attended by President Richard Nixon.
• The first night game was played November 11, 1989, a 19-10 win over Baylor.

FAST FACTS

• When Arkansas plays in Little Rock, it does so in War Memorial Stadium, which seats 53,727 and was dedicated with a 40-6 win over Abilene Christian on September 18, 1948.
• To the north of the stadium is the Broyles Athletic Center, which houses a museum dedicated to Arkansas football. It's named after legendary Arkansas coach/athletic director Frank Broyles.
• Fans flock to Dickson Street before and after games to hang out at a bevy of restaurants and bars. The students have been known to tote a goalpost to Dickson Street after a big victory.
• The Donald W. Reynolds foundation gave $20 million to help overhaul the stadium in 2001.

CAPACITY THROUGH THE YEARS

1938: 13,500	1969: 42,678
1947: 16,000	1985: 51,000
1950: 21,200	2001: 72,000
1957: 26,400	

X MAGIC MOMENTS

in the history of Razorback Stadium

I. THE THRILLER, *December 6, 1969.* Yes, the Hogs lost this one, but it was clearly the game of the year in college football's centennial season. Texas quarterback James Street leads a late drive that gives the top-ranked Longhorns a 15-14 win over the second-rated Razorbacks.

II. DISASTER AVERTED, *October 16, 1965.* No. 3 Arkansas bolts to a 20-0 lead over top-ranked Texas but falls behind, 24-20, only to rally for a late touchdown and pull out a 27-24 triumph en route to a second straight Cotton Bowl berth.

III. STEER ROPING, *October 20, 1951.* Pat Summerall's field goal just before halftime turns out to be the winning margin in Arkansas' 16-14 victory over fourth-ranked Texas. It is the Razorbacks' first win over the Longhorns in Fayetteville.

IV. ORANGE CRUSHED, *November 13, 1999.* Tennessee is ranked third in the nation and gunning for a second consecutive national title when it takes a 24-14 third-quarter lead over unranked Arkansas. But a pair of Clint Stoerner TD passes, the second to Anthony Lucas with 3:44 to go, gives the Razorbacks a 28-24 victory.

V. NO. 1 NO LONGER, *October 17, 1981.* Top-ranked Texas invades Fayetteville to take on Lou Holtz's Razorbacks, and the wily coach pulls off another stinger, leading the unranked Hogs to a 42-11 rout.

VI. SIX TIMES SIX, *September 9, 1995.* Running back Madre Hill explodes onto the national scene by scoring six rushing touchdowns in a 51-21 shellacking of South Carolina.

VII. FIRST TO EIGHT, *November 7 1998.* Houston Nutt becomes the first Arkansas rookie coach to start a season 8-0 when he leads the Razorbacks to a 34-0 conquest of Mississippi.

VIII. GREAT BEGINNINGS, *November 23, 1963.* The Razorbacks didn't know it at the time, but their 12-7 win over Texas Tech in the '63 finale is the beginning of a 22-game winning streak that includes a perfect 1964 campaign.

IX. BIG FOOT, *October 15, 1977.* Although eventual Heisman Trophy winner Earl Campbell and No. 2 Texas claim a 13-9 win over ninth-ranked Arkansas, Razorbacks kicker Steve Little boots a 67-yard field goal, equaling the longest to that date in college football history.

X. THE ROAD TO JACKSONVILLE, *October 31, 1959.* The Razorbacks handle Texas A&M, 12-7, beginning a 5-0 run that produces a Southwest Conference co-championship, Frank Broyles' first title of any kind at Arkansas and a Gator Bowl victory.

IV. ORANGE CRUSHED

SIMPLY UNFORGETTABLE

The 1964 national championship season. To this day, it matters not that Alabama won the AP and UPI versions of the national title in '64. The Crimson Tide lost to Texas in the Orange Bowl and never would have been selected as champion had the two polls saved their final vote for after the bowl games. The Helms Athletic Foundation and the Football Writers Association of America, among others, were smart enough to recognize that the 11-0 Razorbacks, who whipped Nebraska in the Cotton Bowl, were the real champs.

Although the Hogs had finished 5-5 in 1963, the pollsters thought enough of their returning talent to list Arkansas as the 11th-best team in the '64 preseason poll. If the voters didn't have the good sense to cast ballots after the bowls, at least they were sharp enough to expect good things from Broyles' team. And after the Razorbacks charged to a 4-0 start and moved up to eighth in the ratings, the nation was eager to see what Arkansas could do with top-ranked Texas—in Austin.

As it turns out, plenty. Ken Hatfield's 81-yard TD on a punt return and Ronnie Caveness' 25 tackles paved the way for a dramatic 14-13 upset of the defending national champions and lifted Arkansas to fourth in the rankings. From there, it was pretty easy. Or at least it seemed that way. The Hogs shut out their next five opponents and rose to No. 2 in the nation with a 10-0 record. The Cotton Bowl beckoned, and the Hogs didn't disappoint, using an 80-yard fourth-quarter TD drive to overcome a 7-3 deficit and secure a 10-7 triumph over Nebraska. It was a fitting end to a championship season—no matter what the polls said.

MICHIE STADIUM

SATURDAY SHRINES

ARMY

Nestled along the banks of the Hudson River a little more than an hour's drive from Manhattan, Michie Stadium sits as one of the most dramatic and picturesque settings in college football. Tailgating takes place throughout the campus, and the school draws an eclectic mix of fans from the tri-state area of New York, Connecticut and New Jersey. Some even arrive via boat on the Hudson. Strolling through the tailgaters, you'll see everything from fine china and candelabra to Budweiser in a cooler with hot dogs cooking on the grill. All fans are sure to be in their seats to see a skydiver descend with the game ball before kickoff.

SETTING The stadium is located on a western bend of the Hudson River because the academy site was chosen for strategic reasons during the Revolutionary War. One of the most dramatic pregame traditions in football is the full-dress cadet parade, which takes place on The Plain, between Washington Hall and Trophy Point, three hours before kickoff. The fall foliage is spectacular, and fans are able to see neighboring burgs across the river. Pregame excitement is built as fans watch the players conduct their pregame Black Knight Walk.

STRUCTURE Michie Stadium is an old concrete facility—with a second deck on one side—that's highlighted by a series of arcs and columns. It's a majestic building that drips with history—including having produced three Heisman winners. As players run onto the field, they touch a plaque near the southeast corner of the stadium that is emblazoned with a quote from Gen. George C. Marshall, chief of staff of the U.S. Army in World War II: "I want an officer for a secret and dangerous mission. I want a West Point football player."

FANS A large part of the crowd is the Corps of Cadets, which stands throughout the game and is referred to as the 12th man. Cannons and fireworks are fired after scores.

Before the game, bagpipers precede the team onto the field, and cadets line up as the team runs past them. The team has live mules—Army's mascot because of their usefulness in military operations—on the sideline before games. After games, the Corps sings the alma mater while the team faces it. If Army wins, everyone sings "On Brave Old Army Team," and the squad goes into the stands to sing the song with the Corps.

MAJOR RENOVATIONS

In 1962, permanent stands on the east side were completed. An upper deck was built in 1969. Recently, the school built the Kimsey Athletic Center, a multipurpose facility, in the south end zone.

MILESTONE MOMENTS

• In 1999, the playing surface was named Blaik Field in honor of Army's legendary coach Earl "Red" Blaik.
• The school switched from grass to turf in 1977.
• The first night game was November 3,

1984, a 24-12 victory over Air Force.
• In the first game at Michie Stadium, Army downed Saint Louis University, 17-0, on October 4, 1924.

FAST FACTS

• The stadium is named for Dennis Mahan Michie, who is credited with introducing football at the academy.
• Army won 39 games in a row at Michie Stadium from 1925-31.
• Only 15 Division I-A stadiums are older than Michie.

CAPACITY THROUGH THE YEARS

```
1924:  21,000
1962:  26,491
1969:  41,684*
```

*Army slightly reconfigured some seating after 1969 to adjust the capacity to 40,000.

X MAGIC MOMENTS
in the history of Michie Stadium

SIMPLY UNFORGETTABLE

Doc Blanchard and **Glenn Davis**. They were known as "Mr. Inside" and "Mr. Outside," and even if you confused the players with their nicknames, there was no question about the prosperity the two players brought to Army during the mid-1940s.

Blanchard (above right) was the strong man, a player who could burst through the interior line and then outrun many a defensive halfback. Davis was the shifty one, capable of turning a routine end run into a magnificent scoring bolt. Blanchard won the Heisman in 1945, and Davis took it in '46. During their three seasons together, they helped the Cadets to a 27-0-1 record and two national championships (plus a claim to a third one). George Trevor of the *New York Sun* said it best: "Ashes to ashes, dust to dust; If Blanchard don't get you, then Davis must."

In '45, Blanchard rushed for 718 yards and gained 7.1 yards per carry as Army recorded its second straight 9-0 season. He scored 19 times in just nine games but was unwilling to take much credit. When he won the Heisman, he said, "I'd have voted for Glenn Davis." The following year, Blanchard rushed for 613 yards and scored 10 times for the 9-0-1 Cadets, who tied Notre Dame in a thriller at Yankee Stadium.

Davis finished second in the Heisman voting in 1944 and '45, averaging 11.5 yards per carry in both seasons. He scored 20 touchdowns as a sophomore and 18 as a junior. And though he managed "just" 5.8 yards per rush as a senior in 1946 and scored only 13 touchdowns, he captured the Heisman. If he received the award out of respect for his career achievements, that was just fine because few players had enjoyed such a remarkable span of college football success.

I. STILL PERFECT, *November 9, 1996.* Army improves to 9-0 for the first time since 1949 with a 23-7 win over Air Force. It's the first triumph over the Falcons in eight years and is the first step on Army's march to the Commander in Chief's Trophy, which it also hasn't won in eight seasons.

II. SUPER SUB, *November 9, 1974.* Mike Marquez, called to action when regular kicker Mike Castelli is hurt on Army's first score and playing in his first game, boots a 33-yard field goal with 17 seconds to play in the Cadets' 17-16 win over Air Force.

III. THE LONELY END, *September 27, 1958.* Legendary coach Red Blaik unveils the "Lonely End" in the Cadets' season-opening 45-8 win over a strong South Carolina squad. Bill Carpenter splits out wide and doesn't return to the huddle after plays, instead watching quarterback Joe Caldwellfor signals. The Cadets go on to an 8-0-1 record.

IV. DOUBLE THE FUN, *October 7, 1999.* Fullback Michael Wallace rushes for a school-record 269 yards, and Army survives a furious comeback by Louisville to prevail, 59-52, in a Thursday night double-overtime thrill ride.

V. BONING UP, *November 3, 1984.* Coach **Jim Young** (right, with quarterback **Nate Sassaman**) installs the wishbone, and the Cadets tear up the field all season en route to the first bowl bid in academy history—the Cherry Bowl. Along the way, Army lays a 24-

12 defeat on Air Force, snapping a three-game losing streak to the Falcons.

VI. MR. CLUTCH, *October 10, 1992.* Senior Patmon Malcom's 43-yard field goal with 5 seconds to play propels Army to a 38-36 win over Lafayette. Later that year, Malcom would drill a 49-yarder with 12 seconds left to beat Navy.

VII. HOME SWEET HOME, *September 19, 1998.* In its first game as a conference member, Army hands Cincinnati a 37-20 loss, christening its affiliation with Conference USA.

VIII. HALL OF A PERFORMANCE, *September 10, 1977.* Rifle-armed senior passer Leamon Hall throws five touchdown passes in a 34-10 rout of Massachusetts, including three to freshman Mike Fahnestock. The win is Army's 500th.

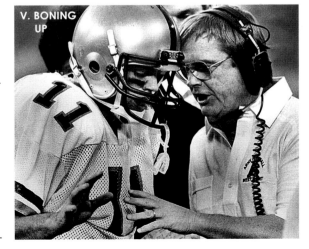

V. BONING UP

IX. MR. CHARLIE, *November 9, 1968.* The Cadets bury Boston College, 58-25. Charlie Jarvis leads the way with a then-school record 253 yards rushing on just 22 carries. He also scores two touchdowns.

X. THRILLS AND CHILLS, *November 13, 1971.* In a season that includes plenty of exciting finishes, Jim Barclay hits a field goal with less than a minute remaining to give the Cadets a 17-14 triumph over Pittsburgh. Earlier in the year, Barclay had beaten Georgia Tech in Atlanta with a late boot.

JORDAN-HARE STADIUM

SATURDAY SHRINES

AUBURN

46

J ordan-Hare is one of college football's most energetic atmospheres, complete with the color and pageantry that punctuate SEC football. Tailgating is king, as RVs take over many areas around the stadium, including the nearby

hayfields. The excitement begins with the Tiger Walk, a tradition that began in the early 1960s and involves the players walking to the field through rows of fans lining the streets. In fact, it's such a big part of the Auburn experience that the team and fans do it even on the road. Mascot Aubie keeps the crowd fired up throughout the game-day activites.

SETTING The word Auburn comes from a line in the poem *The Deserted Village,* but this place is anything but barren on a Saturday afternoon. The surrounding area is largely flat, but that doesn't diminish the charm and personality of one of college football's hotbeds. Fans get pumped up as the players enter the field through plumes of smoke with "Eye of the Tiger" blasting over the P.A. Adding to the excitement is one of the most startling sights on any sideline: Auburn's eagle, who is named Tiger. Before games, the eagle circles the stadium with fans chanting: "War Eagle!" The cheer is the school's battle cry, which dates to 1864 during the Civil War Battle of the Wilderness in Virginia.

STRUCTURE Jordan-Hare is a massive concrete structure that features a second deck on both sides of the field, helping make it one of the most intimidating facilities in the Southeastern Conference. Walkways criss-cross on each side of the facility, and oval-shaped ramps dot each corner, giving the venue a signature look.

On the exterior, the rich history of Auburn football is chronicled on a series of murals.

FANS They bring their lungs and scream from the opening kickoff to the end. "Rolling" Toomer's Corner, the area where the campus meets the city, is tradition after wins. Fans drape the trees (among other things) of Toomer's Corner with toilet paper. In Toomer's Corner, you will find Toomer's Drug Store, an Auburn landmark that serves world-famous lemonade. No doubt fans will be crying "War-r-r-r-r-r Eagle!"

MAJOR RENOVATIONS During Ralph "Shug" Jordan's tenure from 1951-75, the stadium underwent three major overhauls. The work raised capacity by almost 40,000 seats, nearly half of the stadium's present capacity.

MILESTONE MOMENTS
• The stadium was dedicated on November 30, 1939, as Auburn tied Florida, 7-7.
• The facility's first name was Auburn Stadium, and it became Cliff Hare Stadium in 1949, named after Clifford Leroy Hare, a member of the school's first football team and later on the academic staff. The stadium changed its name to Jordan-Hare Stadium in 1973. Ralph "Shug""Jordan coached at Auburn for 25 seasons and is its all-time winningest coach. When Jordan's name was added to the facility, it became the first

major college stadium named for an active coach.

• The first night game was played on September 19, 1981, when the Tigers lost to Wake Forest, 24-21.

FAST FACTS

• On game days, Jordan-Hare Stadium becomes the fifth-largest city in Alabama.

• John Heisman, for whom the Heisman Trophy is named, coached at Auburn from 1895-99, posting a 12-4-2 record. The Tigers have produced two Heisman winners: Pat Sullivan in 1971 and Bo Jackson in 1985.

• Auburn won 30 home games in a row

over a nine-year period that began in 1952.

• Jordan-Hare is the eighth largest on-campus stadium in the country.

CAPACITY THROUGH THE YEARS

1939:	7,500	1980:	72,169
1949:	21,500	1987:	85,214
1955:	34,500	2000:	85,612
1960:	44,500	2001:	86,063
1970:	61,261	2004:	87,451

When the Tigers aren't firing up Auburn fans, mascot Aubie usually is.

SIMPLY UNFORGETTABLE

December 2, 1989. They said it never would happen. Bear Bryant wouldn't allow it, and Ray Perkins didn't want it, either. But the Auburn community never quit believing. And in 1989, it happened: Alabama's Crimson Tide came to The Loveliest Village on the Plains.

From the time the two schools started playing each other, they never had clashed at Auburn. There were contests in Tuscaloosa—the Crimson Tide's home—in 1895 and 1901, and several meetings in Montgomery. But for the most part, the games were played in Birmingham. The Alabama administrators always maintained that Legion Field and its predecessors were a "neutral" site. But since Alabama played so many of its games in Birmingham and sold season tickets that included top-shelf seats at the site, Auburn was always something of a visitor.

When Pat Dye arrived at Auburn in 1981, he said things would change. Told there was a contract to have Tigers-Tide games in Birmingham through 1988, Dye said, "Then we'll play in Auburn in 1989." And that's what happened.

When the big day finally arrived, people in Auburn were so charged up that the game almost became secondary to Alabama's visit. Almost. But there was pure ecstasy when Auburn—led by passer Reggie Slack and runners Stacy Danley and James Joseph—roared from a 10-7 halftime deficit to a 30-20 victory. Although the next three games were played in Birmingham, and Alabama continued to play its home games in the series there until the late '90s, Alabama and Auburn finally began true home-and-home play in 2000.

X MAGIC MOMENTS
in the history of Jordan-Hare Stadium

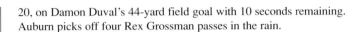

I. PERFECTION, *November 20, 1993.* The pollsters said Auburn couldn't be the national champion because of NCAA probation, so the Tigers went out and did the next best thing—they won 'em all. The finale came against Alabama and was a 22-14 victory, thanks to tailback James Bostic and quarterback Patrick Nix.

II. A STRONG FINISH, *November 18, 1995.* Alabama came to Auburn ranked 17th and left with a 31-27 defeat. It was the third victory in a row for the Tigers, who had bumped off Georgia the week before.

III. STEALING ONE, *September 17, 1994.* It's wild enough that Auburn overcame a 23-9 fourth-quarter deficit to beat LSU in this one, but the method of execution was absolutely unbelievable. Three Tigers returned final-quarter interceptions for touchdowns in a 30-26 victory. In all, Auburn intercepted five LSU passes in the last quarter.

IV. ON THEIR WAY, *September 18, 2004.* Jason Campbell's 16-yard TD pass to **Courtney Taylor** with 1:14 to play and John Vaughn's second-chance PAT gave Auburn a 10-9 victory over No. 5 LSU. It was a huge victory for **Tommy Tuberville**'s team, which would go on to win the Sugar Bowl, finish 13-0 and wind up No. 2 (behind USC) in the final polls.

V. STUNNING NO. 1, *October 13, 2001.* Florida comes to the Plains unbeaten and ranked No. 1, but the unranked Tigers stun the Gators, 23-20, on Damon Duval's 44-yard field goal with 10 seconds remaining. Auburn picks off four Rex Grossman passes in the rain.

VI. STICKING AROUND, *November 22, 2003.* Earlier in the week, Auburn's president and athletic director had flown secretly to Louisville to interview another coach for Tuberville's job. Auburn had lost two straight, and the vultures were circling. But Tuberville directed the Tigers to a 28-23 win over Alabama to keep his job.

VII. CHAMPIONS, *November 2, 1957.* In its only national championship season, Auburn whips No. 19 Florida, 13-0, behind a stout defense. The Tigers wind up shutting out six of their 10 opponents and not allowing more than one touchdown to any team.

VIII. RARE AIR, *October 29, 1983.* In just Pat Dye's third year at Auburn, the Tigers climb the polls to the fourth spot and meet No. 5 Florida. Auburn holds down the high-powered Gators offense in a 28-21 victory.

IX. STANDING ROOM ONLY, *October 31, 1953.* An extra 10,000 people crowd into the stadium to see the Tigers play Florida, and Auburn wins, 16-7. It's a season in which Auburn crashes the AP rankings for the first time since 1942.

X. NICE DEBUT, *September 20, 1969.* Pat Sullivan begins his legendary tenure as Auburn quarterback by throwing for one touchdown and running for two more in a 57-0 rout of Wake Forest. Wideout Terry Beasley, who would be Sullivan's favorite target for three seasons, catches four passes for 72 yards.

IV. ON THEIR WAY
Early in the 2004 season, coach Tommy Tuberville celebrated Auburn's 10-9 win over No. 5 LSU, a game in which Courtney Taylor (left) snared a tying TD pass in the late going and the Tigers tacked on the winning PAT. Auburn went on to a 13-0 record.

SATURDAY
SHRINES

LAVELL EDWARDS STADIUM

BRIGHAM YOUNG

The Cougars play in one of the most majestic settings in the nation, with the Wasatch Mountains serving as a breathtaking backdrop. Many fans arrive from Salt Lake

City—a 45-minute drive—via I-15, and the traffic can get heavy as they exit onto University Parkway. The band, called the Power of the Wasatch, marches down Canyon Road into the stadium as a prelude to an electric pregame show that is highlighted by the band spelling out "Cougars." After wins, the band plays "Popcorn Popping on the Apricot Tree," a popular song for Mormon youth. During the tune, the tuba players, along with the fans, pop up and down in a festive celebration.

SETTING LaVell Edwards Stadium is set in a hilly area that looks as if it just jumped off a postcard. Looking east from the press box, you can see Y Mountain, which has a large Y set into its side. It's not uncommon for pranksters to try to paint it. During the week of the Utah game, BYU ROTC students guard the rock to prevent Utes supporters from splashing it with red paint. Outside the stadium is a statue of a cougar, which is a popular place for fans to take pictures. Before games, the players run through a cloud of smoke, through a lane of band members. Then the school mascot, Cosmo, leads the team onto the field. Inside the stadium, it gets loud after BYU scores—and not just because Cougar fans are vocal. Members of the BYU Army ROTC shoot off George Q, a vintage World War II 75mm howitzer.

STRUCTURE The stadium itself isn't a pretty facility; the support beams are visible. Regardless, it's an imposing structure because of its size (64,045-seat capacity) and significant because of its symbolism (all of the steel used to build it was manufactured in Utah

County). The stadium isn't a complete bowl, as the corners of each end are open in the single-deck structure. In the concourse, there are posters commemorating great players, teams and moments in BYU history. On the side of the massive press box, all of BYU's bowl teams are chronicled, and the retired jerseys of former greats, such as Steve Young, are displayed.

FANS Most followers trickle to the game via Canyon Road. On the west side of the stadium, there's a big parking lot suited for tailgating, but there isn't a lot of traditional tailgating in Provo. Fans don't arrive hours before kickoff or linger afterward. Still, this is a passionate fan base; scoring BYU tickets still is tough, even when the Cougars are losing, and the Cougars rank among the top 25 in attendance every year. Adding to the fans' experiences are the Cougarettes, BYU's nationally renowned dance team.

LaVell Edwards coached BYU to a national title and won 257 games in 29 seasons—feats worthy enough to have the stadium bear his name.

BRIGHAM YOUNG

MAJOR RENOVATIONS Big changes took place in 1982, when stands were added to the north and south end zones. The field also was lowered eight feet. Club seating was added in 2003.

MILESTONE MOMENTS

• The first game was played October 2, 1964. The Cougars lost to New Mexico, 26-14.

• After wins, BYU rings the Victory Bell, which hangs in a tower dedicated in 1959. In 1973, the bell dropped and shattered but was repaired, and in 1978 it was moved to another site, where it still hangs from an arch.

• Before the stadium was renovated in 1982, two NCAA track championships were held in the facility. O.J. Simpson helped USC win the 4 X 100 relay at the 1967 event. That track was removed during the 1982 renovations.

FAST FACTS

• Stored underneath the bleachers are boxes of dinosaur bones, which are awaiting their turn in BYU's earth science museum.

• Every Fourth of July, the Stadium of Fire, a large fireworks display and concert, is held at the facility.

• The facility is now called LaVell Edwards Stadium, but before 2000 it bore the name Cougar Stadium. During the last home game of the legendary coach's career, on November 18, 2000, the stadium was dedicated to him so he could coach one game in the edifice that bears his name. BYU beat New Mexico, enabling Edwards to go 1-0 in the stadium.

CAPACITY THROUGH THE YEARS

1964: 26,812   1982: 65,000   2003: 64,045

X MAGIC MOMENTS

in the history of LaVell Edwards Stadium

SIMPLY UNFORGETTABLE

September 8, 1990. It was judgment day, the chance for Brigham Young to prove itself once and for all on the national stage. The Cougars had won the 1984 national championship, but many scoffed at BYU's claim to the crown because the Cougars had played a "soft" Western Athletic Conference schedule and defeated a 6-5 Michigan team in the Holiday Bowl—and needed some late magic to do it.

Six years later, here came top-ranked Miami, symbol of the big time in college football. The mighty Hurricanes boasted the model for gridiron success. Their defense was fast and nasty and the offense capable of scoring quickly and often. The national TV cameras were on hand to find out if Brigham Young had the essentials necessary to compete with the national powers.

At first, it appeared as if the Hurricanes were in charge. Stephen McGuire's touchdown run gave Miami a 7-0 lead. But the 14th-ranked Cougars evened things in the second quarter, when quarterback Ty Detmer hooked up with Matt Bellini on a 14-yard touchdown pass. BYU went up 10-7 and then 17-14 by halftime and looked strong, despite having turned the ball over four times.

In the third quarter, Leonard Conley's touchdown run gave the Hurricanes a 21-17 lead. That would be all Miami would get. Detmer led the Cougars on a pair of scoring drives, the second culminating in a TD pass to Mike Salido and a two-point conversion that pushed the BYU advantage to 28-21 late in the third quarter. Miami drove deep into Brigham Young territory but squandered the opportunities with two turnovers. With less than 2 minutes left, the Hurricanes made it to the BYU 25, but the Cougars defense stiffened, and Brigham Young took over on downs and ran out the clock. The big boys had come, and BYU had sent them home beaten.

I. THE ROAD TO PERFECTION, *October 13, 1984.* BYU quarterback Robbie Bosco leads an 80-yard drive in the fourth quarter and throws his fifth TD pass of the game to rally the Cougars from a 38-33 deficit to a 41-38 win over Wyoming, keeping Brigham Young undefeated in its national championship season.

II. STORMING BACK, *November 17, 2001.* The Cougars spot Utah a 21-10 lead but come back in the fourth quarter to win on a Luke Staley 30-yard TD run, 24-21. The win keeps BYU's hopes for an unbeaten season alive and gives the Cougars the Mountain West title.

III. TAMING THE LIONS, *October 31, 1992.* National power Penn State comes to Provo and takes a 3-0 lead before Brigham Young reels off 30 unanswered points to beat the Nittany Lions, 30-17, for the first time in school history.

IV. GREAT BEGINNINGS, *August 24, 1996.* **Steve Sarkisian** passes for 536 yards and six touchdowns, including one with just 1:03 left. The BYU defense forces a fumble with a minute to play, giving Brigham Young a 41-37 win over Texas A&M in the Pigskin Classic. BYU goes on to win 14 games that season.

IV. GREAT BEGINNINGS
Steve Sarkisian had reason to exult in the 14-win 1996 season. In the opener, he threw six TD passes.

V. DEAD DUCKS, *November 4, 1989.* It doesn't matter that Oregon flies out to a 33-14 lead. BYU rides the strong arm of sophomore Ty Detmer and beats the Ducks, 45-41. Detmer leads a 95-yard drive in the final minutes to clinch the win in a game that features 1,276 yards of offense.

VI. LIVING DANGEROUSLY, *September 9, 1999.* Kevin Feterik leads a touchdown drive that culminates with a pass to freshman Chris Hale with just over a minute remaining, and the BYU defense stands strong deep in its own territory, lifting the Cougars to a 35-28 win over Washington.

VII. GREAT START, *August 25, 2001.* After the Cougars had spent 29 years under LaVell Edwards' direction, Gary Crowton takes over as coach and authors a dream debut. BYU piles up 734 yards of offense in a 70-35 mauling of Tulane.

VIII. HOW SWEET IT IS, *November 19, 1983.* The Cougars always enjoy beating rival Utah, but nothing tops a humbling rout. In the final game of the regular season, thanks to six Steve Young touchdown passes, BYU beat Utah, 55-7.

IX. A BIG STEP, *November 9, 1974.* Gary Scheide's 9-yard touchdown pass to Tim Mahoney gives Brigham Young a 21-18 win over defending WAC co-champion Arizona State and paves the way for LaVell Edwards' first conference title at BYU.

X. STARTING ANEW, *September 14, 1985.* One week after losing to UCLA to snap a 25-game win streak, BYU rebounds to beat Washington, the 1984 national runner-up, 31-3.

SATURDAY
SHRINES

MEMORIAL STADIUM

CALIFORNIA

It begins with Cal players' March to Victory almost three hours before games and continues with the Cal Band and its high-stepping marchers spelling out the script Cal and blaring out the classic songs "Big C" and "Hail to California." Memorial Stadium is a college football jewel located in an area known as Strawberry Canyon.

The stadium is treasured for its breathtaking views and underrated history in one of the most beautiful regions of America. This is college football meets National Geographic.

SETTING Offering sweeping views of the San Francisco Bay, Memorial Stadium is nestled next to classic old homes. On a clear day, three bridges are visible to the west of the stadium: Golden Gate, Bay and San Rafael. To the east are views of the pines in the Berkeley Hills. And just outside Memorial Stadium is one of college football's most unique areas: Tightwad Hill. Those not wanting to buy a ticket hike up to Tightwad Hill above the northeast corner of the stadium, where they can see the game and the spectacular San Francisco Bay for free.

STRUCTURE Memorial Stadium is a concrete and steel single-level bowl. It has a classic look—it was patterned after Rome's Colosseum. The sightlines are unmatched, and in an intimate atmosphere, fans are right on top of the action. Arches mark Memorial Stadium's white facade, and pine trees surround its perimeter. A word of caution to those visiting the stadi-

um: It sits on the Hayward Fault. However, school officials are making structural upgrades so the stadium can withstand any future earthquakes.

FANS The team draws its fans from a large alumni base in the Bay Area and has the advantage of being a school where the spirit and history run deep. Berkeley is the birthplace of the card stunts, in which students hold up cards to depict various words and symbols. It's a tradition that began in 1910 for the Big Game vs. Stanford—although back then the teams played rugby. Students perform as many as 10 stunts with more than 5,000 cards each game, with coordinating efforts simplified by computers. Fans have little room to tailgate because the stadium is built on a hill, but the best spot is Maxwell Family Field, where it is common to hear fans greet one another with a classic yell of: "Go Bears!"

MAJOR RENOVATIONS In 1981, training quarters were added and outdated weight and locker rooms were overhauled, in addition to the installation of turf. More major updates are on the horizon.

SATURDAY SHRINES

CALIFORNIA

MILESTONE MOMENTS
• The first game was played on November 24, 1923, a 9-0 victory over Stanford.
• The first night was played October 30, 2004. Cal drubbed Arizona State, 27-0.
• Cal won 21 games in a row at Memorial Stadium from 1947-50.
• Artificial turf was installed in 1981. In 1995, grass was reinstalled. Turf was reinstalled before the 2003 campaign.

FAST FACTS
• The California Victory Cannon is located on Tightwad Hill. It is shot off before games, after Cal scores and after victories.

• Located on Charter Hill above Memorial Stadium is Big C, a large stone that was installed in 1905. A school organization is in charge of painting and protecting it.
• The stadium was built to honor those who lost their lives in World War I.

CAPACITY THROUGH THE YEARS

1923:	80,000	1962:	76,780
1928:	82,000	1982:	75,662
1947:	83,000	2001:	73,347

X MAGIC MOMENTS

in the history of Memorial Stadium

I. MAGICAL UPSET, *November 1, 1975.* The unranked Golden Bears, led by quarterback Joe Roth and running back Chuck Muncie, stun fourth-ranked USC, 28-14, in front of a national TV audience. Muncie runs for 143 yards on just 18 carries.

II. SALVAGING A SEASON, *November 22, 1986.* Despite entering the game 1-9, Cal shocks No. 16 Stanford, 17-11, in coach Joe Kapp's final game. It remains the greatest upset in Big Game history.

III. REMEMBERING A STAR, *October 29, 1977.* Two years after Joe Roth had engineered a huge upset of USC, the Bears retire his No. 12 jersey at halftime, after Roth had died of cancer. Unranked Cal honors its fallen hero by whipping the No. 10 Trojans, 17-14.

IV. WORKING OVERTIME, *September 27, 2003.* **Tyler Frederickson**'s 38-yard field goal in the third overtime period gives California a stunning 34-31 upset of third-ranked USC. Cal forces four Trojans turnovers and capitalizes on a big opportunity when USC's Ryan Killeen misses a 39-yard field-goal attempt in the third OT.

V. COAST TO COAST, *October 15, 1949.* Frank Brunk returns a kickoff 102 yards for a touchdown to give the ninth-ranked Golden Bears a 16-10, come-from-behind win over No. 12 USC. The win propels the Bears to a 10-0 regular season and a Rose Bowl berth.

VI. SURPRISE ENDING, *November 24, 1945.* UCLA blocks a California punt, but the Bears recover the ball and take it in for a touchdown. It's the only score in a 6-0 win over the 12th-ranked Bruins.

VII. RALLY TIME, *November 13, 1993.* Unranked California falls behind No. 13 Arizona, 20-0, before roaring back to win, 24-20. The victory sparks a three-game season-ending win streak and an Aloha Bowl invitation.

In the third overtime of a stirring 2003 game, Cal's Tyler Frederickson nailed a 38-yard field goal to give the opportunistic Bears an upset of No. 3 USC.

IV. WORKING OVERTIME

VIII. BARNES STORMING, *November 2, 1996.* Pat Barnes tosses a Pac-10-record eight touchdown passes in California's wild, 56-55 four-overtime win over Arizona.

IX. NO. 1 IN THE COUNTRY, *October 23, 1937.* California celebrates its first No. 1 AP ranking by beating No. 11 USC, 20-6. The Bears finish the season 10-0-1 and beat Alabama in the Rose Bowl.

X. BIG GAME BREAKTHROUGH, *November 23, 2002.* After losing in seven straight meetings with Stanford, California finally breaks through in the Big Game, walloping the Cardinal, 30-7. The victory gave the Bears their first winning season since 1993.

SIMPLY UNFORGETTABLE

November 20, 1982. It remains a staple of blooper shows and ranks at the top of every "miracle" list. Neither Cal nor Stanford entered this game with much of a national profile. Despite boasting star quarterback John Elway, the Cardinal was 5-5. Cal was just 6-4 but had made strides in Joe Kapp's first season as coach.

With 4 seconds left in the game, Stanford had just seized a 20-19 lead on a field goal and was preparing to kick off. The ensuing final play lasted what seemed like an eternity—it included five laterals. In the end, Kevin Moen, who had received the kick to begin with, caught a pitch and headed toward the goal. He sprinted past a couple of dazed members of the Stanford kickoff team and toward the end zone, which was now filled by the Cardinal band. As he crossed the goal line, Moen crashed into trombone player Gary Tyrrell and into Cal legend. The final call on the play? Moen to Richard Rodgers to Dwight Garner to Rodgers to Mariet Ford to Moen to history (and a 25-20 Cal victory).

MEMORIAL STADIUM

CLEMSON

| | CLEMSON | | : | | U S C |
| BALL ON | | DOWN | | TO GO | | QTR |

TIME OUTS LEFT

Rubbing Howard's Rock is Clemson's way of leaving no stone unturned in the quest for inspiration.

Saturdays are intense in Clemson, a tiny town located in the northwestern tip of South Carolina. Helping build the fever is one of the grandest stadium entrances in college football. After a short trip on two buses, the players enter from the top of a hill at the east end of the facility. A cannon is fired, and the players run en masse 100 feet down the hill toward the field, rubbing Howard's Rock—named for legendary Clemson coach Frank Howard—for inspiration before sprinting through a lane formed by the band.

SETTING Taking in a Clemson game is the ultimate small college town experience. The campus is nestled in the foothills of the Blue Ridge Mountains, and rolling hills highlight the landscape. Lake Hartwell sits nearby. It's easy for fans to find their way to campus, thanks to a series of orange Tiger paws painted on highways around the area.

STRUCTURE They call Clemson Death Valley. Why? In the 1940s, Lonnie McMillian routinely took his Presbyterian College teams to Clemson—and routinely got thumped. He remarked to the press one year that he was taking his team to play in Death Valley. The nickname was heard here and there until Howard popularized it in the '50s, and it has stuck. Now a sign reading "Clemson Welcomes You To Death Valley" screams out from a second-deck overhang on the stadium. Also dis-

'Florida was loud in the Swamp. But the loudest, not only the stadium, but the loudest place I have been around in my life was definitely Death Valley. I was yelling at the top of my lungs in that first series, and I couldn't even hear what I was saying.' *–Florida State QB Chris Rix*

CLEMSON

played are the names of the Tiger athletes who have been enshrined in Clemson's Ring of Honor.

FANS The Tiger following is a rabid group that takes its tailgating as seriously as it does its football. There's a spacious tailgating spot behind the west end zone, and a lot of folks tailgate on the parking lot of Littlejohn Coliseum. Tiger tailgating fare often includes low country stew and boiled peanuts, and many fans often make the short walk from the stadium to the Esso Club. The club once was a gas station, but now bartenders serve food and cans of beer. Perhaps the most rabid Tiger fan is Dick Herbert of Anderson, S.C., who drives The Paw Bearer, a purple and orange hearse, to every game. During the game, the band often strikes up "Tiger Rag."

MAJOR RENOVATIONS A south upper deck was added in 1978 and a north upper deck in 1983, push-

ing capacity to more than 80,000. There's a $52 million west end zone project in the works that will include the additions of premium seating, upscale cuisine, locker rooms and training rooms.

MILESTONE MOMENTS
- Players rubbed Howard's Rock for the first time on September 23, 1967, before a 23-6 win over Wake Forest.
- On October 23, 1999, Florida State coach Bobby Bowden squared off with son Tommy, the first time a father and son faced off as head coaches in a major college game. Daddy won, 17-14.
- The first game in Memorial Stadium was September 19, 1942, as the Tigers beat Presbyterian, 32-13.

FAST FACTS
- On game days, Clemson becomes the third-largest city in South Carolina.
- Memorial Stadium was the home field for the NFL's Carolina Panthers in 1995.
- Howard's Rock was retrieved from Death Valley, Calif., by a Clemson graduate and given to Howard.
- John Heisman coached the Tigers to their first perfect season in 1900. He coached at the school from 1900-03.
- Clemson has one of the most successful fund-raising clubs in the nation in I.P.T.A.Y., which originally meant I Pay $10 A Year. Now, the sum is generally considerably more.

CAPACITY THROUGH THE YEARS

Year	Capacity
1942:	20,000
1958:	38,000
1960:	53,000
1978:	63,000
1983:	81,473

X MAGIC MOMENTS

in the history of Memorial Stadium

I. DEATH (VALLEY) DEFYING, *November 18, 2000.* **Rod Gardner** hauls in a 50-yard pass with just 10 seconds remaining to set up Aaron Hunt's 25-yard field goal with 0:03 left in a thrilling 16-14 win over South Carolina.

II. TURNOVER CRAZY, *September 19, 1981.* It doesn't matter that defending national champion Georgia has mighty running back Herschel Walker. The fourth-ranked Bulldogs cough it up nine times and fall to Clemson, 13-3.

III. ROCK AND ROLL, *September 24, 1966.* In the first game at Death Valley with Howard's Rock present, Clemson overcomes a 35-17 late-third-quarter deficit and bumps off Virginia, 40-35. Jimmy Addison's 74-yard TD pass to Jackie Jackson in the fourth quarter is the game-winner.

IV. WELCOME TO CLEMSON, *November 12, 1960.* After refusing to play the Tigers at Clemson throughout the teams' rivalry (dating to 1896), South Carolina finally pays a visit and gets whipped, 12-2, in front of a wild Memorial Stadium crowd.

V. THE FIRST, *November 24, 1956.* Eight days after Vice President Richard Nixon watches Clemson lose to Miami in south Florida, the Tigers rebound with a 7-0 victory over Virginia that clinches the school's first ACC championship.

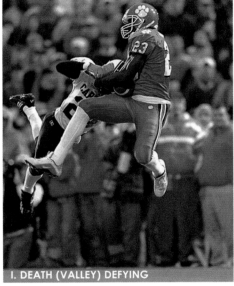

I. DEATH (VALLEY) DEFYING

Rod Gardner was Clemson's go-to guy in a wild finish against South Carolina in 2000.

One week later, the Tigers earn an Orange Bowl berth by beating Furman.

VI. HOWARD'S LAST, *November 1, 1969.* It is legendary coach Frank Howard's final game at Memorial Stadium, and Clemson sends him out properly by handing Maryland a 40-0 defeat. It remains the Tigers' largest margin of victory over the Terps.

VII. THREE HUNDREDS, *November 25, 1978.* Three Clemson backs go over the 100-yard mark in the Tigers' 41-23 triumph over South Carolina that clinches the Tigers' first 10-win season since 1948 and marks the opening of the upper deck on Death Valley's south side.

VIII. FANCY FOOTWEAR, *November 18, 1967.* After noticing that North Carolina State's defense wears white shoes, Clemson's team paints its shoes orange and then goes on to spank the 10th-ranked Wolfpack, 14-6, giving Howard his sixth and final ACC title.

IX. SIXTY YEARS IN THE MAKING, *October 5, 1974.* Clemson knocks off Georgia, 28-24, giving it victories over the Bulldogs and Georgia Tech (21-17) in the same season for the first time since 1914.

X. ERUPTION, *October 31, 1981.* Clemson sets 21 records and piles up 756 yards of offense in an 84-24 drubbing of Wake Forest. Clemson scores 49 first-half points and then adds a TD on its first possession of the second half. Included in the blitz are 536 rushing yards.

SIMPLY UNFORGETTABLE

November 8, 2003. It's called the Bowden Bowl, and each year, Ann Bowden has to choose sides between her son Tommy, the Clemson coach, and her husband Bobby, the Florida State coach. It wasn't that hard a choice; Ann took Tommy—and then watched her husband beat up on the Tigers the first four times father and son met.

Well, 2003 was different—not that it gave any indications of that. Clemson had just dropped a 45-17 decision to Wake Forest, its second defeat in three games. Tigers fans and alumni weren't too happy with Tommy Bowden, and word was out that only a huge finish would save him. Since the final three regular-season games included the third-ranked, 8-1 Seminoles and a trip to in-state rival South Carolina, things didn't look bright for Clemson and Bowden.

But the Tigers bolted to a 13-0 halftime lead against Florida State and didn't let up, adding a field goal to start the third quarter. Charlie Whitehurst connected on a 58-yard TD pass to Derrick Hamilton later in that quarter, putting the game away. The final was 26-10, making FSU the highest-ranked opponent Clemson had ever vanquished.

Things got even better after that. The Tigers crushed Duke the following week and then blasted South Carolina, 63-17. They closed the year with a 27-14 victory over Tennessee in the Peach Bowl. The 4-0 finish did more than just make Clemson 9-4. It also saved Bowden's job. And it all began with an improbable win in Ann Bowden's least-favorite game of the season.

SATURDAY SHRINES

FOLSOM FIELD

COLORADO

62

There are few settings as breathtaking as the one surrounding Folsom Field in Boulder. The Flatirons serve as the backdrop, and on a clear day, fans can see the Continental Divide. Parking is at a premium.

Through the years, fans have been forced to be resourceful, and season-ticket holders have found nooks and crannies to park their vehicles. You'll find the high rollers in the Gold Lot, but the best place to tailgate is Lot 169, which butts up against Boulder Creek.

SETTING Anyone would be hard-pressed to find a stadium that blends in better with its surroundings. The facility's stone facade is striking, and the stadium is one of college football's most intimate settings because fans are seated right upon the action. Colorado's mascot, Ralphie, a 1,300-pound buffalo who leads the team onto the field before each half, provides a unique CU tradition. The buffalo and her handlers charging onto the field is one of the best opening acts in the nation.

STRUCTURE Folsom Field isn't a massive structure, and it's design is fairly simple. In fact, you could be standing next to it and not even know it's a football stadium—it looks like a collection of curved two-story buildings. However, a unique aspect of the structure is the fact it is a sunken stadium, having been carved out of a hillside. The rooftops of the stadium buildings are made of the same stone and red tile as the other buildings on campus, which are based on an Italian architectural style, so the stadium blends in as a part of the university. Built

Everything is up-tempo for Ralphie, the Colorado Buffaloes and Buffs fans on an autumn Saturday in Boulder.

in 1924, the stadium is one of the oldest in the country. In 1956, a second deck was constructed, and before the 1968 season, the west side, with donor seating and a press box, was added. In the north end zone is the Dal Ward Center, added in 1979, which houses the football offices, weight room and locker room, among other things.

FANS Colorado's following isn't rabid, but the Buffaloes have a solid core of fans. Getting to Folsom Field can be difficult because there's only one major road into Boulder from Denver: U.S. 36, which also is known as the Boulder Turnpike. When back on campus, many fans flock to the Harvest House hotel and its vast outdoor seating area. After games, its common for fans to gather on Pearl Street, an area with an eclectic mix of restaurants, bars and shops.

MAJOR RENOVATIONS There haven't been massive changes since the stadium opened. The biggest came in 1956, when a second deck was added around two-thirds of the stadium. In 1967, the running track was removed, which helped create more seating. A six-tier press box was built before the 1968 season, and wooden bleachers were replaced with aluminum ones in 1976.

MILESTONE MOMENTS
• The stadium was dedicated on October 11, 1924, as the Buffs beat Regis College, 39-0.

COLORADO

• The facility originally was called Colorado Stadium, but the name changed to Folsom Field after the death of former great Colorado coach Frederick Folsom in 1944.

• The first game on artificial surface was played September 18, 1971, a 56-13 win over Wyoming. Grass was reinstalled in 1999.

FAST FACTS

• In the 1970s and early 1980s, Folsom played host to Grateful Dead weekends. The largest crowd ever (61,500) was in 1977 for a show by Fleetwood Mac, Bob Seger, Santana and Country Joe McDonald. Paul McCartney also packed the stadium for a concert in the early 1990s.

• There's a stature of Frank Shorter, who cofounded the Bolder Boulder, at the corner of Stadium Drive and Folsom Street. The Bolder Boulder, the world's third-largest timed road race, includes nearly 50,000 participants and takes place on Memorial Day, concluding in Folsom Field.

• There's a bronze bust of Fred Folsom, one of the school's most successful coaches, on the south side of the stadium. It was carved by his grandson. In the suite area, there's a life-size sculpture of CU great Byron "Whizzer" White.

CAPACITY THROUGH THE YEARS

1924: 26,000	1991: 51,748
1956: 45,000	1995: 51,655
1967: 51,000	2001: 50,942
1976: 52,005	2003: 53,750
1979: 51,463	

Nebraska's defense couldn't keep up with Chris Brown and the rest of the Buffaloes in a 2001 game. Brown ran for 198 yards and six touchdowns in a 62-36 Colorado romp.

II. HOW SWEET IT IS

X MAGIC MOMENTS
in the history of Folsom Field

I. THE TURNING POINT, *October 25, 1986.* After a 19-year drought, Colorado finally beats Nebraska, 20-10. The victory over the third-ranked Huskers marks CU's return as a player on the national scene.

II. HOW SWEET IT IS, *November 23, 2001.* **Chris Brown** rushes for 198 yards and six touchdowns, and the Buffaloes torch the proud Nebraska "Black Shirt" defense in a 62-36 blowout. It was the most points ever scored against the Cornhuskers to that point in time.

III. ORANGES ALL AROUND, *November 4, 1989.* The win three years earlier announced Colorado was back. This one cemented the Buffaloes' stature. Despite passing for only 22 yards, the Buffaloes topple Nebraska, 27-21, to all but clinch the Big Eight title and an Orange Bowl berth.

IV. TWO AND DONE, *October 21, 1972.* The Buffaloes spank second-ranked Oklahoma, 20-14, holding the vaunted OU attack to just 238 yards. The Sooners are the highest-ranked opponent ever defeated by CU.

V. THE RALLY, *September 22, 1990.* Reeling from a come-from-ahead loss to Illinois the week before, Colorado stages the rally this time and hands Texas a 29-22 defeat. In overcoming a 22-14 fourth-quarter deficit, the Buffs generate momentum that carries over to an eventual national title.

VI. STREAK STOPPER, *September 26, 1970.* Fourth-ranked Penn State brings its 31-game unbeaten streak and 23-game winning streak to Boulder and leaves with a 41-13 beating and the win-o-meter reset to zero. Afterward, Phil Irwin is on the cover of *Sports Illustrated*, the first time a CU athlete earns that distinction.

VII. THE BLEMISH, *September 27, 1952.* In what has to be considered one of the most pleasing ties in college football history, the Buffaloes fight No. 4 Oklahoma to a 21-21 deadlock, providing one of only two stains on an OU conference unbeaten streak that eventually would reach 74 games.

VIII. MILESTONE DAY, *November 19, 1994.* Tailback Rashaan Salaam goes over 2,000 yards for the season, quarterback Kordell Stewart sets the all-time Big Eight total-offense mark and Bill McCartney announces his forthcoming retirement after a 41-20 win over Iowa State.

IX. RANKED NO MORE, *October 6, 1951.* Despite being outgained, Colorado stuns No. 20 Kansas, 35-27, for the school's first victory over a ranked opponent.

X. HESSLER'S MAGIC, *September 23, 1995.* Starting quarterback Koy Detmer gets hurt, but John Hessler comes off the bench to rally Colorado to a 29-21 win over No. 3 Texas A&M.

SIMPLY UNFORGETTABLE

1990. There was doubt when the season started— some thought the team's 11-1 run in '89 was fueled mostly by emotion after the death of former quarterback Sal Aunese. Could the Buffs win big again? Many thought no.

Those cynics appeared to be right when the Buffaloes staggered out of the blocks at 1-1-1. Included was a 23-22 loss to Illinois in which CU collapsed after building a 17-3 second-quarter lead. Yes, it looked as if Colorado was a one-hit wonder. After the Buffaloes developed some momentum and pushed their record to 3-1-1, controversy lay ahead.

The Buffs stampeded into Columbia in week six to meet Missouri in a game that would become one of the most infamous in college football history. As time expired, CU quarterback Charles Johnson scored the winning touchdown. One problem: It came on fifth down. The referees, the Missouri staff and practically every fan in attendance lost count of the downs. By the time the Tigers realized what had happened, the game was over, and Colorado had the victory, 33-31—and plenty of negative attention.

That didn't stop coach Bill McCartney's team from moving forward. The wins continued to pile up, including a dramatic, emotional 27-12 victory at Nebraska on November 3. A week later, Oklahoma State came to Boulder. The Buffs piled up 444 yards of offense and whipped the Cowboys, 41-22. Kansas State then fell, 64-3, and it was on to the Orange Bowl for the Big Eight champion Buffs. A season that had featured so much turmoil had ended in great style. Colorado would defeat Notre Dame in Miami, securing its first national championship and quieting the critics.

COTTON BOWL

F
ew facilities can match the tradition and history of the Cotton Bowl. Sitting on the east side of Dallas, the Cotton Bowl is a classic stadium that offers fans good sightlines.

It lacks a lot of the amenities that make modern stadiums palatial, but this grand ol' place is a monument to college football and has been host to many great events, including bowl games and the annual Texas-Oklahoma matchup.

STRUCTURE The stadium is a stately structure. The main entrance is on the plaza of the state fairgrounds, and it's a place where people like to meet and congregate. The entrance is the most recognizable aspect of the stadium; it features a wide staircase, the words Cotton Bowl and two images of cotton emerging from a bloom. The lower level of the Cotton Bowl is a bowl, and each side features an upper deck that extends the length of the field.

SETTING Located on the grounds of Fair Park, the Cotton Bowl is a massive concrete structure. The stadium's atmosphere is at its best when Oklahoma and Texas meet in their annual Red River Shootout. The teams tangle during the Texas State Fair, making for a festive and lively environment. The game takes place amid a gamut of rides, livestock judging and the smell of Fletcher's corny dogs. With the fair and football crowds, traffic and parking can be a challenge—but fighting the droves is worth it.

FANS The Friday night before the OU-Texas game, it's a custom for fans to mingle—nicely—in the trendy West End area of Dallas. During the Red River

Shootout, it's easy to tell where the Texas fans are sitting and where Oklahoma's crowd is. In fact, you can split the crowd at the 50-yard line. The north horseshoe always is reserved for Texas faithful, while the south horseshoe is where the Oklahoma fans sit. The south horseshoe also happens to be where the tunnel leading onto the field is located, which means Texas players are subjected to boos and catcalls.

MAJOR RENOVATIONS The Cotton Bowl has been expanded and contracted on several occasions. It underwent a $2.8 million overhaul in 1993-94, in which the field was expanded and grass replaced the artificial turf. Chairbacks were added in 1968 to keep the NFL Cowboys as a tenant. But the biggest change came in the late 1940s, when upper decks were added to both sides of the stadium.

MILESTONE MOMENTS
• The Cotton Bowl stadium, then named Fair Park Bowl, hosted its first game on October 25, 1930. SMU beat Indiana, 27-0.
• The Cotton Bowl served as the SMU Mustangs' primary home from 1949-1978 and from 1995-1999.
• The first Cotton Bowl was played in 1937, as TCU beat Marquette, 16-6.
• Oklahoma and Texas first played in Dallas in 1912, a 21-6 Sooners win. The annual Red River Shootout rivalry began on October 19, 1929, with Texas winning the inaugural game, 21-0.

FAST FACTS

• In 1994, the Cotton Bowl was one of six U.S. venues that played host to World Cup soccer.
• The Dallas Cowboys played their home games in the Cotton Bowl from 1960-70. The AFL Dallas Texans also played three seasons in the Cotton Bowl until moving to Kansas City and becoming the Chiefs.
• When Notre Dame played Texas in the 1970 Cotton Bowl, it was the first bowl for the Irish since 1925. The Longhorns won, 21-17, to claim the national title.

CAPACITY THROUGH THE YEARS

Year	Capacity
1930:	42,600
1948:	57,431
1949:	75,504
1968:	72,032
1994:	68,252

X MAGIC MOMENTS
in the history of the Cotton Bowl

I. A ROYAL WELCOME, *January 1, 1970.* After a self-imposed 45-year absence from bowl play, No. 9 Notre Dame meets top-ranked Texas and coach Darrell Royal in the Cotton Bowl. The Irish hold a late 17-14 lead, but Texas quarterback James Street engineers a scoring drive that includes two fourth-down conversions and gives the Longhorns a 21-17 win and the national title.

II. QUITE A TWINBILL, *October 14, 1950.* Third-ranked Oklahoma gets its 24th consecutive win by whipping No. 4 Texas, 14-13, in the afternoon game. That evening, No. 2 Southern Methodist stomps Oklahoma A&M, 56-0.

III. CLIMBING THE CHARTS, *January 1, 1978.* Notre Dame enters the Cotton Bowl game ranked fifth, but after beating top-ranked Texas, 38-10, and shackling Heisman Trophy winner Earl Campbell, the Irish vault all the way to No. 1.

IV. STRAIGHT TO THE TOP, *October 12, 1963.* In a matchup dubbed the "Game of the Century," Scott Appleton makes 18 tackles and joins sophomore Tommy Nobis on a stingy defense that shuts down No. 1 Oklahoma and gives the second-ranked Longhorns a 28-7 victory.

V. THE FEUD BOWL, *October 11, 1975.* Texas coach Darrell Royal complains about Oklahoma boss Barry Switzer's recruiting practices in the days leading up to the annual Red River Shootout. Although the two are cordial before the game, the second-ranked Sooners are not so hospitable in a 24-17 win over No. 5 Texas.

VI. SUPERSUB, *October 8, 1977.* After Texas quarterbacks Mark McBath and John Aune go down in the first quarter with season-ending injuries, third-stringer Randy McEachern comes in and engineers a 13-6 upset of second-ranked Oklahoma. The No. 5 Longhorns shut down the mighty OU attack, and Earl Campbell runs for 124 yards and Texas' only touchdown.

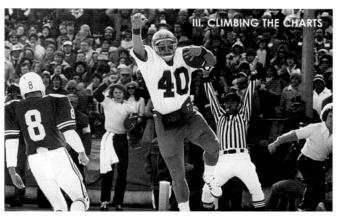

III. CLIMBING THE CHARTS

Two TDs by Terry Eurick (40) in the 1978 Cotton Bowl helped vault No. 5 Notre Dame past Texas and to the No. 1 ranking.

VII. SINKING NAVY, *January 1, 1964.* Navy and Heisman Trophy winner Roger Staubach come to the Cotton Bowl 9-1 and ranked second in the nation. But the top-ranked Longhorns roll to a 28-6 win and claim their first national championship.

VIII. TWICE AS NICE, *October 11, 1958.* After fighting hard to keep the 2-point conversion out of college football, Texas coach Darrell Royal uses it in the contest with second-ranked Oklahoma, and it turns out to be the margin of victory in a 15-14 game.

IX. ILLEGAL PROCEDURE, *January 1, 1954.* Rice's 28-6 win over Alabama lacks much drama, except for a crazy play involving Owl back Dick Maegle. Maegle breaks loose along the right sideline and looks as if he'll score, but Alabama's Tommy Lewis comes off the bench, runs down the sideline and tackles Maegle. The referees award Maegle a 95-yard touchdown.

X. BETTER LATE, PART II, *October 13, 1990.* For the second straight year, Texas mounts a late-fourth-quarter drive to beat Oklahoma. This time, Longhorns quarterback Peter Gardere connects with Keith Cash for the winning touchdown, and Wayne Clements hits the extra point to pull the unranked Longhorns ahead of No. 4 Oklahoma, 14-13. Sooners kicker R.D. Lashar misses a 46-yard field-goal try in the waning seconds, and Texas holds on to win.

SIMPLY UNFORGETTABLE

January 1, 1979. Joe Montana already had engineered magical victories and a national title for Notre Dame. Now, he went a step beyond in the Cotton Bowl.

It was around 20 degrees in Dallas, with icy rain mixing with sleet. A year earlier, the Fighting Irish had won a national crown there by upsetting Texas. This time, the No. 10 Irish were pitted against Southwest Conference champion Houston and its vaunted veer offense.

The No. 9 Cougars rolled to a 20-12 lead in the first half. And things got worse for Notre Dame in the third quarter, when Montana left the game with a low body temperature. Houston piled on two more TDs and led, 34-12, entering the fourth quarter. Things looked bleak.

But Montana returned and led a miraculous rally over the final 7:37. It began when Steve Cichy scooped up a punt blocked by Tony Belden and dashed 33 yards for a TD. Montana's conversion pass made it 34-20. The Irish defense then forced a Houston punt, and Notre Dame regained possession on its own 39 with 5:40 to play. It took just 1:25 for Montana to get the Irish into the end zone, a drive he capped with a 2-yard scoring run. Another conversion pass drew the Irish within 34-28. A Montana fumble later in the quarter dampened Irish hopes, but when Houston opted to go for it on fourth down from its 29 with 28 seconds left, the Irish stuffed the play and took over.

Montana ran for 11 yards. He hit Haines for 10 more. Then an incomplete pass left 2 seconds on the clock, and the Irish had the ball on the 8. On the game's final play, Montana hit Haines for the score. Joe Unis' kick was good, but a procedure penalty forced him to kick again. So, he did. And Notre Dame had a 35-34 win that still defies description.

FLORIDA FIELD

FLORIDA

FLORIDA FIELD

Nothing fancy. It's all about function, and the function here is to play football. Few schools do it better.

Before former Heisman Trophy winner Steve Spurrier returned to his alma mater as coach, the Gators were underachievers and games were often just social events. In fact, Alabama coach Bear Bryant once viewed the Florida program as a sleeping giant, envisioning what the Gators might become with the right supervision. In 12 years under supervisor Spurrier, Florida compiled a 69-5 record at The Swamp. The atmosphere is not unlike a heavy metal concert—except that a Gators home game is louder. Much louder.

SETTING No great scenery here. Gainesville is land-locked in the upper part of the state and receives no cooling ocean breeze. But that's part of the so-called charm of a Gators home game. The heat and humidity reach suffocating levels on the field, and it's no picnic in the stands, either. Players and fans alike have to deal with it—and they do. Much credit must be given to Spurrier for creating a hostile environment at Florida Field. Amazingly successful at Florida, he led the Gators to the 1996 national title and groomed quarterback Danny Wuerffel for Heisman Trophy

honors, which Wuerffel won in the same season.

STRUCTURE It's right there on an interior wall of the stadium: "This is ... THE SWAMP." It's a moniker that Spurrier coined at the end of the 1991 season. And it's fitting. Various renovations over the years have resulted in an 83,000-seat configuration unlike a typical bowl. Both end zones are enclosed, and there's no buffer from the field to the stands (less than 10 feet in some areas), creating a sense of fans being right on top of the action. The north end zone Touchdown Terrace is deafening for opposing teams. And this place wouldn't be complete without a statue of a gator out front.

FANS Mean. Noisy. Relentless. That's the Gators faithful. And then the game begins. Nothing can prepare the opposition for the game-day experience at The Swamp. It's eardrum-breaking and sweltering, and the intensity and emotion never let up. There's nothing quite like the scene at the end of the third quarter, when Florida fans sway back and forth while singing "We Are the Boys."

MAJOR RENOVATIONS In 1982, the

> '**I think it is an atmosphere that is just incredible. The electricity and the environment make it just a phenomenal place to play.'**
>
> —*1996 Heisman Trophy winner Danny Wuerffel*

FLORIDA

SIMPLY UNFORGETTABLE

Steve Spurrier, I and II. It started in 1964, when a gunslinger out of Tennessee came to Gainesville to play for Ray Graves and create the kind of sustained excitement that hadn't been seen at Florida. Spurrier never led UF to an SEC title as a player, but he did win the Heisman Trophy and thrill fans with his late-game heroics.

Perhaps his most amazing performance came in a loss. Florida fell behind Missouri in the 1966 Sugar Bowl, 20-0, but Spurrier went on a tear in the final 10:32, throwing three touchdown passes. But the Gators missed three consecutive two-point conversions and lost, 20-18. Spurrier finished with 352 yards passing. As a senior, he led Florida to a 7-0 start, but a loss to Georgia cost the Gators a shot at their first conference crown. He passed for 2,012 yards and 16 TDs that year and won the Heisman by a two-to-one margin over Purdue's Bob Griese.

Spurrier's second act in Gainesville came in 1990, when he took over as coach at his alma mater. In '91, he led Florida to the first SEC title in school history. Spurrier brought five more conference championship trophies to the school, and in 1996 he authored the greatest season in school history. The Gators went 10-1 in the regular campaign, whipped Alabama in the SEC title game and then avenged their only defeat of the year in the Sugar Bowl, winning the national championship with a 52-20 pasting of Florida State. By the time he was done at Florida, after the 2001 season, Spurrier had won 122 games in 12 years and lifted the Gators to heights that even he couldn't achieve as a highly decorated player.

10,000-seat south end zone expansion increased the capacity to 72,000 and also included an athletic training center and skybox tower. Nearly 10 years later, the north end zone Touchdown Terrace club seating pushed the capacity to 83,000. A two-year, $50 million expansion/renovation was finished before the 2003 season that added premium seating.

MILESTONE MOMENTS

• The first game was played November 8, 1930. Red Barber called the play-by-play as the Gators lost, 20-0, to Alabama.
• On September 23, 1950, the first night game was played at Florida Field, a 7-3 win over The Citadel.
• Artificial turf was installed in 1971. It was replaced by grass in 1990.

FAST FACTS

• On October 13, 1934, Florida Field was dedicated to the memory of military personnel who died in World War I.
• In 1989, the facility was named Ben Hill Griffin Stadium at Florida Field to honor a longtime Gators supporter.
• Florida won 30 games in a row at Florida Field from October 1994 to September 1999.

CAPACITY THROUGH THE YEARS

Year	Capacity
1930:	21,769
1965:	56,164
1966:	62,800
1950:	40,116
1982:	72,000
1991:	83,000
2003:	88,548

X MAGIC MOMENTS
in the history of Florida Field

I. FINALLY!—*November 16, 1991.* After decades of disappointment, Florida wins its first SEC title with a 35-26 victory over Kentucky. Steve Spurrier, who had come close to winning a league crown as a player, directs the Gators to the championship in just his second year as head coach.

II. NOT THIS YEAR, *September 20, 1997.* Tennessee quarterback Peyton Manning returns for his senior season to chase an SEC title and the Heisman Trophy, but Florida jolts his hopes for both with a decisive 33-20 win over the Volunteers that lifts UF to No. 1 in both polls.

III. THE EXPLOSION, *September 16, 1995.* Florida falls behind Tennessee, 30-21, at the half but erupts for six second-half touchdowns in a wild 62-37 victory. Quarterback Danny Wuerffel leads the way by completing 29 of 39 passes for 381 yards and six touchdowns.

IV. THE BIG BOOT, *October 29, 1966.* Steve Spurrier, not known for his kicking skills, nails a 40-yard field goal that barely clears the crossbar late in the fourth quarter to give the Gators a 30-27 win over Auburn. He passes for 259 yards and punts for a 46.9-yard average.

V. TWO BIG POINTS, *October 1, 1960.* Larry Libertore tosses a two-point conversion pass to Jon MacBeth with 33 seconds to play, giving the Gators an 18-17 win over 10th-ranked Georgia Tech during Ray Graves' first season as Florida coach. Lindy Infante had scored on a fourth-down run to set up the winning conversion.

VI. THE BELL TOLLS, *November 1, 1986.* Kerwin Bell comes off the bench to lead Florida back from a 17-0 deficit against Auburn. He hits Ricky Nattiel with a 5-yard scoring pass with 36 seconds to play, then runs it in on a two-point conversion to give the Gators an 18-17 victory.

VII. TWO BAD, *September 18, 1999.* No. 2 Tennessee, the defending national champion, comes to Gainesville but can't overcome the fourth-ranked Gators, who earn a 23-21 victory and take a key early step toward another SEC East title.

VIII. THE MAESTRO, *November 2, 1974.* The Gators move up to sixth in the AP poll after a 25-14 win over Auburn. The hero is QB Don Gaffney, who runs the wishbone to perfection. One newspaper account says he operated the offense "like he had invented it."

IX. A BIG START, *September 8, 1990.* After losing four of their last five games the season before, the Gators burst forth in the first game under new coach Spurrier and blast Oklahoma State, 50-7, to move into the top 25. Florida would not be out of the rankings again under Spurrier.

X. MAKING A STATEMENT, *October 2, 1965.* The Gators lose to No. 8 Mississippi State but rebound the next week to take down fifth-ranked LSU, 14-7, and re-enter the national rankings at No. 10.

The Steve Spurrier-coached Gators dominated most opponents—including Tennessee and Peyton Manning—in Spurrier's 12 seasons at the helm. Manning, wrapped up in a 1997 game at Florida Field in which a 33-20 Gators win thrust Florida into the top spot in the polls, never defeated UF, which went 122-27-1 overall under Spurrier and won a national championship in 1996.

DOAK CAMPBELL STADIUM

FLORIDA STATE

This facility has grown in stature with each step the team has taken under Bobby Bowden, and that's a whopping distance. Now, it's one of the finest stadiums anywhere, providing the Seminoles with one of the best home-field advantages in the nation. For a relatively young program, Florida State has plenty of history

and tradition. One highlight is the "H" goalposts, which are called "Pete's Posts" in homage to former Seminoles coach Bill Peterson, who kick-started the program in the 1960s with an innovative offense. Peterson's teams came onto the field by running between the goalposts, a stirring entry that Bowden has revived.

SETTING Just after the coin toss, one of college football's most compelling traditions takes place. That's when Osceola rides Renegade, an appaloosa, from the south end of the stadium and thunders to the middle of the field. The horse rears up and Osceola plunges a flaming spear into the FSU logo at the 50-yard line. When the Florida Gators are in town, Osceola dismounts Renegade, raises the spear, shows it to each side of the stands and tosses it into the logo. After the team has concluded pregame warmups, the Marching Chiefs strike up "The Good, the Bad and the Ugly." The players hold up their helmets and walk to the locker room.

STRUCTURE The stadium used to be called the "Erector Set" because so many support beams were visible. Now, the facility is resplendent in brick, giving it a stately look. In 2004, a statue of Bobby Bowden

was dedicated and sits on the north side of the stadium. Also, a stained-glass window, one of the largest in America at 30 feet high, 20 feet wide, bears Bowden's likeness and is part of an adjacent athletic center. The field also was dedicated to Bowden, Division I-A's all-time winningest coach.

FANS This is a loyal and knowledgeable base that enjoys a good defensive effort as well as offensive pyrotechnics. Throughout the game, fans will break into the FSU

Seminoles football has been a flaming success since Bobby Bowden's arrival in Tallahassee.

"war chant," which is punctuated by fans making a chopping motion with one arm. Credit the Marching Chiefs with developing the chant during a game with Auburn in 1984, though its roots can be traced to the 1960s. Fans assemble in the baseball stadium adjacent to Doak Campbell for a pregame concert with the Marching Chiefs. After that, the band marches into the stadium. Tailgaters have an abundance of space around the stadium in which to set up their grills and tables. There's also Langford Green, a big, grassy area where games are arranged for kids.

MAJOR RENOVATIONS Where to begin. One of the biggest ones in the early years was a 15,500-seat addition prior to the 1964 season. One of the more recent changes was a brick facade that matches the architectural design of most of the other buildings on campus.

MILESTONE MOMENTS
• On September 16, 1978, in a game vs. Oklahoma State, Chief Osceola first threw a flaming spear into the field. A tradition was born.
• The sod cemetery, near the stadium but moved a slight distance in the spring of 2005 when practice fields were expanded, was begun in 1962 following an 18-0 victory over Georgia. Since Florida State was

FLORIDA STATE

a road underdog in that game and won, it decided to take a piece of sod back home, plant it in the cemetery and erect a tombstone to commemorate the event. The Seminoles often were underdogs early in the Bobby Bowden regime, which began in 1976, but that's rarely the case these days. Hence, the rules have changed—any landmark road victory and all bowl games are now "sod games."

• The first game at Doak Campbell was a 40-7 win over Randolph-Macon on October 7, 1950.

FAST FACTS

• Florida State's first football facility was called Centennial Field, which was the Seminoles' home for three years before they moved into Doak Campbell in 1950.

• Doak Campbell was the Florida State University president who pushed to form a football team when it wasn't popular to do so.

• Burt Reynolds Hall is a short pass from the stadium. You won't find the former Seminole football player-turned-actor there, however. At one time, the entire team lived in the hall. Now, it's just for the freshmen and select sophomores.

CAPACITY THROUGH THE YEARS

1950:	15,000	1992:	70,123
1954:	19,000	1993:	72,589
1961:	25,000	1994:	75,000
1964:	40,500	1995:	77,500
1978:	47,413	1996:	80,000
1980:	51,094	2001:	82,000
1982:	55,246	2003:	82,300
1985:	60,519		

Florida State fans turned a 1996 home win over Florida into their own version of a "sod game," digging up some souvenir turf after the No. 1-ranked Gators had fallen. (The real thing—FSU's sod cemetery—is top left.)

III. MAKING THE MOST OF IT

X MAGIC MOMENTS
in the history of Doak Campbell Stadium

I. A BIG STEP, *October 9, 1993*. After having lost three straight to Miami by a total of 13 points (with the 1991 defeat coming on a missed field goal), Florida State whips the Hurricanes, 28-10, and keeps its top ranking en route to its first national title.

II. FIVE IN A ROW, *October 9, 1999*. The Seminoles get 332 yards passing from Chris Weinke and blast No. 19 Miami for the fifth straight time, 31-21. The victory keeps the Seminoles ranked No. 1 in the nation and continues the team's wire-to-wire run to the national title.

III. MAKING THE MOST OF IT, *November 30, 1996*. Despite being outgained, 443 yards to 317, and managing only 16 first downs, No. 2 Florida State edges top-ranked Florida, 24-21, thanks to three interceptions. The teams meet again a month later in the Sugar Bowl, but the Gators prevail.

IV. AT LAST, *November 21, 1964*. Led by the "Seven Magnificents" on defense, coach Bill Peterson's team stuffs Florida, 16-7. It is the first time in school history the Seminoles have defeated the Gators and the first time UF has deigned to play in Tallahassee.

V. PICKIN' AND WINNIN', *October 28, 1989*. After four consecutive losses to Miami, including an embarrassing 31-0 season-opening defeat in 1988, the 'Noles pick off four Gino Torretta passes and defeat the second-ranked Hurricanes, 24-10.

VI. THE DEFENSE DOESN'T REST, *November 21, 1998*. FSU holds Florida's Fun 'n' Gun offense to 204 total yards and picks off three passes to whip Steve Spurrier's fourth-ranked club, 23-12.

VII. TOP 20 BOUND, *October 22, 1977*. Florida State's defense puts the clamps on Auburn,

and the FSU rushing attack grinds out 240 yards in a 24-3 victory. The following Monday, 5-1 FSU breaks into the AP rankings—at No. 20—for the first time in school history.

VIII. GATOR HUNTERS, *November 18, 2000*. Chris Weinke throws three touchdown passes, and the FSU defense holds fourth-ranked Florida to just 37 rushing yards in 20 carries. It's a 30-7 romp that carries Florida State into the national championship game.

IX. TAKE THAT, *October 4, 1997*. Even though Miami is reeling from the effects of rebuilding after probation, the Seminoles delight in a 47-0 thrashing of their hated rival. FSU's defense holds the Hurricanes to minus-33 yards rushing in 27 carries.

X. HOLDING ON, *December 1, 1990*. Despite surrendering 484 yards of total

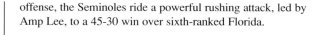

offense, the Seminoles ride a powerful rushing attack, led by Amp Lee, to a 45-30 win over sixth-ranked Florida.

SIMPLY UNFORGETTABLE

1987-2000. There is nothing that compares to it in recent college football in terms of amazing numbers and unparalleled success. The Seminoles were ranked in the final AP top five 14 straight times in this stretch, won nine consecutive ACC crowns (FSU didn't join the league until 1992), captured two national championships and ran up a 152-19-1 record (.887 winning percentage).

Florida State went 11-3 in bowl games, lost only five times at home and was pretty much on everybody's national title short list at the beginning of each season.

Coach Bobby Bowden's team could be counted on for explosive offense and teeth-rocking defense, a good reason why the team was so successful for so long.

Of course, the two national title teams stand out. The first was the 1993 edition, which entered a November 13 game at Notre Dame ranked first but dropped a heartbreaker to the Irish. But since ND lost the following week, to Boston College, FSU climbed back into the top spot and then secured the national championship with wins over Florida in the regular-season finale and Nebraska in the Orange Bowl.

Six years later, the 'Noles left no doubt, going wire-to-wire at the top of the polls and capping matters with a 46-29 spanking of Virginia Tech in the Sugar Bowl. The 12-0 record said it all. And though FSU sagged somewhat in the years after the second championship, it will be a long while—if ever—before another team is capable of replicating the Seminoles' 14-year run.

SATURDAY SHRINES

SANFORD STADIUM

GEORGIA

78

Sanford Stadium is a true Southern classic. The facility is in the middle of campus, which creates a festive atmosphere in one of America's best college towns.

Most fans arrive from Atlanta, following I-85 before forking off on Highway 316 about 35 miles from Athens. The road gets crowded, but attending a game is worth the effort. And there are few pregame rituals more memorable than the Dawg Walk. The team is dropped off on Lumpkin Street and makes its way through the crowd, getting bombarded with backslaps and cheers before entering the stadium. The surrounding tailgating is second-to-none, with RVs dotting the landscape, making this one of college football's most festive venues.

SETTING It doesn't get any better than hunkering down between the renowned English privet hedges that line the field at Sanford Stadium. It's believed famed Atlanta sportswriter Grantland Rice coined the phrase "between the hedges," a now-legendary reference to the position in which opponents find themselves when they face the Bulldogs at Sanford. Mascot Uga, a live English bulldog, roams the sideline and has become one of the nation's most popular mascots. He's also as fierce as Georgia's football players; he once lunged at an Auburn receiver. And when the Ugas die, they aren't forgotten. They are entombed in marble vaults near the west end zone. Another unique aspect of

the venue is the Sanford Bridge outside the stadium's main gate. The bridge allows fans to peer into the facility from the street. Adding to the ambience are lively off-campus nightspots and restaurants. Many fans enjoy getting a 50-cent ice cream cone from Hodgson's Pharmacy on Milledge Avenue.

STRUCTURE Sanford Stadium is a massive concrete and steel facility with two upper decks, which extend around three-quarters of the stadium. The lower level is built into the ground, which means the stadium doesn't jut high like others of its capacity. A creek runs under the facility, which has helped maintain the playing surface during water-restriction times.

FANS The fight song, which was sung at games as early as the late 1800s, is "Glory, Glory," sung to the tune of the "Battle Hymn of the Republic." With about eight minutes left before kickoff and the team in the locker room, a trumpet soloist moves to the southwest corner of the upper deck and plays the first few strains of the song. While this is taking place, a montage of great Georgia moments, narrated by legendary Bulldogs announcer Larry Munson, plays on the stadium's big screen. Now, it's game time, and plenty of shouts of "How 'bout them Dawgs!" can be heard.

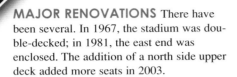

GEORGIA

MAJOR RENOVATIONS There have been several. In 1967, the stadium was double-decked; in 1981, the east end was enclosed. The addition of a north side upper deck added more seats in 2003.

MILESTONE MOMENTS
• In the first game at Sanford Stadium, Georgia beat Yale, 15-0, on October 12, 1929.
• The first night game was October 26, 1940, when the Bulldogs tied Kentucky, 7-7.
• Georgia won 24 games in a row at Sanford Stadium from September 13, 1980, to November 12, 1983.

FAST FACTS
• The stadium is named for Dr. Steadman V. Sanford, who served the university in many capacities, including dean, president and chancellor. He was largely responsible for coaxing Yale to make its first trip south of the Mason-Dixon Line to play in the stadium's dedication game.
• Sanford Stadium was the site of the medal rounds for men's and women's soccer for the 1996 Olympics. To accommodate the larger field, the famed hedges had to be torn out, but offshoots of the originals were replanted.

CAPACITY THROUGH THE YEARS

1929: 30,000	1991: 85,434
1949: 36,000	1994: 86,117
1964: 43,621	2000: 86,520
1967: 59,000	2003: 92,058
1981: 82,122	2004: 92,746

When the Georgia Bulldogs take the field at venerable Sanford, they're ready to defend their turf "between the hedges."

SIMPLY UNFORGETTABLE

November 29, 1980. It had been an amazing year. Herschel Walker had been the player everybody had hoped he would be, even if he was just a freshman. A finely chiseled, faster-than-lightning freshman but a fresh-man nonetheless. Everything had gone right, from the nail-biting season opener against Tennessee, right through the miracle finish against Florida, 1980 was outstanding.

And on November 29, in the regu-lar-season finale, it all came together. The Bulldogs had climbed steadily to the No. 1 ranking and were playing host to Georgia Tech. Could there be any better way to close out a perfect season and advance to the precipice of a second national championship than by dismantling the Wreck?

Georgia had survived all the SEC tests, the toughest coming on November 8 against Florida, when a last-minute Buck Belue-to-Lindsay Scott touchdown pass propelled the Bulldogs to the top spot in the rank-ings. Now, it was time to finish the job. Nobody cared that Tech was 1-8-1. Just three weeks earlier, the Yellow Jackets had tied Notre Dame, 3-3.

But Georgia was ready. And although Tech managed 20 points, it wasn't nearly enough. Georgia put up 38 and could have had more. Walker set a national freshman rushing record of 1,616 yards. Georgia's celebration began, and it wouldn't end until New Year's Day, when Georgia capped a 12-0 season with a 17-10 win over No. 2 Notre Dame in the Sugar Bowl. The Bulldogs were the consensus national champions.

X MAGIC MOMENTS
in the history of Sanford Stadium

I. **KA-BOOM**, *September 22, 1984.* Sanford Stadium turns into a house of bedlam when Kevin Butler drills an SEC-record-tying 60-yard field goal with just 11 seconds remaining in the game to give the 20th-ranked Bulldogs an improbable 26-23 victory over No. 2 Clemson.

II. **FRAN THE MAN**, *November 14, 1959.* In a finish as wild as any in Georgia history, **Fran Tarkenton** fakes right, then throws a fourth-down touchdown pass to **Bill Herron** with just 30 seconds remaining, and the extra point gives the Bulldogs a 14-13 win over Auburn and the SEC title.

III. **LEAVITT-TATION**, *November 27, 1976.* The Bulldogs had locked up the SEC title a week before in Auburn, but Allan Leavitt gave them bragging rights when he hit a 33-yard field goal with 5 seconds left in a 13-10 win over Georgia Tech.

IV. **ANOTHER CLOSE CALL**, *October 2, 1999.* Georgia wins its second one-point decision in as many weeks when Will Witherspoon knocks away an LSU two-point conversion pass with 18 seconds left, giving the Bulldogs a 23-22 win.

V. **WRECKING THE WRECK**, *November 26, 1966.* During a season in which the Bulldogs allow no team to score more than 17 points, No. 7 Georgia shackles fifth-ranked Georgia Tech, 23-14, in the season finale to clinch a Cotton Bowl berth.

VI. **LOW TIDE**, *October 2, 1976.* Vince Dooley's third SEC title team sets the stage for its run through the league by whip-ping five-time defending SEC champ Alabama, 21-0. It's the Bulldogs' first win over the Tide in 11 years.

VII. **CRIMSON TEARS**, *September 18, 1965.* Even though Alabama's team will go on to win a second consecutive AP national title, it stumbles out of the gate, dropping an 18-17 decision to the Bulldogs. It would be the Tide's only loss that season.

VIII. **GOING OUT IN STYLE**, *November 26, 1960.* The Bulldogs send legendary coach Wallace Butts out with a victory when they edge Georgia Tech, 7-6, in Butts' final game. Butts finishes with a 140-86-9 record at Georgia.

IX. **THE ROAD TO PASADENA**, *November 28, 1942.* Despite dropping a tough decision at Auburn the week before, No. 5 Georgia rips second-ranked Georgia Tech, 34-0, in the season finale and earns its first trip to the Rose Bowl. Ranked No. 2 in the final AP poll (but voted No. 1 by some rating services), the Bulldogs beat UCLA at Pasadena.

X. **GOLDEN MOMENT**, *August 1, 1996.* Playing in front of the largest crowd ever to see a women's soccer game anywhere (76,481), the United States beats China, 2-1, to win the gold medal in the 1996 Olympic Games.

Fran Tarkenton and Bill Herron combined on late heroics against Auburn in 1959, helping Georgia to the SEC crown.

II. FRAN THE MAN

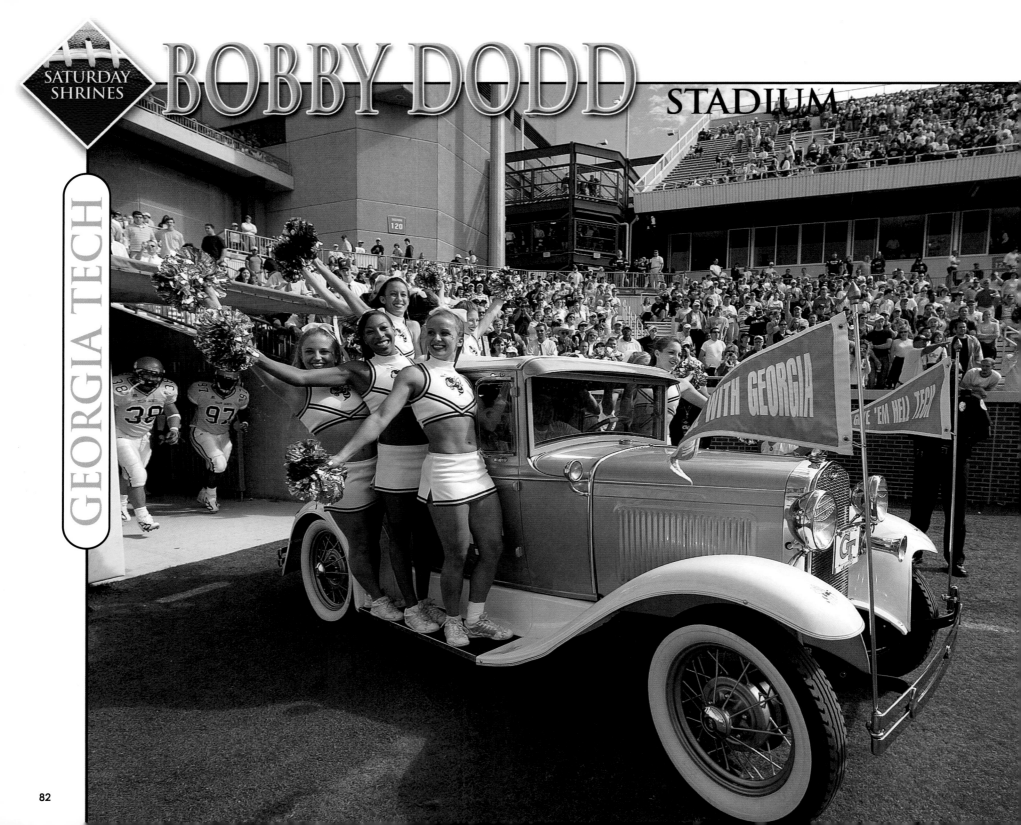

BOBBY DODD STADIUM

GEORGIA TECH

WITH GEORGIA

GIVE 'EM HELL TECH

If you like history, Bobby Dodd Stadium at Historic Grant Field is your place. This is the oldest on-campus stadium in NCAA Division I-A and is packed with tradition. There's even a statue of John Heisman, who coached Georgia

Tech from 1904-1919, inside the football offices in the south end zone of the stadium. But that's just the beginning, as fans line Yellow Jacket Alley before games to watch the parade of players, who a few hours later are led onto the field by the Rambling Wreck, a 1930 Model-A Ford. It's time to play football.

SETTING It's within a few long punts of the skyscrapers of downtown Atlanta. Indeed, this is an urban setting that's contrary to the traditional college campus. Because of that, most fans like it when Tech plays at night amid the glow of the city's brightly lit buildings. This is an intimate campus with the stadium located in the heart of it, just off the interstate.

STRUCTURE Oh, if this place could talk. Great players like Clint Castleberry, Randy Rhino and Maxie Baughan have run, tackled and blocked on this hallowed ground. The first stands—the concrete west stands—were built in 1913, mostly by students. In fact, the old stands are underneath the current ones. The stadium is named for Bobby Dodd, who served as Tech

head coach (1945-66), athletic director (1950-76) and alumni consultant until his death in 1988 at age 79.

FANS Tailgating isn't top-notch because of a lack of space. Mostly, it is limited to parking decks. Plus, Tech doesn't have a lot of fans who drive four or five hours to tailgate. This is a group that largely lives in Atlanta. The heavy hitters can be found on Peter's parking deck right across from the stadium. Before the game, you'll find many fans grabbing something to eat at the Varsity, a short walk from the stadium. Between the third and fourth quarters, you'll hear fans sing the "Bud" song.

MAJOR RENOVATIONS There have been many alterations over the years. The east side of the stadium was double-decked in 1962, with the west side getting a second tier in 1967. But the biggest overhaul was completed in 2003, with a new north end zone structure and revamped seating in the south end zone and in lower stands on the east side. Also, suites and club seats were added.

MILESTONE MOMENTS
• In 1995, grass was installed

GEORGIA TECH

for the first time in 24 seasons. Bobby Dodd Stadium had turf installed in 1971 and was resurfaced with the fake stuff in 1979 and 1988.

• Bobby Dodd Stadium was home of national-championship Tech teams in 1990, 1952, 1928 and 1917.

• The Yellow Jackets won the first game at the present site of Grant Field, 54-0, over Dahlonega in 1905. In 1913, the year the first stands were erected, Georgia Tech won its opener against Fort McPherson, 19-0.

• A great game it wasn't; unforgettable it was: Georgia Tech 222, Cumberland 0. "We were sort of getting to 'em in that last quarter," cracked a Cumberland player, whose team trailed, 180-0, after three quarters in the 1916 clash.

FAST FACTS

• Bobby Dodd Stadium has played host to the Rolling Stones and Nelson Mandela.

• For 43 years, radios around the stadium buzzed with the voice of play-by-play man Al Ciraldo, who was known for expressions like "toe meets leather."

• The stadium was a practice site during the 1996 Olympics, while the adjacent campus served as the Olympic Village.

• The stadium initially was named for Hugh Inman Grant, whose family gave the first $15,000 to build the first permanent concrete stands. Bobby Dodd had his name added in 1988.

CAPACITY THROUGH THE YEARS

1913:	5,000	1962:	53,300
1924:	18,000	1967:	58,121
1925:	30,000	1986:	46,000
1947:	40,000	2003:	55,000
1958:	44,105		

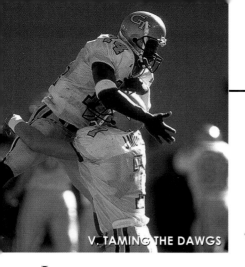
V. TAMING THE DAWGS

X MAGIC MOMENTS

in the history of Bobby Dodd Stadium

I. BEAR HUNTING, *November 17, 1962.* Alabama comes to Atlanta ranked first and riding a 26-game unbeaten streak, but the Yellow Jackets make Mike McNames' second-quarter touchdown stand up in a 7-6 win. Don Toner's end-zone interception of a Joe Namath pass with 1:05 clinches the win.

II. TWO STRAIGHT HEARTSTOPPERS, *September 19, 1991.* One year after beating top-ranked Virginia in Charlottesville on the game's last play, Scott Sisson does it again when he boots a 33-yard field goal as time runs out to give Tech a 24-21 win.

III. PASS-FREE OVER ND, *November 6, 1976.* Unranked Georgia Tech's wishbone rushing attack does all the work in a 23-14 win over 11th-ranked Notre Dame, in which Jackets QB Gary Lanier doesn't throw a pass. David Sims rushes for 122 yards, and Eddie Lee Ivery adds 81.

IV. STREAKBUSTERS, *September 29, 1984.* Georgia Tech leads 21-0 at halftime, but Clemson ties the game with 10 minutes left. The Jackets get a 1-yard touchdown run from Chuck Easley with 33 seconds left and defeat No. 12 Clemson, 28-21. The victory ends the Tigers' 20-game ACC winning streak.

V. TAMING THE DAWGS, *November 27, 1999.* Tech surrenders a 41-24 lead to Georgia, but **Joe Hamilton** completes a touchdown pass to Will Glover that ties the game at 48 in the closing minutes. The game goes to overtime when Georgia fum-

bles on its last possession in regulation, and Tech's Luke Manget drills a 38-yard field goal in overtime to give the Wreck a wild 51-48 triumph.

VI. DENYING AUBURN, *September 6, 2003.* Some had considered Auburn the favorite to win the 2003 national crown, but the Tigers lost their opener to Southern California and came to Atlanta hoping to rebound. But 19th-ranked Tech allowed the No. 17 Tigers just 230 yards of offense in a 17-3 win.

VII. DEFENSE DOESN'T REST, *November 5, 1960.* The Yellow Jackets don't put on an offensive show, but their defense holds eighth-ranked Tennessee to 58 yards in the last three quarters and just 139 for the game in a 14-7 upset.

VIII. FINALLY, *October 7, 1989.* It had been 16 long, ugly games since Georgia Tech had notched an ACC win.

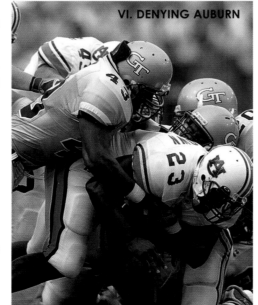
VI. DENYING AUBURN

But the Wreck snapped the streak when Shawn Jones threw four touchdown passes—three of which came in the third quarter—to lead Georgia Tech to a 28-24 win over Maryland.

IX. BLANKING THE BULLDOGS, *November 29, 1969.* Bubba Hoats picks off three Georgia passes, and Jeff Ford intercepts a Bulldog pass in the end zone with 6 minutes remaining to preserve a 6-0 win over the bowl-bound Bulldogs.

X. EFFICIENT WIN, *October 8, 1966.* Tennessee outgains the Jackets, 244-127, but ninth-ranked Tech earns a 6-3 win over the No. 8 Volunteers. W.J. Blane intercepts two passes, including one deep in Tech territory in the last 2 minutes to preserve the win.

SIMPLY UNFORGETTABLE

1990. When North Carolina State came to Atlanta to open the '90 campaign, the Yellow Jackets weren't ranked, much less a part of national championship discussions. In fact, it took three wins before Tech made it into the top 25—when they debuted 23rd after a win over South Carolina. From there, they climbed slowly in the rankings until November 3, when the No. 16 Wreck—its record stained only by a tie with unranked North Carolina—visited top-ranked Virginia for what was supposed to be the Cavaliers' biggest test of the year. It turned out to be much more.

In what some consider the top game in ACC history, Georgia Tech overcame a 28-14 halftime deficit and waged a wild fourth-quarter battle with Virginia that ended on Scott Sisson's 37-yard field goal with 7 seconds left. With the win, the Jackets moved up to No. 7 in the polls. One week later, Sisson was called upon again, this time against Virginia Tech. The Jackets' offense sputtered, so Sisson drilled a pair of field goals in the final 5 minutes, the last coming from 38 yards with 8 seconds left to give Tech a 6-3 win. Subsequent triumphs over Wake Forest and Georgia gave the Wreck a bid to the Florida Citrus Bowl, against Nebraska.

Though some wondered whether the Jackets were worthy contenders for the national crown, they proved everybody wrong by ripping through the Cornhuskers, who were favored despite being ranked 19th in the AP poll. William Bell had three touchdowns, and quarterback Shawn Jones accounted for 318 yards of offense in a resounding 45-21 win. The next day, the Jackets jumped from second in the UPI poll to the top spot, ahead of Colorado, which had narrowly defeated Notre Dame, 10-9, in the Orange Bowl. Colorado remained first in the AP poll. For Georgia Tech, it was a perfect ending to a near-perfect season and the high point of a football history with plenty of highlights.

HARVARD STADIUM

It's as if you've been transported back in time when you walk into this place. Heck, you almost expect the players to run out in leather helmets. The facility is shaped like a horseshoe and features elements of a Greek stadium and

a Roman circus. And there isn't a bad seat in the house for a structure that celebrated its centennial in 2003. Space is at a premium around the stadium, which actually is located in Allston, not Cambridge. The stadium is just across a bridge (over the Charles River) that leads to Cambridge. Simply put, this is college football in its purest form.

SETTING The backdrop is among the best in college football, with the stadium located adjacent to the Charles River and the skyline of Boston looming in the background. There's a throwback environment, complete with cheerleaders doing pushups after touchdowns. After wins, the team gathers to sing the school fight song, "10,000 Men of Harvard." And get this—they do it in English and Latin. Hey, this is Harvard. The songs are followed by a count of how many points the team scored that day, with the coach leading the way.

STRUCTURE The stadium is noted for the exterior arches that are stacked on top of each other. Inside, classic columns ring the upper region in what was the world's first massive reinforced concrete structure and first large permanent arena for American college sports. Here's more history: The fact fans sit close to the action helped change football. There was a movement in the early 20th century to overhaul what had become a violent game. One idea was to widen playing

fields 40 feet. But that would have been too costly for Harvard. Rather, it was agreed that the forward pass would be implemented in college football, which came about in 1906.

FANS Most fans have some connection to the college. They went to school here or know someone who did. Still, a large number of alums no longer live in the Northeast, so there's a huge following nationally. When it comes to tailgating, this isn't a hot dog and hamburger crowd. You'll find some of that, yes, but you'll also find banquet-style tables decked with linen tablecloths. Before and after games, many fans eat and drink at nearby Harvard Square.

MAJOR RENOVATIONS Steel stands in the north end zone were removed in the early 1950s. Prior to the 1982 season, Harvard Stadium underwent an $8 million overhaul that included concrete seating and new steel supports, among other things. In 1998, the field was re-centered, which enhanced the view for spectators seated in the horseshoe end and accommodated construction of the Murr Center athletic facility at the other end.

MILESTONE MOMENTS
• The firt game was played November 14, 1903, when Dartmouth topped the Crimson, 11-0.
• On November 22, 1919, Harvard nipped Yale, 10-3, to earn a trip to the Rose

HARVARD

Bowl, where the Crimson defeated Oregon, 7-6, to finish 9-0-1.

• The U.S. track and field trials for the 1916 and 1920 Olympics were held in Harvard Stadium, which also played host to Olympic Games soccer quarterfinals in 1984.

FAST FACTS

• The then-Boston Patriots played their 1962 home opener at Harvard Stadium and upset the Houston Oilers.

• The Little Red Flag is brought out for the Harvard-Yale game. It's in the possession of the person judged to be the university's greatest fan. Each year, the Harvard Varsity Club selects the best fan, and that person waves the flag whenever Harvard scores.

• Before moving into Harvard Stadium, the Crimson played games at a dilapidated wooden structure that sat on Soldiers Field. (The stadium was built on the same site.)

• Soon after it opened, the stadium served as home of Harvard's ice hockey team for three seasons —and the Crimson skaters never lost a game there.

CAPACITY THROUGH THE YEARS

1903: 40,000   1953: 30,323
1929: 57,750

X MAGIC MOMENTS
in the history of Harvard Stadium

SIMPLY UNFORGETTABLE

November 23, 1968. The headline in the *Harvard Crimson* the next day said it all: "Harvard Beats Yale, 29-29."

Yale was an undefeated and untied team that featured stalwarts Calvin Hill and Brian Dowling. Each was an Eli legend, but both would go on to greater renown after leaving New Haven. Hill became a Pro Bowl running back for the Dallas Cowboys; Dowling became the impetus for Garry Trudeau's famous "B.D." character in the comic strip "Doonesbury."

Harvard, like Yale, was 8-0 entering the regular-season finale. Still, the Crimson figured to come up short on this day. And, for three-plus quarters, it struggled. Yale took a commanding 29-13 lead and looked ready to celebrate an Ivy title on Harvard's turf, a great way to end a season.

But the Crimson had Frank Champi working under center, and he was dangerous. Champi had struggled throughout his career at Harvard, adjusting slowly to campus life and finding only sporadic work on the gridiron. But Champi could throw. With 42 seconds remaining in the game, he hit Bruce Freeman with a 15-yard TD pass, and Gus Crim ran in the two-point conversion, making it 29-21. It was closer, but Harvard still needed a miracle. It got one when the Crimson recovered the ensuing onside kick.

Champi went to work. He ran 14 yards to the Yale 35. A facemask penalty added 15 more yards. First and 10 from the 20. After two incomplete passes, Champi sent Crim up the middle to the Yale 6. First down, with 14 seconds to go. After Champi was thrown for a 2-yard loss, Harvard had just 4 seconds left. Champi dropped back and was flushed from the pocket. Just as the Bulldogs were about to get him, he spotted Vic Gatto alone in the end zone. Touchdown. With no time remaining, 6-4 receiver **Pete Varney** (No. 80, top) outjumped a Yale defender for the two-point conversion. Harvard 29, Yale 29. Bedlam. History. Legend.

I. **SPOILING FOR A TITLE**, *November 23, 1974.* Quarterback Milt Holt leads the Crimson to a come-from-behind 21-16 victory over Yale, ruining the Bulldogs' bid for a perfect season and earning Harvard a share of the Ivy League championship. Holt scores the winning touchdown with 15 seconds to play.

II. **THE CATCH**, *November 10, 2001.* Defending Ivy champion Pennsylvania bolts to a 14-point lead, but Harvard comes back to win, 28-21, thanks in large part to a spectacular 62-yard catch and run by **Carl Morris**. The victory comes in the next-to-last game of the Crimson's first perfect season in 88 years.

III. **PASADENA BOUND**, *November 22, 1919.* Harvard advances to its first and only Rose Bowl by whipping Yale, 10-3, to complete an 8-0-1 regular season that features seven shutouts. The Crimson edges Oregon, 7-6, in Pasadena to capture the last of its seven national titles.

IV. **THUMPING THORPE**, *November 7, 1908.* Jim Thorpe and Pop Warner's mighty Carlisle team pay Harvard a visit, but the undefeated Crimson shut down the legendary back and roll to a 17-0 triumph.

V. **BRICK(LEY) HOUSE**, *November 22, 1913.* Charlie Brickley kicks five field goals to lead Harvard to a 15-5 win over Yale. The win caps a 9-0 season for the Crimson, its last undefeated,

untied campaign until 2001, and secures the national championship.

VI. **THE PRAYING COLONELS**, *October 29, 1921.* Tiny Centre College of Danville, Ky., springs what was considered the greatest college football upset of the first 50 years of the 20th century. Bo McMillin's second-half run accounts for all the scoring in a 6-0 win over Harvard, which entered the game with a 25-game unbeaten streak.

VII. **FIVE TO SCORE**, *November 17, 1951.* Harvard gets five touchdowns from Tom Ossman in a 34-21 win over Brown.

VIII. **STREAK STARTERS**, *November 18, 1911.* A 5-3 win over Dartmouth begins a 33-game unbeaten streak that isn't ended until 1915 by Cornell.

IX. **HAPPY RETURNS**, *November 20, 2004.* Ricky Williamson returns an interception 100 yards for a score and Brian Edwards takes a punt 53 yards for a touchdown in Harvard's 35-3 romp over Yale. The triumph completes a 10-0 campaign for the Crimson—its second perfect season in four years.

X. **(FAR) EASTERN CHAMPIONS**, *June 22, 1991.* Harvard Stadium plays host to the first Japanese collegiate football game played on American soil. Keio University, coached by Crimson staffers, defeats Yale-directed Waseda University, 21-19.

II. THE CATCH

SATURDAY SHRINES

MEMORIAL STADIUM

ILLINOIS

Cars whiz by cornfields and past towns called Decatur, Mattoon, Kankakee and Galesburg, trunks packed with coolers and grills on their way to worship Illinois football in Champaign. And why not? History oozes from the red bricks of Memorial Stadium.

Illinois has four national titles to its credit: 1914, 1919, 1923 and 1927, with Memorial Stadium serving as home of the Fighting Illini for the last two. In fact, the facility opened during the 1923 title run. But the championships alone haven't made this venue special. It's the players who have stood out—the likes of Red Grange, Dick Butkus, George Halas and Jim Grabowski. If you close your eyes, you can see them prowling the hallowed turf at this Midwestern shrine.

SETTING Yes, this is the Prairie State. Yet there is a charm about it. Memorial Stadium is located in one of America's classic college towns, and things are even better inside the facility. One notable moment is when Chief Illiniwek performs an authentic dance, although the Chief's appearance has sparked protests by Native American groups. Also, fans sing the "Three-in-One," a medley of fight songs. Adding to the tradition is the pregame Illini Walk. Players mosey along Irwin Drive just north of the stadium on their way to the game.

STRUCTURE Memorial Stadium is an American gem. About 70 percent of the seats are between the end zones. The double-deck behemoth is dedicated to the Illinois men and women who gave their lives in World War I. Their names appear on the 200 columns that support the east and west sides of the stadium. In 1994, the 70th anniversary of the stadium's dedication, Grange's widow returned to help dedicate Grange Rock at the north end of the field, which is named for legendary Illini coach Bob Zuppke.

FANS The tailgating starts early, with myriad tents set up along Kirby Avenue and First Street. And two hours before games, there's a Street Fest located at the north end of Lot A along Kirby Avenue between Oak and First streets. There's live music, food and games. To keep the

ILLINOIS

spirit high during games, fans from one section will shout: "I-L-L!" and another section will answer "I-N-I!" Adding to the color is the Block I, a group of orange-clad students who pump up the crowd with cheers and perform card stunts.

MAJOR RENOVATIONS Memorial Stadium's appearance has changed little over the years. Upgrades have included the installation of aluminum bleachers in 1972 and a new color matrix scoreboard in 1994. In 1985, an air-tight vacuum dome that covered the field was installed. Locals called it the "Bubble," which allowed Illinois to practice in bad weather. Today, the Illini use the Irwin Indoor Practice

Facility when Mother Nature doesn't cooperate.

MILESTONE MOMENTS
• Memorial Stadium opened on November 3, 1923, when the Illini beat Chicago, 7-0, in a Homecoming game. The stadium was dedicated on October 18, 1924, in one of college football's most famous games as Grange accounted for six touchdowns in a 39-14 triumph over Michigan.
• Artificial turf was installed in 1974 and there has been no grass since. Lights also were added that year.

FAST FACTS
• Illinois is the birthplace of Homecoming. The first

was held in October 1910.
• In the 1980s, Illinois sold out 27 consecutive games.
• Vandals burned a 40-yard section of the artificial turf in the early-morning hours of September 24, 1989. The field was repaired in time for a game against Ohio State on October 7.
• The first Farm Aid was held in Memorial Stadium in 1985.

CAPACITY THROUGH THE YEARS

1923: 69,249

X MAGIC MOMENTS

in the history of Memorial Stadium

SIMPLY UNFORGETTABLE

October 18, 1924. Memorial Stadium was less than a year old when Michigan invaded for the structure's dedication, but the performance staged by Red Grange that day topped anything that happened after it.

In 1923, the Fighting Illini and the Wolverines were undefeated scourges of the Big Ten, but the teams didn't play each other. Grange was a consensus All-American—well, with one exception. *The Michigan Daily* chose him second team. And Wolverines coach Fielding "Hurry Up" Yost predicted trouble for the Illinois star when the two teams met in '24.

"Mister Grange will be carefully watched," Yost said. "Every time he takes the ball, there will be 11 hard, clean Michigan tacklers headed for him at the same time. I know he is a great runner. But great runners have the hardest time gaining ground when met by special preparation."

That they do. But Grange was no ordinary runner, and it took him about 15 seconds to prove that to Michigan. Taking the opening kickoff on his 5, Grange blasted straight up the center and cut hard right to avoid a collection of Wolverines. He stopped in the Michigan end zone, untouched. On Illinois' next possession, Grange went 67 yards around left end to score—again untouched. His third touchdown was a 56-yard bolt the next time the Illini had the ball, and he finished his opening salvo by dashing 44 yards for a score. In 12 minutes of action, Grange had amassed 265 yards of offense on six touches. In the third quarter, Grange ran 13 yards for his fifth and final score. In the fourth quarter, he passed for a TD.

Illinois had a 39-14 win, and Yost had learned about the legend of Red Grange. Not everyone was impressed. *The Michigan Daily* grumped, "All Red Grange can do is run." To that, Illinois coach Bob Zuppke said, "And all (opera sensation) Galli-Curci can do is sing."

I. NO. 1 NO MORE, *November 18, 1950.* Ohio State enters the game ranked No. 1 in the nation but falls, 14-7, to Illinois to set up a four-way final sprint for the Big Ten title. The race is decided when Michigan subdues the Buckeyes in the snow the following weekend and the Illini are upset by Northwestern.

II. ROSES, AT LAST, *November 16, 1946.* The ninth-rated Illini earn a 16-7 decision over 13th-ranked Ohio State to set the stage for Illinois' first trip to the Rose Bowl. Star running backs Julius Rykovich and Buddy Young lead the Fighting Illini charge.

III. THANKSGIVING FEAST, *November 22, 2001.* Quarterback Kurt Kittner throws four touchdown passes, leading the Illini to a thrilling 34-28 win over Northwestern. Due to an agreement with the BCS that sends the "national championship" game to the Rose Bowl, Illinois' league title is worth a berth in the Sugar Bowl and the school's first postseason trip to New Orleans.

IV. TURNING MICHIGAN BLUE, *October 29, 1983.* Sophomore Jack Trudeau's two TD passes lead Illinois to a 16-6 victory over eighth-ranked Michigan, setting up the Illini's return to the Rose Bowl. Two weeks earlier, Illinois had upset sixth-ranked Ohio State in Champaign.

V. RED LEAVES HOME, *November 14, 1925.* **Red Grange** bids farewell to the Illini faithful in a 21-0 victory over Wabash. He plays his final game for Illinois the following week, at Ohio State, and then heads out on a professional barnstorming tour that nets him $100,000 in three months.

V. RED LEAVES HOME

VI. COOL CUSTOMERS, *November 3, 1951.* A freak blizzard hits Champaign and grinds the Michigan and Illinois attacks to a halt, until Tommy O'Connell hits Rex Smith with a late-fourth-quarter TD pass to give Illinois a 7-0 triumph and a big step on the road to its second Rose Bowl appearance.

VII. PLENTY OF ROAR IN THE LIONS, *November 12, 1994.* Penn State enters the game undefeated and falls behind 21-0 in the first quarter. Though the Illini counter a PSU charge and still lead 28-14 at halftime, they can't hold back the Lions on a last-ditch, 96-yard TD drive. With 57 seconds left in the game, Brian Milne's TD run gives Penn State a remarkable 35-31 win.

VIII. THE FIRST, *November 3, 1923.* A teeming crowd of 60,632 shows up for the first game at Memorial Stadium, so named to honor the Illinois residents who gave their lives in World War I. The assembled go home happy after the Illini earn a 7-0 win over Chicago en route to an 8-0 mark.

IX. UPSET CITY, *October 27, 1956.* After climbing to 13th in the national rankings, Illinois loses three straight before a visit from top-ranked Michigan State, which is fresh off a 47-14 thumping of Notre Dame. The 1-3 Illini spring a 20-13 surprise on the Spartans, but they don't win again in '56.

X. MAIZE BLUES, *November 5, 1955.* Despite having lost two in a row and three of four, Illinois handles third-ranked Michigan, 25-6. The mighty Wolverines had entered the game 6-0 and had held four opponents to seven or fewer points.

SATURDAY SHRINES

IOWA

KINNICK STADIUM

Kinnick Stadium sits as a beacon to Hawkeye fans across the state, a symbol of pride for Iowa football, the No. 1 sport in the state. Few states are as passionate about their teams, a fact that is accentuated by lack of big-time pro sports in this slice of heaven in the heartland.

How rabid are Hawkeye fans? They show up for even the bad teams, a fact that amazed former coach Hayden Fry when he took the job in 1979. Fry soon turned Kinnick Stadium into one of the most intimidating environs in the nation, filling the Hawkeye Nation with even more pride.

SETTING If you're looking for a postcard setting, you'll be disappointed. Still, this is a place that is beautiful for its trademark Midwestern friendliness and simplicity. In and around Kinnick, you can see for miles once the leaves have dropped from the trees. Across from the stadium is an expansive medical complex, and guarding one corner of the stadium is a looming water tower that instantly identifies Kinnick. Adding to the charm is the nearby Iowa River. The players' entrance and exit from the field is one of the most compelling in the nation, as they hold hands and trot in what is known as the Swarm.

STRUCTURE If you like red brick, you'll love Kinnick Stadium, which celebrated its 75th anniversary in 2004. It's a single-level facility that is built 30 feet into the hills that once were part of a golf course. Kinnick is perhaps best known for the fans' proximity to the action, which makes it one of the most hostile environ-

ments in college football. Legendary Minnesota coach Bernie Bierman even used to complain about fans shouting obscenities and throwing whiskey bottles at him. However, Kinnick Stadium almost never came to be. Soon after the October 19 stadium dedication, the stock market crashed. If the stadium hadn't been completed at that time, its construction might have been abandoned.

FANS It's a sea of black and gold on Saturdays, with mascot Herky working the crowd. The tailgating is legendary, though there isn't a lot of room for RVs. Still, Hawkeyes fans manage to make do, with Iowa flags flying high and everything from pork steaks to brats to chicken sizzling on grills. And you start smelling it all around 7 a.m. After wins, the band plays "In Heaven There Is No Beer, So That's Why We Drink It Here."

IOWA

MAJOR RENOVATIONS There have been several modifications over the years. But perhaps the most radical changes are taking place now, as Kinnick Stadium is close to finishing a multimillion-dollar renovation. The south end zone was enclosed after the 2004 season. After the 2005 campaign, plans call for a new press box and premium seating, among other things.

MILESTONE MOMENTS

• In the inaugural game on October 5, 1929, Iowa topped Monmouth, 46-0. Two weeks later, the Hawkeyes tied Illinois, 7-7, in the dedication game.
• Artificial turf was installed in 1972 but was ripped out prior to the 1989 season in favor of grass.
• Iowa is in the midst of a school-record 18-game home winning streak, and the current 13-game home Big Ten winning mark also is a school standard.

FAST FACTS

• The stadium's name was switched from Iowa Stadium to Kinnick Stadium in 1972 in honor of the Hawkeyes' 1939 Heisman winner, Nile Kinnick, a Navy pilot who was killed during a training mission when he crashed into the Caribbean Sea in 1943.
• The visitors' locker room is painted pink in an effort get opponents out of an aggressive mind-set.
• Kinnick Stadium is one of the 20 largest college-owned stadiums in the nation.

CAPACITY THROUGH THE YEARS

1950:	53,000
1956:	60,000
1983:	66,000
1990:	70,397

X MAGIC MOMENTS

in the history of Kinnick Stadium

SIMPLY UNFORGETTABLE

Nile Kinnick. By the time Kinnick finished his Heisman Trophy acceptance speech in 1939, those assembled didn't know whether to applaud or vote for him. The Iowa back delivered a poised and eloquent speech that thanked his teammates and coaches and then directed his attention to the burgeoning war. "I thank God I was warring on the gridirons of the Midwest and not on the battlefields of Europe," he said.

A little more than two years later, Kinnick was flying naval aircraft. In 1943, while returning to a carrier after a training mission, Kinnick's plane failed and he plunged into the Caribbean Sea. The Iowa Ironman was gone. It was a great loss for the Iowa community and for football.

From the minute the 1939 season began, Kinnick was marvelous. A great runner, he scored three times in the opener against South Dakota. Then, from the beginning of the Hawkeyes' second game, against Indiana, until he separated his shoulder against Northwestern in the finale, Kinnick didn't come off the field. He played 402 consecutive minutes, a big reason the Hawkeyes went 6-1-1, a dramatic reversal from the previous year's 1-6-1 mark.

Kinnick accounted for 1,012 yards of offense in '39, throwing 11 TD passes and averaging 39.9 yards per punt. He won handily over Michigan's Tom Harmon in the Heisman race, and though he was selected in the second round of the NFL draft by the Brooklyn Dodgers, he chose law school over pro football.

I. MAGIC FOOT, *October 19, 1985.* Top-ranked Iowa gets a 29-yard field goal from Rob Houghtlin with 2 seconds remaining to upend No. 2 Michigan, 12-10, en route to its second Rose Bowl appearance in five years. The Houghtlin kick culminates a last-minute drive that includes a harrowing near-interception.

II. ONE-MAN GANG, *November 11, 1939.* Nile Kinnick averages 46 yards on 16 punts, scores the winning touchdown in the second quarter and adds the extra point to give Iowa a 7-6 win over third-ranked Notre Dame.

III. FIRST ROSES, *November 17, 1956.* Two weeks after absorbing a tough 17-14 Homecoming loss to Michigan, the seventh-ranked Hawkeyes stop Ohio State, 6-0, to clinch their first trip to the Rose Bowl. Ken Ploen's third-quarter touchdown pass decides the game.

IV. BREAKING THE STRING, *November 21, 1981.* Iowa wallops Michigan State, 36-7, to tie for the Big Ten title and become the first team other than Michigan or Ohio State to represent the conference in the Rose Bowl since Indiana's 1967 champions went to Pasadena. The Hawkeyes' Phil Blatcher runs for 247 yards.

V. BIG COMEBACK, *October 4, 2003.* After spotting Michigan a 14-0 advantage, the Hawkeyes storm back behind the fleet feet of running back Fred Russell (110 yards) and a career passing day from Nathan Chandler (17-of-34, 195 yards, two TDs) to deal the Wolverines a 30-27 defeat.

VI. ROAD WARRIORS, *November 17, 1990.* Having beaten Michigan, Michigan State and Illinois on the road, Iowa dumps Purdue, 38-9, in Iowa City on the way to winning a trip to Pasadena.

VII. CRAZY LEGS PODOLAK, *November 9, 1968.* Running back Ed Podolak rushes for 286 yards on just 17 carries to key a 68-34 shellacking of Northwestern and give the Hawkeyes their largest point total in 11 years.

VIII. DOUBLE FIGURES, *November 23, 1991.* The Hawkeyes tear through Minnesota for a 23-8 win, which gives them 10 regular-season victories for only the second time in school history. It also brings the coveted "Floyd of Rosedale" trophy back to Iowa City after a two-year hiatus.

IX. DOUBLE THE FUN, *November 4, 2000.* Playing the first overtime game in Iowa history, the Hawkeyes take Penn State to two extra periods before winning, 26-23. It's the biggest win since Kirk Ferentz took over as coach the previous season and helps set the stage for a winning year in '01.

X. ORANGE BOUND, *November 9, 2002.* The Hawkeyes obliterate Northwestern, 62-10, for their eighth win in a row and penultimate step in an 11-1 regular season that produces a berth in the Orange Bowl.

LEGION FIELD

A sign inside venerable Legion Field says: "Birmingham Football Capital of the South." Indeed, Legion Field has played host to scores of big games, making it one of the most historic stadiums in the nation.

From 1948-88, the Iron Bowl game between Alabama and Auburn was played exclusively at Legion Field. Legion was the Tide's home away from home for years, as Bama played several games there each season. In fact, this is the place where Paul "Bear" Bryant became college football's all-time winningest coach in 1981 when the Crimson Tide defeated Auburn. And the Tide program was changed forever during a season-opening 42-21 loss in 1970 to an integrated USC team led by running back Sam Cunningham. In the aftermath of the defeat, Bryant realized it was time to begin recruiting African-American players.

SETTING Located just west of downtown Birmingham, Legion Field sits in a largely residential area that has fallen on hard times in recent years. But the area could come to life on game days, particularly when Alabama and Auburn played. It was half orange and blue (Auburn) and half crimson and white (Alabama) for the Iron Bowl. You could see the division of fans at the middle of the goalposts. Outside the south end zone on Graymont Avenue is a bar called the Tide & Tiger, which was a destination for many and a jumping joint during the Iron Bowl.

STRUCTURE The facility has fallen into disrepair. But in its day, Legion Field was a noted structure that featured

brick painted green and white. For many years, it was the only stadium in the state big enough to hold a major game. Two spiral walkways on the west side of the stadium are Legion signatures. The facility is shaped like a bowl with one upper deck. However, that 9,000-seat deck on the east side was deemed unsafe due to structural problems, prompting Alabama to abandon the stadium.

FANS UAB calls Legion Field home, but this isn't a rabid fan base for what's still a fledgling program. But Legion rocked when the Iron Bowl was taking place. The conversations between Tide and Tigers fans could get lively in the surrounding parking lots, with shouts of "Roll Tide!" and "War Eagle!" echoing back and forth. The tailgating was festive when Alabama rolled into town for a "home" game, as the smoked billowed off grills and filled the air with smells ranging from hamburgers and hot dogs to catfish and ribs. And the fans showed up early and left late—win or lose. There was a game to be analyzed.

MAJOR RENOVATIONS This has been a work in progress, but there have been few massive changes over the years. One of the biggest alterations occurred in 1961, when an upper deck on the east side was added. Later that decade, Legion grew with work on the north end zone.

This is the place where Paul "Bear" Bryant became college football's all-time winningest coach.

MILESTONE MOMENTS

• Legion Field was the site of the first SEC championship game in 1992. Alabama defeated Florida, 28-21, en route to winning the national title.
• The first game was played November 19, 1927. Howard (now Samford) topped Birmingham Southern, 9-0.

FAST FACTS

• Several pro teams have called Legion Field home: the Birmingham Americans and Birmingham Vulcans of the World Football League, the Birmingham Stallions of the USFL, the Birmingham Barracudas of the CFL, the Birmingham Fire of the World League of American Football and the Birmingham Bolts of the XFL. Legion Field also was home to two postseason college games, the Dixie Bowl and the Hall of Fame Bowl.
• The stadium was named in honor of the American Legion and is a tribute to those who died while serving America.
• In 1972, Billy Graham held a crusade at Legion Field, sharing the dais for one ceremony with Bryant, Joe Namath and Tom Landry, among others.

A late TD by freshman Bo Jackson (34) ended Auburn's frustration against Alabama in 1982. Tide coach Gene Stallings (below) savored a 24-23 win in 1996, his last Iron Bowl.

CAPACITY THROUGH THE YEARS

1927:	25,000	1964:	70,000
1948:	43,000	1978:	76,000
1961:	60,000	1991:	80,500

X MAGIC MOMENTS

in the history of Legion Field

SIMPLY UNFORGETTABLE

December 2, 1972. If you find some Auburn fans who are old enough, they might still have the bumper sticker. It read: "Punt, Bama, Punt," and it became the war cry for Tiger fans for years. The Crimson Tide exacted revenge for the improbable, once-in-a-lifetime Auburn triumph the next season, but "Punt, Bama, Punt" still stings and remains a big part of the Legion Field lore.

Both teams entered the 1972 Iron Bowl in the top 10. Alabama was 10-0 and ranked second behind Nebraska, and the No. 9 Tigers were 9-1, the only blemish coming in a loss at LSU. The usual crowd of zealots filled Legion Field for a classic Iron Bowl showdown.

In the fourth quarter, Alabama had a 16-0 lead and had been so dominant that few could imagine a scenario in which Auburn would win. And nobody really cared that Roger Mitchell had swatted away the Tide's first extra-point attempt. Touchdowns by Wilbur Jackson and Steve Bisceglia and a Bill Davis field goal had given the Tide its overwhelming advantage. The only thing Auburn could muster was a Gardner Jett field goal early in the fourth quarter.

Then came the lightning. Midway through the fourth quarter, Bill Newton blocked an Alabama punt, and David Langner picked up the loose ball. He dashed untouched into the end zone. Jett's kick made it 16-10 with 5:40 remaining. Still, Tide fans weren't too worried. Then Auburn kicked deep, and Alabama was unable to move up the field. So on fourth down, from its own 42, the Tide punted again. And Newton blocked it again. And Langner returned it for a touchdown again. And Jett added the extra point again. Two blocked punts. Two touchdowns. Two extra points. Auburn 17, Alabama 16. Langner intercepted a Tide pass in the final seconds to secure the improbable win.

I. THE KICK, *November 30, 1985.* Van Tiffin's 52-yard field goal in the final seconds gives unranked Alabama a 25-23 win over No. 7 Auburn in one of the wildest games in the schools' histories. Reggie Ware's 1-yard touchdown run with 57 seconds left pulls the Tigers ahead, 23-22, but Auburn misses the 2-point conversion, and Alabama drives 45 yards to set up Tiffin's kick.

II. WELCOME BACK, *December 4, 1948.* After a "41-year timeout," in which the two schools refused to play each other because of a variety of old grudges and arguments, Alabama and Auburn renew the Iron Bowl series at Legion Field. The day is momentous, although the game is a blowout: Alabama 55, Auburn 0.

III. AT LAST, *November 27, 1982.* After losing to Alabama for nine straight years, Auburn finally breaks through with a 23-22 win, when freshman Bo Jackson scores on a fourth-down, 1-yard touchdown run with 2:26 remaining.

IV. THE CALL STANDS, *November 29, 1974.* Officials rule that Auburn receiver Thomas Gossom's second-half touchdown reception was made out of bounds, and second-ranked Alabama goes on to beat No. 7 Auburn, 17-13, by holding off a late Tiger rally. Mike Dubose's fumble recovery

II. WELCOME BACK

finishes off Auburn's last drive. The win gives Alabama its second undefeated regular season and its fourth consecutive SEC championship.

V. SNAKING TO VICTORY, *December 2, 1967.* The field was soggy, and the weather was awful, but that didn't stop Alabama quarterback Ken "Snake" Stabler from scoring on a 47-yard touchdown run down the sideline in the No. 8 Tide's 7-3 win over unranked Auburn.

VI. UPSET, *December 3, 1949.* A 1-4-3 Auburn team enters the game a decided underdog against 6-2-1 Alabama but earns a shocking 14-13 win when Eddie Salem's extra-point attempt after the Tide's last touchdown is no good.

VII. WE'RE NO. 1, *November 30, 1957.* Top-ranked Auburn clinches its first national championship on the back of a great defense. In their final game of the season, the Tigers beat the Crimson Tide, 40-0—one of six Tiger shutouts that season.

VIII. THE SALUTE, *November 30, 1963.* One week after President John F. Kennedy is assassinated, Auburn backup quarterback Mailon Kent's touchdown pass to Tucker Frederickson is the difference in the ninth-ranked Tigers' 10-8 win over No. 6 Alabama. As he is carried off the field, Auburn coach Shug Jordan receives a salute from Bear Bryant.

IX. A TROPHY OF THEIR OWN, *November 27, 1971.* Auburn's Pat Sullivan is crowned the Heisman Trophy winner, but Alabama isn't intimidated. The third-ranked Crimson Tide beat No. 5 Auburn and Sullivan, 31-7.

X. ELITE PROGRAMS FACE OFF, *September 2, 1978.* Nebraska visits Birmingham for a rare showdown with the Crimson Tide, and the No. 10 Huskers are dealt a 20-3 loss by No. 1 Alabama, which goes on to win the national title.

A picture-perfect moment: Saturday night on the Bayou. Local lore has it that LSU plays better in night games—that day games simply don't have that certain magic. There's not much of a difference, really, other than Tiger Stadium is more juiced and seems louder at night.

Plus, more tailgate time means more excitement and anticipation (read: consumption of adult beverages).

SETTING The campus is beautiful, the crowning jewel of Louisiana's capital city. From the moss-draped oaks to the formal gardens and classic Southern architecture, it all rolls into a memorable game day. Adding to the ambience are some of the country's top fight songs, including "Fight for LSU," "Touchdown for LSU" and "Hey, Fightin' Tigers." Before games, mascot Mike the Tiger and his wheeled cage are parked in front of the visitors' locker room, and opponents are forced to pass him. Then, Mike is paraded around the stadium in his cage with the cheerleaders riding on top.

STRUCTURE Few facilities can match the architectural and aesthetic genius of Tiger Stadium, which is a bowl with decks on each side. The stadium recently received a 11,600-seat expansion, complete with an upper deck on the east side that includes luxury suites. The facade on Tiger Stadium looks similar to the Roman Colosseum, complete with myriad archways. It's an imposing structure on fall Saturdays, when the stadium is overtaken by the electricity of game day, the steam of the Bayou and 90,000-plus fans.

FANS There's a reason they call it Death Valley. The fans never let up. Before the game, fans watch the Golden Band from Tigerland march down North Stadium Drive from Broussard Hall while blaring out "Hold That Tiger." And then there's the tailgating, which is legendary. Many fans arrive as early as Thursday, cooking up local favorites that include the likes of shrimp, boudin, muffalettas, fried alligator, jambalaya, pig roast gumbo and crawfish. One of the most chilling moments for fans is when P.A. announcer Dan Borne says "It's Saturday night in Death Valley, and here come your Fighting Tigers of LSU!" as the team runs onto the field.

MAJOR RENOVATIONS There have been more glamorous additions, but none has had as big an impact as the 1953 renovation. It was then that Tiger Stadium's south end was enclosed and nearly 22,000 seats were added, turning the horseshoe into a bowl and giving the facility its "Death Valley" mystique.

MILESTONE MOMENTS
• The first game was November 25, 1924, a 13-0 Homecoming loss to Tulane in the last game of the season.
• The first night game was played on October 3, 1931, as LSU topped Spring Hill, 35-0. T.P. "Skipper" Heard, a graduate manager of athletics and later the school's athletic director, spawned the idea of evening games. The thought was to avoid the heat of the day and to avoid scheduling

LOUISIANA STATE

conflicts with Tulane and Loyola.
• In 1986, the field was moved 11 feet to the south to make room between the back line of the north end zone and the curvature of the fence that surrounds the field.

FAST FACTS
• At one time, Tiger Stadium had 1,500

dorm rooms. It was a way for the school to expand its stadium while filling a need for housing.
• The tradition of wearing white jerseys at home began in 1958, when the school won the national championship. Not wanting to ruin a good thing, the school has maintained the tradition, with some twists over the years.

CAPACITY THROUGH THE YEARS

1924: 12,000	1931: 22,000
1936: 46,000	1953: 67,720
1978: 78,000	1988: 80,150
1994: 80,000	2000: 91,600

X MAGIC MOMENTS

in the history of Tiger Stadium

I. TITLE GAME-BOUND, *December 1, 2001.* An improbable streak of three straight wins has the Tigers back in SEC West contention despite three league losses. LSU whips 25th-ranked Auburn, 27-14, to reach the SEC championship game (and then beats No. 2 Tennessee for the SEC title and No. 7 Illinois in the Sugar Bowl).

II. LAST-SECOND HYSTERIA, *November 4, 1972.* LSU pushes its winning streak to 11 games when Bert Jones hits Brad Davis in the corner of the end zone as time expires against Mississippi, and Rusty Jackson nails the extra point, giving the Tigers a 17-16 come-from-behind victory.

III. THE EARTHQUAKE, *October 8, 1988.* The reaction in Tiger Stadium to Eddie Fuller's touchdown reception from Tommy Hodson is so great that seismologists in the LSU geology department detect vibrations in a seismograph reading at the exact moment of the play. The seismic score is the Tigers' only one in a 7-6 win over Auburn.

IV. ONE IS DONE, *October 11, 1997.* After taking an early lead against No. 1 Florida, LSU holds on while the Gators fight back in the fourth quarter. The Tigers seal the win on Raion Hill's interception with less than 3 minutes left in the game. The 28-21 victory is LSU's first ever over a top-ranked opponent.

V. WHITE-OUT NIGHT, *October 5, 1996.* Vanderbilt refuses to allow LSU to wear its traditional white jerseys, so the Tigers encourage fans to wear white to the game, and

IV. ONE IS DONE

LSU takes the field wearing gold jerseys. LSU wins the psychological game and the football contest, 35-0.

VI. ON TOP, *October 25, 1958.* LSU sneaks past Florida, 10-7, on Homecoming to ascend to the top of the AP rankings for the first time in school history. It's a designation the Tigers won't surrender en route to their first national title.

VII. TAMIN' THE 'DAWGS, *September 20, 2003.* Matt Mauck hits Skyler Green with a 34-yard touchdown pass with just 1:22 to play, breaking a 10-10 tie and giving the Tigers a 17-10 triumph over Georgia, which botches several chances to take a big lead.

VIII. LIGHTS ON, *October 3, 1931.* Interested in avoiding the suffocating heat endemic to Baton Rouge and hoping to increase attendance, LSU plays its first night game. The game is a success, as the Tigers draw a big crowd to watch a 35-0 dismantling of Spring Hill.

IX. LIGHTS OUT, *September 3, 1988.* LSU stuffs No. 10 Texas A&M four times from the 5-yard line in a 27-0 win. While the Tigers are repelling the Aggies, a bank of lights in the end zone goes out, leading to the unit's "lights-out defense" designation.

X. LOUD IN DEFEAT, *September 29, 1979.* Top-ranked USC comes to Baton Rouge and escapes with a 17-12 win, but those in attendance swear that Tiger Stadium is the loudest it has ever been.

SIMPLY UNFORGETTABLE

October 31, 1959. In the span of just a few seconds, **Billy Cannon** went from All-American to LSU legend. From star player to Heisman Trophy winner.

It was Halloween night, and while much of the nation was trick-or-treating, the top-ranked LSU Tigers were locked in a struggle with No. 3 Mississippi. A crowd of more than 67,000 had crammed its way into Tiger Stadium, hoping to see LSU extend its winning streak to 19 games. But the Rebels had locked up LSU all night and held on to a 3-0 lead late in the game.

If Cannon had listened to his coach, Paul Dietzel, what happened next wouldn't have occurred. Dietzel had a hard-and-fast rule: Nobody fields a punt inside the Tigers' 15. But Cannon took the Rebel punt at the LSU 11 and started upfield. He bounced off seven Ole Miss tacklers on the way to an 89-yard touchdown run that gave the Tigers a 7-3 victory. It was the ultimate highlight in a career filled with them.

Cannon becomes a legend.

"Billy isn't the kind who scores five touchdowns against Podunk U," a teammate said of Cannon. "He's the kind who runs 89 yards in the last quarter to beat Mississippi."

The play sealed Cannon's bid for the 1959 Heisman Trophy and his fate as an LSU legend.

SATURDAY SHRINES

MIAMI

It's cramped, lacks amenities and isn't in the greatest part of town—but who cares? This is the Orange Bowl. We're talking about classic bowl games (Nebraska-Miami in 1984), super Super Bowls (III with Joe Namath's guarantee, and

Steelers-over-Cowboys triumphs in X and XIII) and great teams (1972 Dolphins and five Miami Hurricanes national champs). Add it all up, and this arguably is the most famous football venue in the nation.

SETTING The area around the Orange Bowl gets a bad rap. Little Havana is rough around the edges, but it offers fans a chance to experience the great Cuban heritage and cuisine in the neighborhoods surrounding the stadium. Parking is tight, but the locals are willing to help fans find spots—for the right price. Any trip to the Orange Bowl can be enhanced with a trip to Eighth Street (Calle Ocho) for Cuban cuisine. The establishments don't always looks great, but the food and service are. However, the Orange Bowl tailgating experience isn't on par with those at most Midwestern and Southern venues.

STRUCTURE Unlike a lot of stadiums, the Orange Bowl has terrific sight lines. Every seat is angled toward the center of the field, and the stadium was built for football. Plus, fans sit close to the field. From the outside, the stadium doesn't appear to be a fancy place. The exterior is exposed, revealing the support system for the stadium. At the west end is the famous Orange Bowl sign. The east end is open, allowing fans to take in a view of

downtown Miami and the Atlantic Ocean. From the facade of the upper deck, a sign shouts: The City of Miami Welcomes You to the Orange Bowl.

FANS At Miami games, you won't find the typical college fans. In fact, Hurricane followers are cut more from the pro mold, which is why they aren't afraid to occasionally boo the players. Also, because this is a relatively small school, many who attend games at the Orange Bowl aren't students or alumni. And students who do attend games must make the nearly eight-mile trek from campus. But once at the Orange Bowl, fans are treated to one of the best traditions in college football: Miami's smoky entrance. Many teams mimic it, but this is the place that mastered it. Players surge onto the field from the southwest corner of the stadium through a swirl of smoke, a Miami tradition that is more than 50 years old.

MAJOR RENOVATIONS The Orange Bowl has been cobbled together over the years. The biggest change occurred in 1947, when the stadium increased in capacity by more than 24,000 seats. Another major development occurred between 1950 and 1955, when the Orange Bowl added a second deck on each side.

MILESTONE MOMENTS
• From 1985-94, Miami won a national-record 58 home games in a row. The streak lasted through three presidents, two

MIAMI

head coaches and included victories over 17 ranked teams before it ended in a 38-20 loss to Washington.

• On January 1, 1984, Miami beat Nebraska, 31-30, in the Orange Bowl to win its first of five national championships.

• The stadium was dedicated on December 10, 1937, as Georgia beat Miami, 26-0.

FAST FACTS

• The Orange Bowl has played host to five Super Bowls, and 14 national champions have been crowned there.

• The stadium originally was named for one of Miami's pioneers, Roddy Burdine. In 1959, the facility was renamed the Orange Bowl.

• In 1996, the Orange Bowl was the site of Olympic soccer.

CAPACITY THROUGH THE YEARS

Year	Capacity
1937:	23,330
1944:	35,030
1947:	59,578
1950:	64,552
1953:	67,129
1955:	76,286
1977:	75,500
1989:	74,712
1996:	72,319

X MAGIC MOMENTS
in the history of the Orange Bowl

SIMPLY UNFORGETTABLE

January 2, 1984. Nope, Nebraska didn't have to go for two points in the 1984 Orange Bowl, but Cornhuskers coach Tom Osborne wanted to win the national championship without any questions. So he sent quarterback Turner Gill back out to get the one-point lead.

How did it even come to this? Nebraska was the Greatest Team Ever. Everybody knew that. The Huskers had begun the season by trampling Penn State, 44-6, and had rolled past everything else in their path. Even though Miami was rated fifth in the nation and, under coach Howard Schnellenberger, had emerged from years of mediocrity to become a national power, no one considered the Hurricanes a real threat to the Nebraska juggernaut.

Yet, after one quarter, Miami held a stunning 17-0 lead, thanks to a pair of touchdown passes from **Bernie Kosar** (above) to tight end Glenn Dennison. Although the Huskers fought back to tie it at 17 in the third quarter, the Hurricanes scored two more times—on runs by Alonzo Highsmith and Albert Bentley—and entered the final 15 minutes leading 31-17.

All Miami had to do was hold on for one more quarter, which wasn't so easy. Nebraska backup running back Jeff Smith, playing because of an ankle injury to Heisman Trophy-winning tailback Mike Rozier, scored twice; the second time came with just 48 seconds to play, on a fourth-and-8 desperation play from the Nebraska 24. Then came Osborne's decision. He would go for the win.

Gill rolled right and looked for Smith just over the goal line. But Kenny Calhoun deflected the pass, and it glanced off Smith's shoulder pads. Miami had pulled one of the biggest upsets in college football history, 31-30, and would be rewarded with its first national championship.

I. SUPER UPSET, *January 12, 1969.* After brash quarterback Joe Namath predicts victory for his 18-point underdog Jets, New York dominates the "invincible" Baltimore Colts to win Super Bowl III, 16-7, establishing the American Football League as a legitimate competitor of the NFL.

II. HAIL FLUTIE, *November 23, 1984.* With 6 seconds left and Miami ahead, 45-41, Boston College quarterback Doug Flutie's "Hail Mary" pass finds its way into the arms of Gerard Phelan in the end zone, giving BC a 47-45 win in one of the greatest games in college football history.

III. LATER, SOONERS, *January 1, 1988.* Oklahoma enters the Orange Bowl averaging 428.8 rushing yards per game, but the Miami defense stifles the Sooners, limiting them to just 179 yards on the ground as the Hurricanes win their second national title, 20-14.

IV. PAYBACK TIME, *November 25, 1989.* One year after losing a one-point decision at Notre Dame in a raucous, hostile environment, the Hurricanes deal No. 1 Notre Dame a 27-10 defeat. The win moves Miami up to second in the polls and puts it in the Sugar Bowl, where it wins its third national title.

V. HUSKER DON'T, *January 1, 1992.* Miami holds Nebraska's powerful offense to one yard in the first quarter of the Orange Bowl and just 82 yards in the game en route to a 22-0 thumping, which clinches a fourth national title for the Hurricanes.

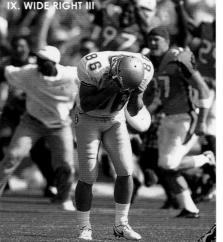

IX. WIDE RIGHT III

Matt Munyon's agony is Miami's ecstasy.

VI. THE BIG ONE, *October 31, 1981.* It was one thing for Miami to whip 19th-ranked Penn State in 1979. Two years later, coach Howard Schnellenberger's team spanks the No. 1 Nittany Lions, 17-14.

VII. WIDE RIGHT II, *October 3, 1992.* One year after Miami defeats Florida State by a field goal in "Wide Right I," Miami fights back from a 16-10 deficit to take a 19-16 lead on Florida State with 1:35 remaining. The Seminoles drive 59 yards to set up a game-tying field goal, but Dan Mowrey's 39-yarder sails right.

VIII. VINNY SMACKS THE BOZ, *September 27, 1986.* Oklahoma brings its heralded linebacker, Brian "The Boz" Bosworth, to Miami, where eventual Heisman winner Vinny Testaverde burns the Sooners with four touchdown passes in a 28-16 win that wasn't even close.

IX. WIDE RIGHT III, *October 7, 2000.* Once again, the Hurricanes fight from behind against Florida State, taking a 27-24 lead with 46 seconds to play on a touchdown pass from Ken Dorsey to tight end Jeremy Shockey. But FSU puts **Matt Munyon** in position to try a 49-yard field goal, which he misses (of course) wide right.

X. SOONERS SOUTH, *January 1, 1956.* After trailing 6-0 after the first half of the Orange Bowl, Oklahoma erupts in the second 30 minutes to win its 30th in a row, claiming a national championship with a 20-6 win over previously undefeated Maryland, which was led by former OU coach Jim Tatum.

MICHIGAN STADIUM

MICHIGAN STADIUM

MICHIGAN	N. DAME
24	0

3 TIME OUTS LEFT   12:30   TIME OUTS LEFT 3

2 DOWN   6 TO GO   BALL ON 24 QTR. 3

	RUSHING	
118	RUSHING	46
166	PASSING	5
284	TOTAL	51

14

1901 1902 1903
1904 1918 1923   HAIL TO THE VICTORS   M

Take a stroll around the place they call the "Big House," but bring your walking shoes. Legendary Wolverines coach and athletic director Fielding Yost wanted the biggest stadium in the land—he actually dreamed of one that seated 150,000.

His wish to be biggest was fulfilled, and a 1998 renovation pushed stadium capacity to its high mark of 107,501.

SETTING Ann Arbor is filled with college charm, especially the quaint downtown area that features myriad restaurants, coffee houses and eclectic shops. But that's just the beginning. Inside the stadium, fans jump to their feet as the players in the famed winged helmets explode onto the field under the "Go Blue" sign, with players jumping like kids to touch it. The pre-kickoff buildup continues with round after round of the band blaring "The Victors," one of the most famous anthems in the collegiate ranks.

STRUCTURE From the exterior, Michigan Stadium isn't an overwhelm-

ing facility. Unlike the other two mammoth stadiums in the nation (Tennessee's Neyland Stadium and Penn State's Beaver Stadium), Michigan Stadium was built deep into the ground. It's a sea of red bricks that doesn't reach very high into the sky. Yost got the inspiration for the stadium from the Yale Bowl, which was patterned after the Rose Bowl. The pitch of the seats, which features the famous "Block M" on the east side, is steady, as the rows slowly glide out, giving the bowl a massive look from the interior.

FANS This is an educated bunch that knows football, and the fans aren't afraid to cheer, regardless of accusations this is the quietest 100,000 you'll ever be around. The Michigan faithful love to shout out "Go Blue!" to passers-by while tailgating. The nearby university golf course serves as a major hot spot for football tossing and cooking out. Many fans also gather at the Varsity Plaza. Inside the stadium, the fans are squeezed in long rows, but they don't seem to mind—especially on a blustery, cold day.

MAJOR RENOVATIONS The growth has been steady, with the biggest leap occurring when the stadium eclipsed the 100,000-seat level in 1956. In 1991, the field was lowered 3½ feet to improve sightlines for those sitting lower. Varsity

MICHIGAN

Plaza, brick and wrought iron fencing were added in 1997, while 5,000 more seats and Wolverine Plaza, among other things, were built in 1998.

MILESTONE MOMENTS

• On October 1, 1927, in the first game at Michigan Stadium, the Wolverines walloped Ohio Wesleyan, 33-0. The stadium was dedicated on October 22 of that same year, with Michigan beating Ohio State, 21-0.

• The Big House drew more than 100,000 fans for the first time on October 6, 1956. Michigan lost, 9-0, to Michigan State.

• An artificial surface was installed in 1969. Grass was reinstalled for the 1991 season before a synthetic surface was put back for the 2003 season.

FAST FACTS

• On November 8, 1975, Michigan shut out Purdue, 28-0, in front of 102,415 fans. Since then, Michigan has always played before at least 100,000 (a stretch of 186 games).

• When the stadium capacity increased to 101,000, a tradition began of ending all Michigan Stadium capacity numbers with the digit 1. The extra seat was in honor of Fritz Crisler, Michigan's legendary director of athletics and football coach. But the location of Crisler's seat remains a mystery.

• In 1930, electronic scoreboards were installed. Michigan Stadium was the first to use electronic timing on the scoreboard as the official game clock.

CAPACITY THROUGH THE YEARS

1927:	72,000	1973:	101,701
1928:	85,753	1992:	102,501
1949:	97,239	1998:	107,501
1956:	101,001		

X MAGIC MOMENTS

in the history of Michigan Stadium

I. PERFECTION, *November 22, 1997.* Michigan clinches the Big Ten title and caps a perfect season with a 20-14 win over Ohio State. The win sends the top-ranked Wolverines to the Rose Bowl, where they capture their first national title in nearly 50 years by beating Washington State.

II. TAKE, THAT, WOODY, *November 22, 1969.* One year after absorbing a 50-14 beating from Ohio State, Michigan and new coach Bo Schembechler spank the top-ranked Buckeyes, 24-12, to earn the Big Ten title.

III. COMEBACK CITY, *October 30, 2004.* After falling 17 points behind Michigan State with 7 minutes remaining in the fourth quarter, No. 12 Michigan stages a furious rally to force overtime.

I. PERFECTION

The Wolverines then pull out a 45-37 win in three extra periods, keeping the team undefeated in Big Ten play.

IV. A.C. POWER, *October 27, 1979.* Indiana seems primed to stun a Homecoming crowd when it ties the Wolverines, 21-21, but Michigan gets to the Hoosier 45 with 6 seconds remaining. On the game's final play, quarterback John Wangler hits freshman Anthony Carter over the middle. Carter shakes off two Hoosier defenders and runs into the end zone to give Michigan a 27-21 win.

V. HOWARD'S MAGIC, *September 14, 1991.* The Wolverines hold a precarious 17-14 lead in the fourth quarter and find themselves with a fourth-and-1 from the Notre Dame 25. Coach Gary Moeller elects to go for it, and quarterback Elvis Grbac floats a pass toward the end zone, where Desmond Howard makes a diving catch for a touchdown. The play ended the Irish's hope for a comeback and kick-started Howard's Heisman Trophy campaign.

VI. HOT, HOT, HOT, *August 26, 1995.* Michigan falls behind Virginia, 17-0, on a scorching afternoon but rallies to close the gap to 17-12. On the game's final play, Wolverines redshirt freshman quarterback Scott Dreisbach finds Mercury Hayes, who makes a leaping, twisting touchdown catch to give Michigan an improbable victory.

VII. HAIL MARY, *September 24, 1994.* With Wolverines fans streaming toward the exits, celebrating an apparent win, Colorado quarterback Kordell Stewart heaves a Hail Mary pass into the end zone on the game's final play. The ball is tipped by Michigan's Ty Law but ends up in the arms of Buffaloes receiver Michael Westbrook for a 64-yard TD that gives the Buffs a 27-26 victory.

VIII. JOHNSON RUNS WILD, *November 16, 1968.* In his final home game, running back Ron Johnson tears through Wisconsin for 347 yards rushing and five touchdowns in a 34-9 win. Johnson ignores a light rain and a muddy track to go over 1,000 yards for the second consecutive season.

IX. SINKING NAVY, *October 3, 1964.* Michigan blanks the sixth-ranked Midshipmen and quarterback Roger Staubach, who had won the Heisman Trophy the previous season, 21-0.

X. SPOILING HARVARD'S FIRST TRIP, *November 9, 1929.* After decades of trampling all comers on the East Coast, Harvard travels to the Midwest for the first time and loses, 14-12, to the Wolverines. Not only is it the first win over the Cantabs for Michigan in five tries, it marks the first time the Wolverines ever score on Harvard.

SIMPLY UNFORGETTABLE

Bo vs. Woody, *1969-1978.* They were gridiron giants, their shadows sprawling over the Big Ten and beyond. Michigan's **Bo Schembechler** and Ohio State's Woody Hayes squared off 10 times, with each game a regular-season-ending contest that decided the league title.

The men were hardly strangers when Schembechler took over at Michigan in 1969. Schembechler had served a stint as an assistant on Hayes' OSU staff before taking head coaching positions at Miami (Ohio) and then Ann Arbor. And though some considered Schembechler Hayes' pupil, it took one November afternoon for the Michigan coach to establish himself as his former mentor's equal.

The Wolverines' 1969 win over the top-ranked and undefeated Buckeyes was a chilling dose of revenge, administered by an angry team still smarting from the previous year's 50-14 Big Game drubbing. From that moment, which came in Schembechler's first season at Michigan, the two were mighty adversaries.

Schembechler went 5-4-1 against Hayes. His presence in Ann Arbor and his rivalry with Hayes shot Michigan to the top of the college football world. Schembechler's influence remained strong following his retirement after the 1989 season. He made the Wolverines great, but his rivalry with Hayes accorded the program a status it had never received before and established Michigan-Ohio State as college football's preeminent matchup.

It's a sea of red on Saturdays, with every corner of the state emptying to worship at the house of the Cornhuskers. This is college football at its essence. Smoke billows from grills circling the stadium, and nearby downtown

Lincoln buzzes in anticipation of kickoff as cars creep into town at parade speed. Game time is drawing near, and you better have a ticket; Memorial Stadium has sold out every game since November 3, 1962, a string of 268 games. There has been a lot to cheer about, including five national championships and Heisman winners in Eric Crouch (2001), Mike Rozier (1983) and Johnny Rodgers (1972).

SETTING Lincoln is located in the heartland of America, about an hour from Omaha. It's a flat region, which is one reason the farming is good. On Saturdays, most Nebraskans break away from the duties at hand and turn their attention to the Cornhuskers. Fans line Stadium Drive before the game to watch the band march to the stadium, while kids in Nebraska replica jerseys toss footballs nearby.

STRUCTURE This has evolved into a palace over the years, with myriad renovations. The latest improvement will be the addition of the Tom and Nancy Osborne Athletic Complex to the north end of the stadium. The complex will house locker and weight rooms, among other things. A unique feature of Memorial Stadium is the inscriptions on the four corners of the facade: Southeast: "In Commendation of the men of Nebraska who served and fell in the Nation's Wars." Southwest: "Not the victory but the action; Not the goal but the game; In the deed of the glory." Northwest: "Courage; Generosity; Fairness; Honor; In these are the true awards of manly sport." Northeast: "Their Lives they held their country's trust; they kept its faith; they died its heroes."

FANS Husker fans might be the most

knowledgeable in college football. They get especially fired up when the team does its traditional pregame "Tunnel Walk" to strains of the Alan Parsons Project song "Sirius." Certainly Nebraska fans are the most polite in college football, as the Cornhusker faithful regularly applaud the opposing team as it leaves the field. Fans often get their pictures taken next to the Husker Legacy statue in front of the stadium. The sculpture features a Kansas State running back being tackled by six Huskers.

MAJOR RENOVATIONS In 1964, a south end zone section was installed, making the stadium a horseshoe. The next year, a center portion of the north end zone section was added. In 1966, both wings of the north end zone were added, which made the facility a bowl.

MILESTONE MOMENTS
• The stadium dedication game was played October 20, 1923, a Homecoming meeting in which Nebraska and Kansas played to a scoreless tie. The Cornhuskers had opened the facility the week before, beating Oklahoma, 24-0.
• The first night game was played September 6, 1986, when the Huskers defeated Florida State, 34-17.
• The field was named for Hall of Fame coach Tom Osborne in 1998.

FAST FACTS
• The facility is named in honor of Nebraskans who served in the Civil War and Spanish-American War and those who died in World War I, World War II, the Korean War and the Vietnam War.
• Nebraska won 47 consecutive games in Memorial Stadium from October 1991 to October 1998. The streak was ended with a 20-16 loss to Texas.
• The Huskers lost just three home games in the 1990s and seven in the 1980s.
• On game days, Memorial Stadium becomes the third-largest city in the state.
• While walking to the field before a game, players touch a lucky horseshoe that hangs above the double doors that open into the tunnel.

CAPACITY THROUGH THE YEARS

1923:	31,000	1972:	73,650
1964:	48,000	1994:	72,700
1965:	53,000	1999:	74,056
1966:	65,000	2000:	73,918

X MAGIC MOMENTS

in the history of Memorial Stadium

I. TAMING THE HORSEMEN, *November 10, 1923.* Dave Noble runs for one touchdown and catches a pass for another to give Nebraska a 14-7 win over Notre Dame and its legendary "Four Horsemen" backfield. It's the second straight triumph for the Huskers over the Fighting Irish.

II. STREAK STOPPING, *October 31, 1959.* In an upset so big it spawned a celebration that prompted Nebraska's president to cancel school the next Monday, unranked Nebraska defeats No. 19 Oklahoma, 25-21, ending the Sooners' 74-game conference unbeaten streak.

III. CROUCHING HUSKER, *October 27, 2001.* **Eric Crouch**, who would win the Heisman Trophy later that year, proves to be a multiple threat in a 20-10 win over second-ranked Oklahoma. The Huskers' quarterback catches a 63-yard TD pass on a trick play to help cement the win.

IV. GROUNDING THE GOPHERS, *October 2, 1937.* After having posted a 1-15-2 record in previous games against mighty Minnesota, the Cornhuskers upend the defending national champs in their first game under coach Biff Jones. A 25-yard TD pass from Harris Andrews to William Callihan gives NU a 14-9 win.

V. ROLLING THE SOONERS, *November 26, 1982.* After losing a controversial heartbreaker to Penn State earlier in the year, the Cornhuskers roll through the Big Eight and end conference play with a 28-24 win over 11th-ranked Oklahoma. The win

against the Sooners is the second in a row for the Huskers. Nebraska went on to beat LSU in the Orange Bowl.

VI. THAT CHAMPIONSHIP SEASON, *October 29, 1994.* The Huskers had come close before but had never won the national championship. But the 1994 Nebraska team does, after the Huskers' 24-7 win over second-ranked Colorado propels NU into the top spot in the rankings.

VII. SNIFFING ROSES, *November 30, 1940.* Nebraska qualifies for its first bowl game—in Pasadena—by whipping Kansas State, 20-0. The win caps an 8-1 regular season and lifts the Huskers to seventh in the AP poll.

VIII. CRIMSON TEARS, *September 17, 1977.* Tom Osborne had accomplished a lot in his first four-plus years as head coach at Nebraska, but he had never beaten a top-five team. That ends when Rick Berns scores on a 1-yard TD run and Jim Pillen intercepts a pair of fourth-quarter passes in a 31-24 win over Bear Bryant's fourth-ranked Crimson Tide.

IX. GO HOME, ND, *November 26, 1925.* An overflow crowd packs the stadium to watch the Huskers beat 7-1-1 Notre Dame, 17-0, in the final game of an annual series that had begun in 1915. It is Nebraska's last game against the Fighting Irish until 1947.

X. GREAT START, *September 12, 1987.* One week after opening the season with a blowout of Utah State, No. 2 Nebraska gets a stronger test from third-ranked UCLA and comes away with a 42-33 victory.

III. CROUCHING HUSKER
Heisman Trophy-bound quarterback Eric Crouch used a little trickery against Oklahoma in 2001, catching a long TD pass.

SIMPLY UNFORGETTABLE

November 11, 1978. There was no doubt **Tom Osborne** (inset) was the right man to coach Nebraska after Bob Devaney retired. It was Osborne, loyal lieutenant to Devaney and hand-picked to be his successor, who, as an assistant under Devaney, implemented the power-I attack that helped the Huskers become the scourge of the Big Eight. Osborne had won at least nine games in each of his first five seasons, guaranteeing there would be no drop-off after Devaney left the sideline.

But Osborne had yet to beat Oklahoma, and that was a problem. No matter how well the Huskers had played or how many bowl wins Osborne had registered, Nebraska hadn't beaten the Sooners during his reign.

In 1978, Oklahoma came to Lincoln ranked No. 1 and expecting another trip to the Orange Bowl. Behind eventual Heisman-winning running back Billy Sims, the Sooners were undefeated. And confident.

Rick Berns ran for 113 yards and scored a touchdown, and I.M. Hipp hit the end zone for the Huskers' second TD. A Billy Todd field goal with 11:51 left made it 17-14. Nebraska recovered six Oklahoma fumbles, including two by Sims late in the fourth quarter. The second came on the NU 3-yard line with 3:27 left and was recovered by Jim Pillen to secure the victory. In the end, Osborne had his first win over the Sooners and security as the Nebraska coach.

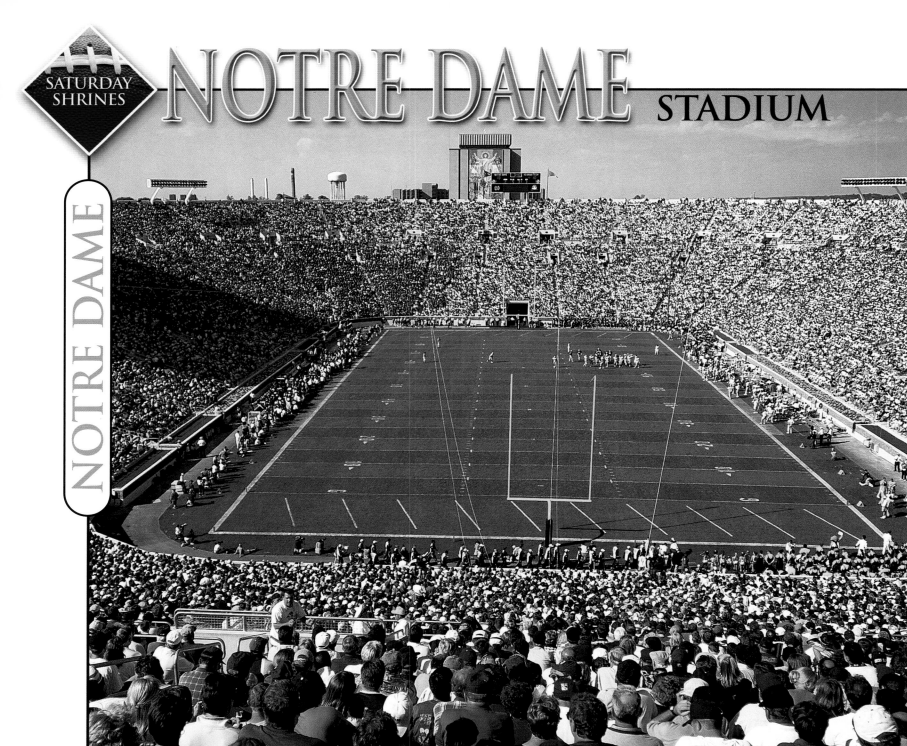

SATURDAY
SHRINES

NOTRE DAME STADIUM

I t's perhaps the most famous sign in college football. As Notre Dame players run toward the field before kickoff, they descend a set of stairs and tap a "Play Like A Champion" sign. It's a tradition that symbolizes college football's most holy ground. Notre Dame has the Four Horsemen, George Gipp and Knute Rockne. Walking the campus on a fall Saturday morning is enough

to prompt anyone to belt out "Cheer, cheer for old Notre Dame!" And don't forget about the seven Heisman winners and 11 national titles. Notre Dame has it all wrapped tightly on a small campus that rests in northern Indiana near the Michigan border in a region known as Michiana.

SETTING The best days for South Bend are in its rearview mirror, but it scores big for being home to the College Football Hall of Fame. But the best part of town is the campus. All within walking distance of the stadium are great venues such as the Golden Dome, the Grotto, the Basilica of the Sacred Heart and the Hesburgh Library, which features "Touchdown Jesus" on its side. Fans are treated to an intimate view of the game, and they can thank Knute Rockne, who insisted that builders keep the area between the field and the stands small to keep sideline wanderers to a minimum. Adding to the pregame excitement is the Irish Guard, which leads the

band onto the field. Members are dressed in kilts and sport bearskin shakos.

STRUCTURE After the renovation that replaced the old facade with a new brick one, the stadium is beautiful. It was patterned after Michigan Stadium but has its own unique touches. The lettering at the north and south canopies, as well as the interlocking ND logo at the top of the press box, are gold laminate, and the landscaping was created to engender a park setting around the stadium. As part of the 1997 renovation, the architects eliminated the first three rows of seats because they had bad sightlines.

FANS Notre Dame Stadium was expanded in 1997 to accommodate the many fans who previously had struggled to find tickets. The school has sold out every game but one since 1964, and the only non-sellout over that time was a Thanksgiving Day game against Air Force in 1973, when students weren't on cam-

pus. Fans show their loyalty by holding rousing pep rallies on Friday nights. And if you happen to be at Notre Dame for the home opener, you'll see students wearing The Shirt—a T-shirt bearing a unique motto. Revenue from the sale of the shirts is used to benefit various projects.

MAJOR RENOVATIONS This place remained relatively unchanged for years until 1997, when Notre Dame unveiled a new-look stadium that increased capacity from 59,075 to 80,232 by adding a rim around the top of the stadium. It was a two-year, $50 million project that added, among other things, a new facade, playing surface, lights and locker rooms.

MILESTONE MOMENTS
• Notre Dame dedicated its stadium by beating Navy, 26-2, on October 11, 1930. However, the first game in the facility was a 20-14 triumph over SMU a week earlier.
• The first night game was against Michigan on September 18, 1982, a season-opening contest. The Irish upset the Wolverines, 23-17.
• The renovated Notre Dame Stadium was rededicated on September 6, 1997, in a 17-13 victory over Georgia Tech.

FAST FACTS

• From November 1942 to September 1950, Notre Dame won 28 consecutive games in Notre Dame Stadium.

• On Friday nights before home games, the school conducts pep rallies in the adjacent Joyce Center, where such celebrities as Regis Philbin, Tommy Lasorda and Wayne Gretzky have spoken.

CAPACITY THROUGH THE YEARS

1930: 59,075

1997: 80,232

2001: 80,795

I. NOT THIS TIME, *October 27, 1973.* The Notre Dame student body issues a warm welcome to Southern California tailback Anthony Davis—whose six touchdowns the year before had headlined a big Trojans win—by hanging him in effigy on campus. Afterward, the Irish defense stifles the star in a 23-14 win that ends USC's 23-game unbeaten streak.

II. TOMAHAWK CHOPPED, *November 13, 1993.* In a classic matchup of Nos. 1 vs. 2 and dueling 16-game winning streaks, Notre Dame bolts to a 21-7 halftime lead and then holds off top-ranked Florida State. With 3 seconds remaining, the score 31-24, the Seminoles are thwarted from the Irish 14-yard line when **Charlie Ward**'s pass is batted away by Shawn Wooden.

III. GREEN MACHINE, *October 22, 1977.* After warming up in the traditional blue jerseys for an annual meeting with Southern California, the Irish return from the locker room for the game wearing green, sending the crowd into a frenzy and stunning the fifth-ranked Trojans, 49-19.

IV. ORDER RESTORED, *November 8, 1952.* Even though Oklahoma holds the best record in the nation over the previous five seasons and enters the game with a 13-game unbeaten streak, the Irish repel three late Sooners charges and come away with a 27-21 victory.

V. THE DAY THE WIND DIED, *September 20, 1980.* Although no one has given a good meteorological reason for it, a swirling wind dies down just in time for Harry Oliver to drill a 51-yard field goal as time runs out to give Notre Dame a 29-27 win against Michigan.

VI. SNOW BOWL, *November 14, 1992.* Down 16-9, with snow swirling down and covering the icy, slick stadium grass, Rick Mirer leads the Irish on a 64-yard scoring drive that culminates with a touchdown pass to Jerome

X MAGIC MOMENTS
in the history of Notre Dame Stadium

Bettis. A two-point conversion toss to Reggie Brooks with 20 second remaining gives Notre Dame a 17-16 victory against Penn State.

VII. THE FINAL CONFLICT, *October 20, 1990.* The football world tunes in to watch the heated struggle between sixth-ranked Notre Dame and second-ranked Miami in what would be the last scheduled game in a heated rivalry. Notre Dame prevails, 29-20, and the Hurricanes struggle mightily to retain their composure.

VIII. WRECKING THE WRECK, *October 24, 1953.* Quarterback John Lattner and fullback Neil Worden spearhead an Irish ground attack that piles up 323 yards in a 27-14 win against Georgia Tech, snapping the Ramblin' Wreck's 31-game unbeaten streak. The Irish prevail even with coach Frank Leahy sidelined after halftime by chest muscle spasms.

II. Tomahawk chopped

IX. "AN-THO-NY, AN-THO-NY!" *September 18, 1982.* In the first night game at Notre Dame Stadium, the Irish bottle up Michigan's Heisman candidate, receiver Anthony Carter, and upset the No. 10-rated Wolverines, 23-17, before a delirious crowd.

X. MADE FOR HOLLYWOOD, *November 8, 1975.* In a moment immortalized by a movie, Daniel "Rudy" Ruettiger, 27 years old, realizes a dream when he takes the field in the closing moments of a 24-3 victory over Georgia Tech. He punctuates his only appearance with a sack. After the game, his teammates carry him off the field.

SIMPLY UNFORGETTABLE

October 15, 1988. In marched Miami, boasting a 36-game regular-season winning streak and swaggering with all the arrogance that could be found. The Hurricanes had not only whipped all comers for 2 1/2 seasons, they also had taken four in a row from the Irish, including a humiliating 58-7 rout in Miami three years earlier.

This wasn't just about taking on the No. 1 team in the country, though the fourth-rated Irish certainly were excited about that. This was about revenge. About Notre Dame's honor. Some even viewed it as good vs. evil.

For three hours at Notre Dame Stadium, the two giants traded haymakers, talked junk and played the game at its most competitive level. The intensity was overwhelming, but the play was sloppy. The teams combined for 10 turnovers, including an astonishing seven by Miami.

Midway through the second quarter, Notre Dame held a 21-7 advantage. But Miami stormed back on the strong arm of quarterback Steve Walsh, who finished with 424 yards and four scores. By halftime, it was 21-21. Notre Dame surged again and took a 31-21 lead in a third quarter that featured three turnovers, a blocked field goal and a failed fake punt. A Miami field goal narrowed the margin to 31-24 early in the fourth quarter, but neither team could do anything until the final 2 minutes.

Miami recovered a Notre Dame fumble at the Irish 14, and four plays later, Walsh hit Andre Brown for a touchdown that narrowed the gap to 31-30. The Hurricanes didn't think twice about trying for the win. But Pat Terrell knocked down Walsh's 2-point pass to tailback Leonard Conley in the end zone. When Anthony Johnson recovered the Hurricanes' onside kick, Notre Dame had vindication and a huge step on the road to another national title.

It's a stunning sight, a massive horseshoe drenched in scarlet as far as the eye can see. It's Ohio Stadium, one of the most intimidating and awe-inspiring venues in the nation. To locals and alums, the building is simply known as the "Shoe."

More than 100,000 fans breathe life into the venerable facility that sits on the banks of the Olentangy River in the heartland of America. And those fans have come to cheer on some of the greats in the game, including Heisman Trophy winners Les Horvath, Vic Janowicz, Howard "Hopalong" Cassady, Archie Griffin and Eddie George, along with legendary coach Woody Hayes. Add it up, and it's enough to make this stadium an American classic.

Hayes

SETTING Look around, they're everywhere, tailgaters fanned out around the perimeter of Ohio Stadium. It's a virtual army of RVs, with most sporting large red Ohio State flags. Street vendors hawk everything from gyros to hot dogs from small silver carts. Adding to the environment is the "Best Damn Band in the Land," which has a grand entrance down a ramp into the stadium and executes one of the best—if not the best—formations in the nation: the "script Ohio." The climax is when the "i" is dotted, usually by a fourth- or fifth-year sousaphone player. But sometimes a famous person has done the honors, including the likes

of Hayes and Bob Hope. During the game, it's popular for the band and fans to break out singing the OSU classic "Hang On Sloopy."

STRUCTURE Despite its mass, Ohio Stadium is an intimate venue because the fans are close to the action. Removal of a running track from around the stadium in 2001 played a major role in putting the fans closer to the action. The double-deck horseshoe makes this place intimidating—it seems as if fans are breathing down your neck. One of the most beautiful aspects of Ohio Stadium is the rotunda entrance. It was styled after the architecture of the Pantheon in Rome. Three stained glass windows were installed in 2001. The entrance gates are made of wrought iron and feature a block "O."

FANS This is a passionate bunch, with some showing their love and devotion by wearing necklaces made of buckeyes. You see a bit of the pregame and postgame craziness at the Varsity Club, the most famous hangout on campus. The fans arrive early to St. John Arena to see the Skull Session—the band's last chance to rehearse before show time, with Jim

OHIO HISTORICAL MARKER

THE OHIO STATE UNIVERSITY

The Ohio Agricultural and Mechanical College grew out of the Cannon Act of March 22, 1870. "But let it be started," Governor Rutherford B. Hayes told the Legislature in 1873, "with the intention of making it, ultimately, a grand State University...."

The little college opened September 17, 1873 with a faculty of seven and twenty-four students. One academic building at first housed everything. The campus, remote from the city, was surrounded by some of the original forest. In May, 1878 the name was changed to The Ohio State University.

It was after 1900 before it really began to realize its educational potential, and its major growth occurred after World War II. By 1970, the Centennial Year, the university had more than met the hopes of its founders. A leading university with great manpower and physical resources, it had earned high standing in many fields covering a wide range of educational and research activities.

1970   5-25

OHIO STATE

Tressel and the team stopping by on the way to the game. And fans leave late to sing the classic "Carmen Ohio" one last time and to hear the Victory Bell (located in the southeast tower of Ohio Stadium) ring one last time. On a calm day, legend has it the bell can be heard from five miles away.

MAJOR RENOVATIONS There have been many over the years. But the most significant came from 1999-2001. Among myriad changes, aisles were added, club seats and suites were installed and the press box was upgraded.

MILESTONE MOMENTS
• The first game was played October 7, 1922, when the Buckeyes topped Ohio Wesleyan, 5-0.
• An artificial surface was installed in 1970. Ohio State reverted to grass in 1990.
• Ohio State played under the lights for the first time on September 14, 1985, notching a 10-7 victory over Pittsburgh.

FAST FACTS
• The venue has played host to several big-name rock acts, including the Rolling Stones and Pink Floyd.
• The Buckeyes played home games at Ohio Field prior to the construction of Ohio Stadium. The great play of Charles "Chic" Harley created a demand for more seats, which was an impetus for a new stadium.
• Outside the stadium is Buckeye Grove, where the school plants a buckeye tree for each of Ohio State's All-Americans.

CAPACITY
THROUGH THE YEARS

1922: 66,210	2000: 99,000
1978: 83,112	2001: 101,568
1997: 89,841	

124

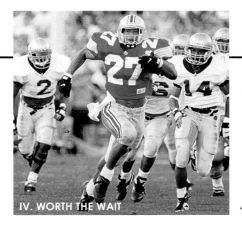

IV. WORTH THE WAIT

X MAGIC MOMENTS
in the history of Ohio Stadium

I. **FIESTA TIME**, *November 23, 2002.* In just the second year of coach Jim Tressel's reign, Ohio State slips past Michigan, 14-9, to win a share of the Big Ten title, cap an undefeated regular season and earn a berth against Miami in the BCS title game in Tempe, Ariz. OSU defeats the Hurricanes, 31-24, in overtime to capture its first national crown since 1968.

II. **WIDE RIGHT, ALL RIGHT**, *November 23, 1974.* Even though undefeated No. 3 Michigan keeps the Buckeyes out of the end zone, four Tom Klaban field goals stake OSU to a 12-10 victory that is secured only when a 33-yard field-goal attempt by UM's Mike Lantry slides just outside the goalpost in the final seconds.

III. **HALF A HUNDRED**, *November 23, 1968.* Woody Hayes elects to go for two points after Ohio State's final touchdown in a 50-14 rout of Michigan that earns the Big Ten title for the Buckeyes, who are bound for the national championship. Although the attempt fails, Wolverine fans are incensed by the move, which reportedly Hayes says he made because he "couldn't go for three."

IV. **WORTH THE WAIT**, *September 30, 1995.* Sixty years after Notre Dame visited No. 1 Ohio State at Ohio Stadium and came away with a stunning 18-13 come-from-behind win in what some say is the greatest game of the first half of the 20th century, the Buckeyes get another crack at the Irish in Columbus and triumph, 45-26.

V. **NOT BAD FOR A FRESHMAN**, *September 30, 1972.* Even though OSU coach Woody Hayes doesn't want to play freshman Archie Griffin because of his fumble the game before, Hayes inserts Griffin against North Carolina and watches the tailback run for a school-record 239 yards in a 29-14 win.

VI. **SNOW BOWL**, *November 25, 1950.* Playing in one of the worst snowstorms ever to hit Columbus, Michigan and Ohio State lock up in a memorable struggle that features 45 punts and 68 combined yards of offense. Michigan wins, 9-3, despite not converting a first down or completing a pass.

VII. **STREAK SNAPPER**, *November 19, 1994.* After going six years without a win against Michigan, the 22nd-ranked Buckeyes pull off a 22-6 upset victory of the No. 15 Wolverines to salvage a season that featured three losses, including a 63-14 defeat at Penn State.

VIII. **NO SHOE, NO PROBLEM**, *October 13, 1984.* Running back Keith Byars scores five touchdowns and rushes for a school-record 274 yards in a 45-38 win over Illinois. On one of his touchdown runs, a 67-yarder, Byars loses a shoe 35 yards from the goal line and covers the remaining distance with one foot clad in only a sock.

I. FIESTA TIME

IX. **"SCRIPT OHIO,"** *October 10, 1936.* The Ohio State Marching Band debuts "script Ohio" during the Buckeyes' 6-0 loss to Pittsburgh. It goes on to become one of the most famous traditions in all of college football.

X. **THE HOUSE THE BUCKEYES BUILT**, *October 21, 1922.* When Ohio Stadium was built, critics had said the 66,000-plus-seat stadium was too big. But the school holds a dedication game against Michigan and has to add temporary seating to handle the 71,138 fans who show up.

SIMPLY UNFORGETTABLE

November 21, 1970. In 1969, Ohio State marched into Ann Arbor as a 17-point favorite with a 22-game winning streak, a No. 1 ranking and the belief that it was headed for a second straight national title. Three hours after kick-off, it was all in smoldering ruins. The Wolverines scored a 24-12 upset, spoiling the Buckeyes' championship dreams and enraging OSU Nation.

By the time November 1970 rolled around, the Buckeyes had been thinking about little other than avenging the Michigan loss for 12 long, sour months. Coach Woody Hayes tried to keep his squad focused from week to week, and Ohio State rolled through its first eight games without a blemish, but the Buckeyes had their minds on revenge. As did virtually everyone else in the state of Ohio.

When game day dawned, a ravenous throng packed the stadium, eager for retribution. Undefeated Michigan held on through the first 20 minutes, forging a 3-3 tie in the second quarter and closing the gap to 10-9 in the third quarter, but the Wolverines never really had a chance on this day. OSU went up 13-9 early in the fourth quarter, then picked off a pass deep in Wolverines territory and converted a touchdown that pushed the margin to 20-9—the final score.

MEMORIAL STADIUM

OKLAHOMA

It shoots high into the Oklahoma sky and serves as home to one of the greatest programs in college football history. There have been great teams (seven national champions),

great players (Heisman winners Billy Vessels, Steve Owens, Billy Sims and Jason White) and great coaches (Bennie Owen, Bud Wilkinson, Barry Switzer and Bob Stoops). Wrap it all up, and you have a special package that makes this one of the best college football experiences in America, complete with color, pageantry, spectacle and excitement.

SETTING If you're looking for a picturesque setting, you'll be disappointed. But if it's an intense football environment, dripping with greatness, that you're after, Memorial Stadium is the place to be on Saturdays in the fall. The stadium sits in the middle of campus, so tailgating takes place all around the area. However, space can be tight. Many folks have to park around the Lloyd Noble Center about a mile south of the stadium and take shuttles to the game. Fans also congregate north of the stadium for FanFest, a whirlwind of bands, games and autograph tents. Not far from the stadium is the Campus Corner area, which is home to a collection of bars, restaurants and shops that attracts many before and after games.

STRUCTURE Memorial Stadium is a beautiful red brick and concrete structure that has seen many improvements in recent years. The stadium once was a horseshoe but since has added upper decks on the east and west sides and the Barry Switzer Center in the south end zone, which houses the coaches' offices, locker room, training room, weight-training facility and OU heritage area. Despite not being enclosed, the stadium still can get very loud.

FANS The OU fans are renowned for getting to the stadium early; they don't want to miss the Sooner Schooner make its loop around the field. And then there's the Sooner band. It typically begins its pregame show by playing the theme from the Broadway musical *Oklahoma!* One of the last songs the band plays before kickoff? "Boomer Sooner," of course. Adding to the color is a student spirit organization called the Ruf Neks, which mans the Sooner Schooner and tends to Boomer and Sooner, the white ponies who pull it.

MAJOR RENOVATIONS This has been a work in progress for years. But a major change took place in 2003, when Memorial Stadium underwent a $65 million overhaul that added 8,000-plus seats, including 27 suites, and remodeled the press box. Another big change came

OKLAHOMA

in 1949, when the school lowered the playing field by 6 feet and eliminated the track that ran around the field.

MILESTONE MOMENTS

• The first game was played at this site on October 20, 1923. The Sooners crushed Washington University (Mo.), 63-7.

• The largest crowd ever to watch a sporting event in the state gathered on November 1, 2003, and saw the Sooners thump Oklahoma State, 52-9, before 84,027.

• The grass playing surface was replaced with an artificial one in 1970, but grass was reinstalled in 1994.

FAST FACTS

• Oklahoma won 25 games in a row at Memorial Stadium from 1947-52 under legendary coach Bud Wilkinson.

• The Sooners ran for a school-record 768 yards against Kansas State in 1988. The Sooners finished the game with 829 yards of offense.

• On a clear day, from the east side upper deck, fans can see all the way to Oklahoma City, which is about 18 miles to the north.

CAPACITY THROUGH THE YEARS

1925:	16,000	1975:	71,187
1929:	32,000	1980:	75,004
1949:	55,000	1982:	72,765
1957:	61,826	2003:	81,207

MAGIC MOMENTS
in the history of Memorial Stadium

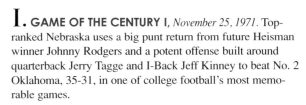

II. GAME OF THE CENTURY II

I. GAME OF THE CENTURY I, *November 25, 1971.* Top-ranked Nebraska uses a big punt return from future Heisman winner Johnny Rodgers and a potent offense built around quarterback Jerry Tagge and I-Back Jeff Kinney to beat No. 2 Oklahoma, 35-31, in one of college football's most memorable games.

II. GAME OF THE CENTURY II, *October 28, 2000.* Third-ranked Oklahoma spots No. 1 Nebraska a 14-0 lead and then rolls to a 31-14 victory, on the strength of a 24-point second quarter and 300 yards from quarterback **Josh Heupel** (above). The win is the centerpiece of a 13-0 national title season.

III. STREAK IS OVER, *November 16, 1957.* With 3:50 remaining in the game, Dick Lynch sweeps around end from 3 yards out for the only touchdown in Notre Dame's 7-0 victory, which snaps Oklahoma's 47-game winning streak. Oklahoma drives deep into ND territory in the waning moments, but Irish quarterback/defensive back Bob Williams intercepts a pass to preserve the win.

IV. TOO MUCH VESSELS, *November 25, 1950.* Sophomore halfback Billy Vessels rushes for 208 yards, scores three touchdowns and passes for a TD in the Sooners' 49-35 win over Nebraska. The win pushes OU's winning streak to 30 games and sets the stage for the Sooners' first national title, clinched the next week with a win over Oklahoma State.

V. SWEET REVENGE, *November 1, 2003.* After losses to Oklahoma State had hurt the Sooners' national title hopes the previous two seasons, OU dominates the Cowboys from the start in a 52-9 win. The Sooners hold OSU to just 161 total yards.

VI. SIMS-PLY AMAZING, *November 24, 1979.* In his last game at Memorial Stadium, Billy Sims rushes for 247 yards to give the Sooners a 17-14 win over Nebraska. Mike Babb intercepts a Cornhusker pass in the final minutes to secure the victory, which gives OU a Big Eight title and an Orange Bowl berth.

VII. GROUND ASSAULT, *October 15, 1988.* In a record-setting performance, Oklahoma rushes for 768 yards in a 70-24 dismantling of Kansas State. Reserve halfback Eric Mitchel leads the way with 161 yards.

VIII. BIG COMEBACK, *October 7, 1950.* After Sooner kicker Jim Weatherall misses an extra-point attempt, Oklahoma is down by one with 3:36 remaining in the game. But Texas A&M was forced to punt with 1:46 left, and Leon Heath's 4-yard TD run, his third of the game, with just 37 seconds remaining gives OU the 34-28 victory. The win is the Sooners' 23rd in a row.

IX. THREE CENTURIES, *November 13, 1976.* Three Sooners—Horace Ivory (159 yards), Kenny King (128) and Thomas Lott (126)—top the 100-yard rushing mark in a 27-20 win over Missouri, one of only five times the Sooners have had a trio of 100-yard rushers.

X. TAKE THAT, AGGIES, *October 23, 1999.* After losing two straight to Texas A&M by a combined score of 80-7, the Sooners exact revenge with a 51-6 romp. OU hits the Aggies with the hook-and-lateral, a fake punt and a fake field goal and formations that used only three interior linemen.

SIMPLY UNFORGETTABLE

1953-57. In 2002, when Miami was preparing to play Ohio State in the BCS title game, college football fans started to do a little math. If the Hurricanes were to beat the Buckeyes for their 35th win in a row, they would be in position to break Oklahoma's record 47-game winning streak in the '03 national title tilt. But the Hurricanes didn't beat Ohio State, didn't reach the 2003 BCS title game and couldn't break the Sooners' record.

Not that you can discredit them. Winning 34 straight is pretty impressive. Winning 47 is outrageous. But that's what Bud Wilkinson's team did, from 1953-57. In a stretch that featured three pristine seasons, a pair of national titles and the kind of domination that permitted only nine of their victims to come within 10 points of them, the Sooners were perfection in helmets and shoulder pads.

It started on October 10, 1953, with a thrilling 19-14 win over Texas on a scorching Dallas afternoon. Not that anyone at the time knew what the Sooners were about to do. Wilkinson's team had started the season with a loss against Notre Dame and a tie at Pittsburgh. But Oklahoma ran off eight more victories after beating the Longhorns, including a 7-0 win over Maryland and former Sooners coach Jim Tatum in the Orange Bowl. The next season brought 10 more wins, and '55 and '56—the national title years—were similarly perfect.

It ended in 1957, in Norman, against Notre Dame. After it was over, the Sooners ran off three more victories, including a 48-21 thrashing of Duke in the Orange Bowl. If you count all the games OU played from 1953 through 1957, it was 50-2-1, an amazing record in itself, even without the 47 straight.

SATURDAY SHRINES

AUTZEN STADIUM

This place might lack the weighty history of Michigan Stadium or the sheer mass of Tennessee's Neyland Stadium, but Autzen Stadium compensates with a megadose of volume. The structure is like an amphitheater cut into the ground. Among the unique

aspects of the stadium are the alternating shades of green that mark each 5-yard segment of the field. The stadium is on a 90-acre lot that sits on the banks of the Willamette River, just a quick jog from campus. And it seems everyone jogs in Eugene, which is 100 miles south of Portland on Interstate 5.

SETTING If you head to Eugene, make sure you pack your bicycle. Heck, you can even ride it to the game—stadium staffers offer valet parking for your two-wheeler. This is a town of naturalists and is home to one of the most picturesque of campuses. Autzen, named for Portland lumberman and philanthropist Thomas J. Autzen, is nestled between the Coburg Hills and Willamette River. Parking can be a pain, as many fans opt to park and take a bus to Autzen. A better, and prettier,

plan is to park near campus and walk to the game. There's a nice path that winds through dense woods before crossing a ⅛-mile footbridge toward the stadium. Get to your seat before kickoff because you won't want to miss a custom Harley Fat Boy leading the Ducks onto the field.

STRUCTURE This is a relatively new facility—it opened in 1967. And it was built just for football. The Ducks' old home was Hayward Field, which still stands and is a famous track and field facility. Since Autzen is football only, it has great sightlines and pushes fans close to the field. Autzen has a novel shape, rising high on each side with the end zones dipping low. The idea is to keep most of the seats between the goal lines. The south side seats are protected by a wood roof, which pays homage to the region's timber production while protecting fans who sit in that area from the notoriously wet Northwest weather.

FANS It's called the Autzen Zoo for a reason. The tailgating is hearty, though parking spots are limited. You won't have to look long to find someone drinking a microbrew, as the state of Oregon produces some of the best beer in the land. Despite seating just 54,000, Autzen is one of the loudest stadiums in the nation. Its unusual shape helps funnel in sound. And the fans do their best, augmenting their high-energy cheering with whistles that mimic duck calls. It can be a deafening

Get to your seat before kickoff because you won't want to miss a custom Harley Fat Boy leading the Ducks onto the field.

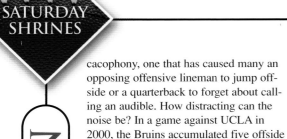
OREGON

cacophony, one that has caused many an opposing offensive lineman to jump off-side or a quarterback to forget about calling an audible. How distracting can the noise be? In a game against UCLA in 2000, the Bruins accumulated five offside penalties in the first half.

MAJOR RENOVATIONS There have been two. The facility underwent a $90 million renovation before the 2002 season that added 12,000-plus seats and 32 luxury boxes. A highlight of the new work was the Club at Autzen, a 10,000-square-foot entertainment center. In 1988, the press box was moved from the north side of the field to the south side. In its place is a three-story box/suite complex.

MILESTONE MOMENTS
• Oregon lost the first game in Autzen, dropping a 17-13 decision to Colorado on September 23, 1967.
• From 1997-2001, Oregon won 23 games in a row at Autzen.
• After just two seasons on grass, the school ripped it out and installed turf in 1969.

FAST FACTS
• The playing field is named for Rich Brooks, who led the Ducks to their first outright Pacific-10 title in 1994 before leaving to coach the St. Louis Rams. Brooks spent 18 years as Oregon's coach and has the most wins (91) of any man to guide the Ducks.
• In 1987, Autzen played host to a concert that featured Bob Dylan and the Grateful Dead.
• In 1983, 4-6 Oregon took on 2-8 Oregon State in the Civil War game. Alas, this Ducks-Beavers clash finished 0-0 and has become known as the forgettable Toilet Bowl.

CAPACITY THROUGH THE YEARS

1967: 41,698   2002: 54,000

X MAGIC MOMENTS
in the history of Autzen Stadium

SIMPLY UNFORGETTABLE

December 1, 2001. Led by quarterback Joey Harrington and an offense that piled up the points, Oregon charged through its 2001 schedule, stumbling only once, when Stanford's offense survived a 49-42 shootout.

On the final Saturday of the regular season, the Ducks were assured a share of the Pac-10 title and a berth in the Fiesta Bowl (that year's BCS "championship" game was being played at the Rose Bowl), but they wanted more. They wanted the conference championship outright and a shot at moving up in the BCS standings to perhaps play for the national crown. All they had to do was win the Civil War against Oregon State, which entered the contest with a 5-5 record and a season of erratic play. But a classic Pacific Northwest rainstorm played havoc with the Oregon attack. Harrington was particularly stymied, completing just 11 of 22 passes for a mere 104 yards. But the Ducks went to work in other ways. Keenan Howry returned a punt 70 yards for a touchdown. And when it came down to it, Oregon's offense was able to deliver. On a crucial late-fourth-quarter drive, with OSU holding a 14-10 lead, Harrington converted a third-and-10 with a 28-yard pass to Howry, and Maurice Morris scored from eight yards out with 4:36 left. Oregon had a 17-14 triumph, the outright Pac-10 title and a 10-1 record. A month later, they made it 11-1 with a 38-16 rout of Colorado in Tempe.

I. STUFFING THE WOLVERINES,
September 20, 2003. Michigan makes its first trip to Eugene and stumbles early in the face of Duck defensive pressure and a delirious Autzen Stadium crowd. Though the Wolverines mount a late charge, Oregon holds on for a thrilling 31-27 win.

II. GOING, GONE ... TO PASADENA,
October 22, 1994. Kenny Wheaton's 97-yard touchdown run off an interception is the big play in the Ducks' 31-20 win over Washington and the second of three consecutive victories against ranked teams that lead to Oregon's Pac-10 championship.

III. AMBUSHED,
October 24, 1970. Tenth-ranked USC comes to Eugene with Rose Bowl dreams and is handed a 10-7 loss at rainy Autzen. It was the Ducks' eighth win in the series, which has been dominated by the Trojans.

IV. BOWLING ALONG,
November 18, 1989. After struggling with mediocre teams throughout his first 12 years at Oregon, Rich Brooks breaks through with an 8-3 regular season. A 30-21 win over Oregon State locks up an Independence Bowl invitation, the Ducks' first bowl berth in 26 years.

V. WORKING OVERTIME,
September 25, 1999. Oregon ties No. 16 USC with a field goal with 30 seconds

V. WORKING OVERTIME

Josh Frankel was the man whose overtime field goal—a 27-yarder—did in USC in 1999.

remaining in regulation, then prevails, 33-30, in a three-overtime marathon that remains the longest game played at Autzen.

VI. GROUND ASSAULT,
September 18, 1971. Bobby Moore, who would later change his name to Ahmad Rashad, rushes for 249 yards—an Autzen record until Onterrio Smith's 285-yard game in 2001—in the Ducks' 36-29 win over Utah.

VII. PILING UP THE YARDS,
September 8, 1990. Bill Musgrave begins the '90 season the right way by throwing for an Autzen-record 443 yards in a 42-21 rout of San Diego State. The record stood until 1995.

VIII. HOUSE WARMING,
October 21, 1967. After beginning the season 0-3 in its new Autzen Stadium home, the team finally christens the house the right way with a 31-6 rout of Idaho.

IX. RARE HONOR,
October 8, 1983. The Ducks' 24-17 win over California isn't greeted with too much notice around the country, until offensive tackle Gary Zimmerman is named Pac-10 Player of the Week for his dominating performance.

X. AIR RAID,
November 7, 1998. Akili Smith erupts for 442 yards passing and three touchdowns in a 27-22 win over Washington.

BEAVER STADIUM

PENN STATE

It's an oasis in the middle of the rolling green hills of central Pennsylvania. Beaver Stadium and the Penn State campus rival any venue in the nation when it comes to tradition. This is hallowed ground, thanks to Joe Paterno's four-

decade body of work. Trips to Beaver Stadium are ritual for thousands of people, with many making the trek through the scenic back roads of the Keystone State to enjoy the company of family and friends, good food and—most of all—Penn State football. It's all part of the lure of Happy Valley, in the shadow of Mount Nittany.

SETTING The stadium rests in a valley surrounded by mountains to the north and south. On Saturdays, it becomes tailgating central. The RVs take over the parking lots around Beaver Stadium, with flags flying high and kids tossing footballs in their Nittany Lion jerseys. The marching Blue Band plays a big part in building an exciting environment. Before games, the drum major will run through the middle of the band. At the 50-yard line, he'll do a forward flip and salute the crowd on the press box side of the field. He'll then run toward the other end zone and do another flip. It's said the outcome of the game hinges on the drum major executing the flips. Then, it's time for the players to enter

the field by running through a tunnel formed by the marching band.

STRUCTURE There's nothing fancy about Beaver Stadium. In fact, it looks like an Erector Set creation. But there's enough substance in this stadium to overcome any style deficiencies, and the $93 million expansion and renovation that was completed in 2001 took some of the rough edges off. Plus, it added a Penn State All-Sports Museum—10,000 square feet of space that house trophies, films, paraphernalia and interactive features preserving the memories of Nittany Lion athletics.

FANS These are among the most loyal fans in the nation. They come from every corner of the state, packing the place to the point where Beaver Stadium becomes the third-largest city in the state on game days. The stadium is a sea of blue

PENN STATE

and white, wailing with a volume that many claim is the highest in the Big Ten. A favorite cheer is when one side of the stands yells "WE ARE!" and the other answers "PENN STATE!" From time to time, the roar of a Nittany Lion will carry over the P.A. system, igniting cheers. After games, many fans like to stroll College Avenue, which divides campus from downtown and hearkens to days gone by. The area features an assortment of shops, bars and restaurants—and there's always the Penn State Creamery, which serves up scoops of Peachy Paterno.

MAJOR RENOVATIONS Expansion has been a frequent occurrence. The most recent facelift made Beaver Stadium the second-largest stadium in the nation.

MILESTONE MOMENTS
• Lights were added to Beaver Stadium in 1984.
• Penn State enjoyed 49 consecutive non-losing seasons from 1939 through 1987.
• The stadium was dedicated in a 20-0 victory over Boston University on September 17, 1960.

FAST FACTS
• The stadium is named for James Beaver, who was a Civil War soldier, superior court judge, governor of Pennsylvania and president of the Penn State Board of Trustees.
• The stadium used to be northeast of Rec Hall on the west side of campus before moving to the east side in 1960. The stadium was dismantled and moved in 700 pieces before being reassembled.
• Fans love to get their picture taken at the Nittany Lion Shrine, which isn't far from the stadium. The area is home to the Nittany Lion, a 13-ton block of Indiana limestone that was dedicated on October 24, 1942.

CAPACITY THROUGH THE YEARS

1960:	46,284	1980:	83,770
1969:	48,284	1985:	83,370
1972:	57,538	1991:	93,967
1976:	60,203	2001:	107,282
1978:	76,639		

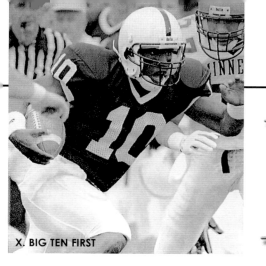

X. BIG TEN FIRST

X MAGIC MOMENTS
in the history of Beaver Stadium

I. COMEBACK CRAZINESS, *September 25, 1982.* In the signature win of Penn State's first national championship season, Joe Paterno's team drives 65 yards in the final 1:18 to beat second-ranked Nebraska, 27-24. With 4 seconds left, quarterback Todd Blackledge hits tight end Kirk Bowman with a 2-yard TD pass. On the final drive, tight end Mike McCloskey catches a 14-yard sideline pass that the Huskers argue was made out of bounds.

II. TURTLE SOUP, *November 4, 1978.* Fifth-ranked Maryland invades Happy Valley with its vaunted ground attack but is dominated by the No. 2 Nittany Lions, who stifle the Terp ground attack (minus-32 yards) on their way to a 27-3 triumph.

III. HEISMAN BOUND, *November 17, 1973.* In a 49-10 win over Ohio, senior tailback John Cappelletti tops the 200-yard mark for the third straight game, shredding the Bobcats for 204 yards and four touchdowns in little over a half of play. The outburst secures the Heisman Trophy for Cappelletti.

IV. PERFECTION, *December 7, 1968.* The thermometer reads just 25 degrees, but the Nittany Lions are plenty hot, ripping Syracuse, 30-12, to secure the school's first perfect regular season since 1947 and become the first Penn State team to win 10 games in one year.

V. TAKE THAT, BUCKEYES, *October 29, 1994.* A year after a demoralizing 24-6 defeat in Columbus, the Lions obliterate the Buckeyes, 63-14—Ohio State's worst loss since 1946—en route to a 12-0 campaign and a Rose Bowl triumph.

VI. WHAT A DIFFERENCE A YEAR MAKES, *October 12, 1985.* Penn State stifles Alabama's vaunted ground attack and forges a 19-17 victory that continues the team's dramatic turnaround from a five-loss '84 campaign.

VII. SUGAR BOUND, *November 26, 1982.* No. 5 Pittsburgh still has national title hopes when it invades Beaver Stadium on the Friday after Thanksgiving, but the Panthers' prospects are dashed by a 19-10 Nittany Lions triumph that features four Nick Gancitano field goals into a strong, swirling wind.

VIII. THE GAMBLERS, *November 24, 1978.* On fourth down with 5 minutes to play and Penn State down by 3, Joe Paterno, thinking the Lions need 4 yards for a first down, sends kicker Matt Bahr onto the field. Quarterback Chuck Fusina tells Paterno that Penn State needs 2 feet for a first down. It is more like 2 yards, but Bahr leaves the field and Penn State goes for it anyway. Mike Guman cuts into the end zone to put the Lions ahead, and Bahr tacks on an insurance field goal to give the top-ranked Lions a 17-10 win over Pittsburgh and a perfect regular season.

IX. STUFFED, *November 21, 1987.* Coming off a national title in 1986, Penn State already had lost three times when No. 7 Notre Dame came to town. But the unranked Nittany Lions improve their season with an upset of the Fighting Irish, 21-20, on a biting cold day when Pete Curkendall and Keith Karpinski stop Tony Rice short of the goal line in the Irish's last-minute 2-point conversion attempt.

X. BIG TEN FIRST, *September 4, 1993.* In their first game as a Big Ten Conference—or any other conference—member, the Lions thump Minnesota, 38-20, behind four receiving touchdowns by **Bobby Engram** (top).

SIMPLY UNFORGETTABLE
October 27, 2001. It wasn't a great season. The previous year wasn't much fun, either. Penn State was struggling, and there had been calls for an end to the Paterno regime.

But for two weeks in 2001, all was perfect again in Happy Valley. First, Penn State whipped 22nd-ranked Northwestern, 38-35. Although it was the first win of the season after four losses, it still created a buzz. PSU fans knew what was next: the Bear. The Lions' victory over the Wildcats tied **Joe Paterno** with Bear Bryant for the top spot on the all-time Division I coaching wins list. With one more victory, JoePa would stand alone.

But it wouldn't be easy. Ohio State bolted to a 27-9 lead, and it appeared Paterno's record would have to wait. But the Lions fought back. Penn State stole the momentum, powered by redshirt freshman quarterback Zach Mills, and earned a 29-27 triumph in front of 108,327 fans. Paterno had the record—324 wins—and a postgame celebration fit for a king. As he stood at midfield afterward, surrounded by players, family members and friends, Paterno choked up, and all of Penn State Nation joined him. The man who had given his life to the school and helped give it a national identity was finally being recognized as the best.

SATURDAY SHRINES

FRANKLIN FIELD

PENNSYLVANIA

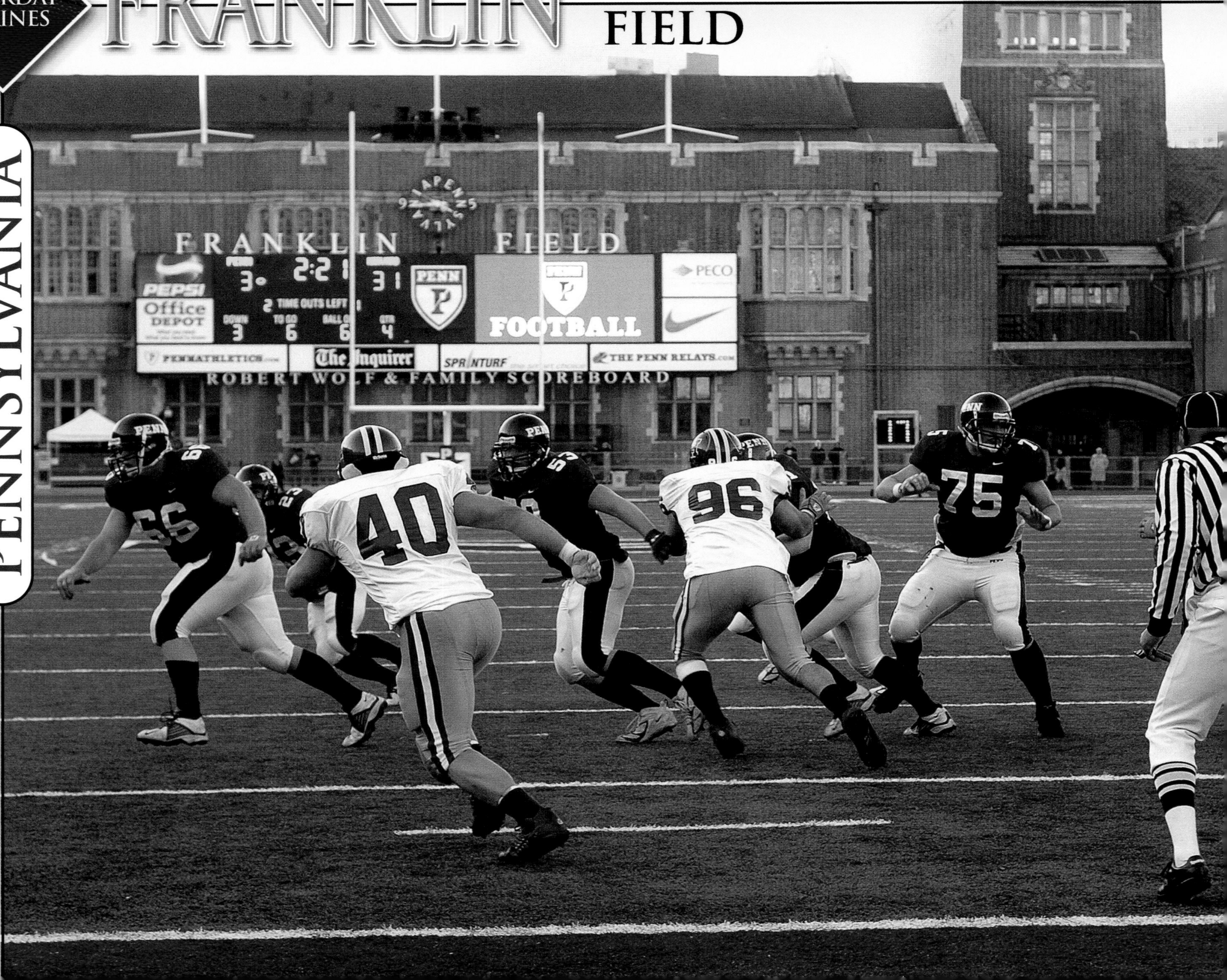

This place just feels like Ivy League football. Yes, Franklin Field is in an urban setting, as downtown Philadelphia is just a few miles away. But you'd never know it walking the campus on a crisp autumn Saturday morning.

And the football played inside this hallowed site has been among the best in Ancient Eight annals. In fact, Penn has claimed 12 Ivy crowns in the past 23 years. Venerable Franklin Field has seen its share of Quakers greats, headed by Pro Football Hall of Famer Chuck Bednarik.

STRUCTURE Sitting on the outskirts of the campus southwest of Philadelphia, Franklin Field opened in 1895 and is recognized by the NCAA as the oldest stadium still operating for football games. Franklin Field became the first permanent horseshoe college stadium in 1903. In 1925, a second tier was added, making Franklin Field the country's first double-decked stadium. The stadium is attached to Weightman Hall, which houses offices and a basketball practice court.

SETTING Franklin Field has the best of both worlds—an intimate collegiate feel with the Philadelphia skyline off in the distance. Parking is at a premium. Still, folks make do and enjoy some of the best tailgating in the Ivy League.

People put together their own version of the Philadelphia cheese steak sandwich for which the City of Brotherly Love is so well-known. But there also is plenty of hot dog and sausage fare to keep fans warm and full on a cool fall day at a stadium that's just a few blocks from another college: Drexel.

FANS They come far and wide to attend games, with many alums arriving from New York, Baltimore, Boston and throughout Pennsylvania. Many arrive via I-76, getting off at the South Street exit and rolling toward the stadium located at the corner of 33rd and Spruce adjacent to the university hospital. And they know how to have fun, especially the students. At the end of the third quarter, students sing "Drink a Highball." As the last line is sung ("Here's a toast to dear old Penn"), they toss toast—real bread, often burned—into the air. To pick up the toast littering the sideline and track, the school altered a turf cleaner so it could snatch up larger objects, earning it the moniker "Toast Zamboni."

PENNSYLVANIA

MAJOR RENOVATIONS This gem has been altered many times over the years. Franklin Field was opened in 1895 but totally redone in 1903. A big change occurred in 1922, when the stands were razed and the currents ones were constructed. Three years later, a second deck was added.

MILESTONE MOMENTS
• The dedication of expanded Franklin Field was on October 28, 1922, as Penn beat Navy, 13-7.
• The 1960 NFL championship game was played at Franklin Field. The Philadelphia Eagles defeated the Green Bay Packers, 17-13.
• Artificial turf was installed prior to the 1969 season.
• The first college scoreboard was erected here (1895) and the first local college football telecast (October 5, 1940) originated from Franklin Field.

FAST FACTS
• The Penn Relays, the oldest organized relay competition in the nation (debut: 1895), are held here every April. Great events in Penn Relays history are commemorated on plaques around the stadium. Greats like Carl Lewis and Michael Johnson have competed in the Relays.
• The Philadelphia Eagles called Franklin Field home from 1958-70. The Philadelphia Stars of the USFL played at Franklin Field in 1984. Eighteen Army-Navy games also have taken place here.
• Vice President Calvin Coolidge attended the 1922 Army-Navy game at Franklin Field.

CAPACITY THROUGH THE YEARS

1903: 20,000	1922: 54,500	1925: 63,000

X MAGIC MOMENTS
in the history of Franklin Field

SIMPLY UNFORGETTABLE

November 13, 1982. It had been 23 years since Penn's last Ivy League title. That was the scenario when Dave Shulman lined up to attempt a game-winning field goal against Harvard. It would clinch a tie for the Ivy crown.

For a school with a rich tradition, it had been a difficult period. Under coach Harry Gamble, the Quakers had been solid at times from 1971 through 1980 but never made it to the top. In 1972, a 48-30 win over Yale and a 20-14 victory over Columbia had set up a big season-ender with Dartmouth. Win, and a share of the title was Penn's. But although the Quakers took an early lead, Dartmouth won, 31-17. It would be 10 years before another chance arose.

The opportunity came under Jerry Berndt, who had promised great things, even as his first team, the '81 Quakers, finished 1-9. But Pennsylvania gathered momentum throughout 1982, and when Harvard came to Franklin Field, the Quakers were ready. Not that history was on Penn's side. Harvard had won eight straight over Penn and hadn't lost at Franklin Field since 1973. In the fourth quarter, it seemed Penn's misery was over—the Quakers led, 20-0. But Harvard rebounded to score three touchdowns and seized a 21-20 edge with 1:24 left.

Penn seemed to have blown its big chance, but quarterback Gary Vura drove the Quakers downfield, giving Shulman a chance to save the day with a 37-yard field goal. But with 3 seconds to play, Shulman was horribly wide left. Harvard celebrated—until it saw the flag. *Roughing the kicker.* Shulman lined up again, with no time left on the clock and a crowd of 34,746 awash in anxiety. This time, his kick was true. Penn had won a share of the Ivy crown with a 23-21 victory. Students poured from the bleachers, tore down the goalposts and threw them into the Schuylkill River.

I. CONCRETE CHAMPIONSHIP, *December 26, 1960.*
This Christmas present to the city of Philadelphia was a day late, but it was well-received nonetheless. The Eagles, led by "Concrete Charlie" Bednarik, defeat Green Bay, 17-13, to win the NFL championship.

II. PERFECTION, *November 15, 1986.* Ed Zubrow, taking over as coach for a Quakers program that had won four consecutive Ivy titles, guides Penn to a 10-0 record and another crown. It's the university's first perfect season since 1904. In their final home game of the year, the Quakers improve to 9-0 by downing Harvard, 17-10.

III. NATIONAL AUDIENCE, *November 16, 2002.* With ESPN's *GameDay* crew in the house, Penn throttles Harvard, 44-9, avenging a loss to the Crimson a year earlier and clinching at least a tie for the Ivy crown.

IV. THE FIRST ONE, *November 26, 1959.* The Quakers celebrate Thanksgiving in style by whipping Cornell, 28-13, and winning their first Ivy title in the fourth year of round-robin league play.

V. FINE FIFTEEN, *November 25, 1897.* Legendary coach George Woodruff leads the Quakers to a 4-0 win over Cornell on Thanksgiving Day to cap a 15-0 season.

III. NATIONAL AUDIENCE

Standout Harvard receiver Carl Morris is about to be brought down from behind by Penn's Michael Johns (33) in the 2002 game that lured ESPN's *GameDay* contingent to Franklin Field.

VI. DYNASTIC INTENTIONS, *November 22, 2003.*
Pennsylvania, already having clinched its second straight Ivy League title and third in four years, crushes Cornell, 59-7. It's the 15th straight Ivy victory for the Quakers, who eventually extend the streak to 20 games.

VII. GATHERING STEAM, *November 11, 2000.* After struggling with consistency in a 3-3 start, the Quakers start rolling and end up winning the Ivy title. The key victory is a thrilling 36-35 triumph over Harvard.

VIII. GHOST SIGHTING, *October 31, 1925.* Red Grange and Illinois come East, and the Galloping Ghost puts on quite a show, rushing for 331 yards in a 24-2 shellacking of Pennsylvania.

IX BEDNARIK, THE EARLY DAYS, *November 27, 1947.* Long before he led the Eagles to the NFL title, Bednarik was an All-American terror with Penn. On Thanksgiving, he helped the Quakers to a 21-0 win over Cornell, capping a 7-0-1 season marred only by a tie with Army.

X. THE FIRST, THE BEST, *April 1895.* The Penn Relays debut in Franklin Field. By the time their first century is up, the Relays have become the nation's largest track-and field carnival, with more than 10,000 participants and crowds that reach 45,000.

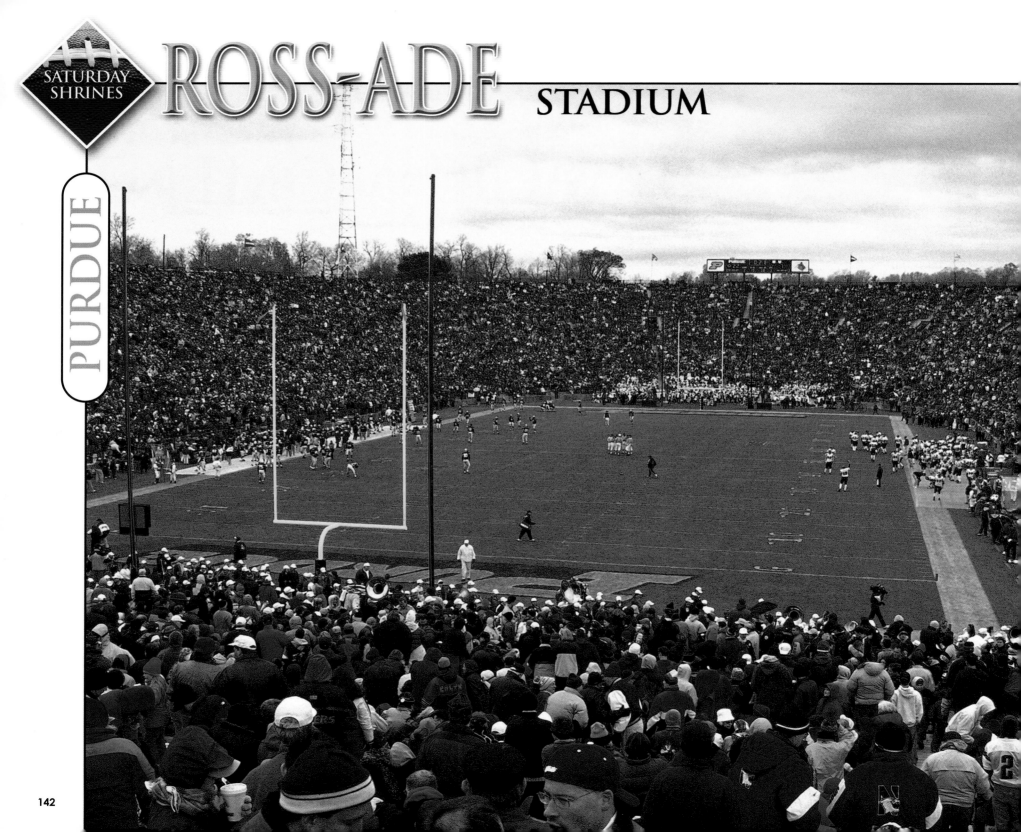

ROSS-ADE STADIUM

SATURDAY SHRINES

Built into the side of a hill, Ross-Ade Stadium sits like a red-bricked beacon on the north edge of Purdue's campus. The place has seen its share of great moments and standout players,

including the likes of Mike Alstott, Otis Armstrong, Dave Butz, Rod Woodson and Leroy Keyes. But Ross-Ade is best known as the "Cradle of Quarterbacks"—the school has produced such players as Bob Griese, Len Dawson, Mike Phipps, Gary Danielson, Jim Everett and Drew Brees. But from hard hat-wearing Purdue Pete wielding his sledgehammer to the Boilermaker Special blasting its horn as the team enters the field, it's what goes on in and around the stadium that makes Ross-Ade special.

SETTING No one ever has confused West Lafayette with Chapel Hill, Charlottesville or Provo, but it has a Midwestern charm and appeal. And the fans are more intense than given credit for in what's considered a basketball-mad state. Playing a big role in the atmosphere is the All-American Marching Band, a massive unit that features what's billed as the world's largest drum. But the most famous aspect of the band is the Golden Girl, a sequined baton twirler who is joined by the Silver Twins and the Girl in Black, all of whom add flash and dash to the Saturday experience.

STRUCTURE Prior to a major renovation that was completed in 2003, Ross-Ade Stadium had its unseemly girders exposed to the world. But now, the facility has been wrapped by a brick facade that meshes with the overall look of this staid campus. An oversized scoreboard with a train whistle affixed to the top anchors the south end zone. The fans are given an up-close look at the players in one of the Big Ten's most

intimate environments; in fact, fans are right on top of the action, almost able to reach from the first row and touch the players on the sideline. And there are no obstructed views in what has become one of the league's best venues.

FANS They are a loyal lot who enjoy their football as much as the basketball played next door in Mackey Arena. The fans arrive early, with cars lining the streets of adjacent neighborhoods and locals selling parking spots on their front yards. The tailgating is top-notch, with a massive parking lot north of the stadium and nearby Slayter Hill being popular places to set up chairs and grills to prepare Midwestern fare that ranges from burgers to pork to

A drumroll (a really big one), please: Here comes Purdue's All-American Marching Band.

PURDUE

> One of the most moving moments occurs before games, when the P.A. announcer reads a tribute to freedom called "I Am An American," with the crowd shouting those four words in unison.

corn on the cob. One of the most moving moments occurs before games, when the P.A. announcer reads a tribute to freedom called "I Am An American," with the crowd shouting those four words in unison. After wins, players serenade fans with the school's fight song: "Hail Purdue."

MAJOR RENOVATIONS This has been a work in progress since opening. Capacity more than doubled in 1949 when temporary bleachers were ditched for permanent steel grandstands on the west side. At the end of 2003, work was done on a $70 million facelift that saw, among other things, capacity dip but a new brick facade added, in addition to a massive press box that features lots of premium seating.

MILESTONE MOMENTS
• The first game was played November 22, 1924. The Boilermakers scored a 26-7 Homecoming victory over Indiana.

• The first night game was held October 18, 1986, with Ohio State claiming a 39-11 triumph.

FAST FACTS
• Purdue is the birthplace of Prescription Athletic Turf, which was installed in 1975 and later became widely used at venues across the nation.
• The stadium is named for David Ross, former president of the Board of Trustees, and George Ade, a writer/humorist who conceived the idea for the stadium and selected its site. The duo purchased the land and gave it to the school.
• The Golden Girl was created in the 1950 as a complement to Boilermakers star Dawson, who was dubbed the Golden Boy.

CAPACITY THROUGH THE YEARS

1924:	13,500	1969:	68,000
1930:	23,074	1970:	67,332
1949:	51,295	2001:	66,295
1955:	55,500	2003:	62,500
1964:	60,000		

X MAGIC MOMENTS

in the history of Ross-Ade Stadium

SIMPLY UNFORGETTABLE

November 6, 1976. Michigan was undefeated, ranked first in the nation and hungry for its first national championship under Bo Schembechler. The Boilermakers, meanwhile, were 3-5 and stuck among the dregs of the Big Ten. It seemed like a done deal. Michigan would roll on toward its inevitable showdown with Ohio State, and Purdue would continue its season as a Big Ten bottom-feeder.

Fans thought so, too. Just 57,205 showed up for the game, nearly 10,000 short of capacity. But those who did show up witnessed one of the greatest games in Purdue history. The "Spoilermakers" sprung a mammoth upset on the mighty Wolverines, whipping UM, 16-14, behind a running back with a sore ankle, a defense that rose to the occasion and a little bit of luck.

Running back Scott Dierking, who had suffered tendon damage to his ankle against Wisconsin, led the Boilermakers attack with 162 yards on eight carries. Purdue dominated the usually rugged Michigan defense with its power running game, and the Wolverine offense wasn't clicking, so the game stayed close until the end.

In the fourth quarter, with Michigan up 14-13, the Wolverines' Rob Lytle fumbled on the Purdue 29, the Boilermakers recovered, and Rock Supan eventually capitalized on the opportunity with a game-winning field goal. It gave Purdue a monumental win and triggered a wild celebration through Ross-Ade Stadium and West Lafayette.

I. PASADENA BOUND, *November 19, 1966.* Despite having won or shared six previous Big Ten titles, Purdue never played into the Rose Bowl until Bob Griese and coach Jack Mollenkopf's team cap a 8-2 regular season with a 51-6 thrashing of Indiana. Though the Boilermakers finish second in the league, they go bowling because of a Big Ten rule that prohibits the champion—Michigan State in this case—from making two straight Rose Bowl trips.

II. ROSE, TAKE 2, *October 28, 2000.* In one of the most electrifying plays in stadium annals, Drew Brees fires a game-winning 64-yard TD pass to Seth Morales with 1:55 remaining in a 31-27 victory over No. 12 Ohio State. Moments earlier, the game/Big Ten title hopes seemed lost after Brees tossed his fourth interception. The triumph serves as a catapult to the Rose Bowl.

III. DOWN GOES NO. 1, *September 30, 1967.* Notre Dame is ranked first in the nation and is fresh off a national title when it invades Ross-Ade for a meeting with the 10th-ranked Boilermakers. Before a then-record crowd of 62,316, Purdue mounts a 28-21 upset, thanks to four interceptions, two TD passes by Mike Phipps and two scoring runs by Perry Williams.

IV. CRUSHING THE BUCKEYES, *October 6, 1984.* After opening the season with an upset of eighth-ranked Notre Dame, Purdue beats No. 2 Ohio State, 28-23, behind the arm of junior quarterback **Jim Everett**, who passes for 257 yards and three touchdowns. The Boilermakers trail the Buckeyes, 17-14, early in the fourth quarter but score twice—both after interceptions of

IV. CRUSHING THE BUCKEYES

Jim Everett, who burned Ohio State in '84, continued a sterling quarterback tradition.

Ohio State quarterback Mike Tomczak.

V. PILING UP YARDS, *October 3, 1998.* Sophomore quarterback Drew Brees sets a school record with 522 passing yards and connects for six touchdowns in Purdue's 56-21 rout of Minnesota in the most efficient example of second-year coach Joe Tiller's spread attack.

VI. 2 FOR 2, *September 27, 1969.* Two years after upsetting top-ranked Notre Dame, the Boilermakers do in the Irish once again, this time 28-14. Quarterback Mike Phipps leads the way for the No. 16 Boilers, who deal ninth-ranked Notre Dame its only loss of the regular season.

VII. ON THE MAP, *October 14, 1978.* Despite opening the season 3-1 under second-year coach Jim Young, Purdue doesn't receive national attention until it beats 16th-ranked Ohio State, 27-16.

VIII. BACK TO EARTH, *September 22, 1979.* One week after having knocked off Michigan in Ann Arbor, Notre Dame visits West Lafayette and loses to Purdue, 28-22. The Boilers rebound from an upset loss the week before to UCLA to bump off No. 5 ND.

IX. CHAMPS, *November 16, 1929.* Before a Homecoming crowd of 26,000, the Boilermakers conclude their home schedule by whipping Iowa, 7-0, to remain undefeated. One week later, the Boilermakers clinch their first outright Big Ten title by routing Indiana, 32-0.

X. REBOUNDING IN STYLE, *October 3, 1959.* After being bounced from the rankings by a season-opening scoreless tie at unranked UCLA, the Boilers deal No. 8 Notre Dame a 28-7 loss that catapults Purdue to seventh in the polls.

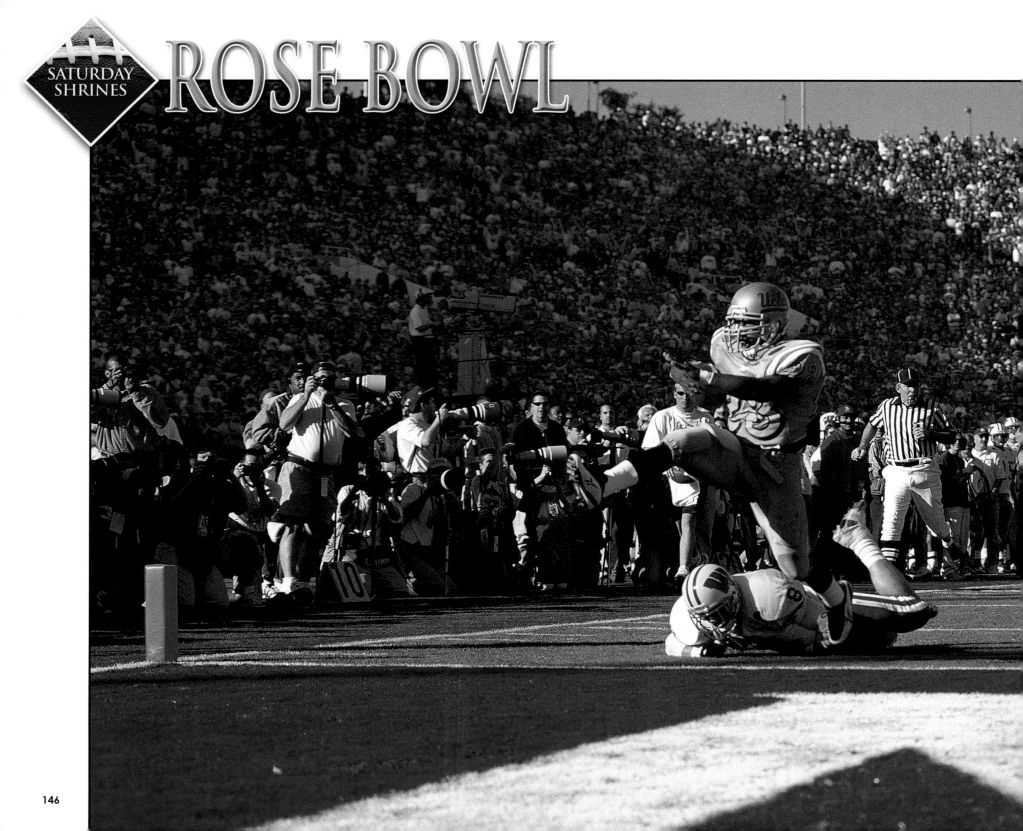

SATURDAY SHRINES

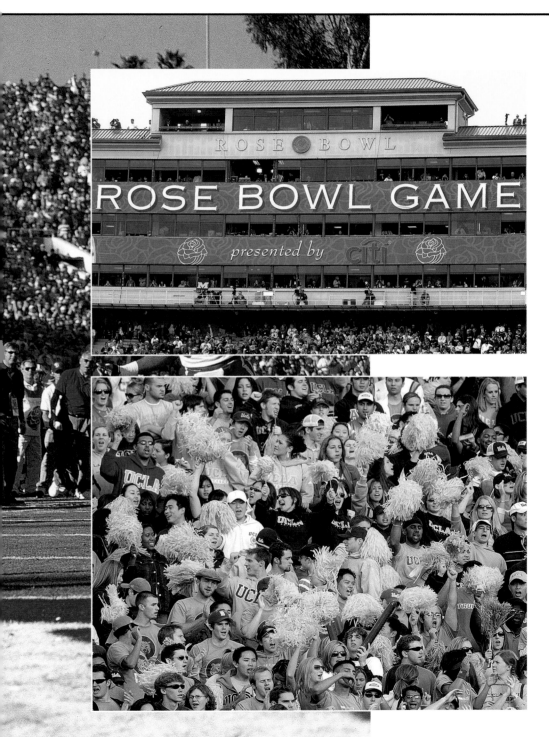

This is the place little boys dream about while playing football in the back yard. Why? Because this is where legends are made.

It's the Rose Bowl, home to the UCLA Bruins and the bowl game known as the Grand Daddy of Them All. A venue this gorgeous has to be in southern California, among the palm trees, multimillion-dollar houses, Mercedes-Benz owners and beautiful people. Shivering Midwesterners sitting in the dark rub their eyes in disbelief on New Year's Day while watching the sun-drenched Rose Bowl, swearing no place in American can be that nice in the dead of winter. Well, it is. But the Rose Bowl's appeal goes beyond the setting and weather. It's history that makes this venue an American treasure and one of the most famous stadiums on the globe.

SETTING Sit back and soak it all in. There's green everywhere, with the inspiring San Gabriel Mountains serving as a backdrop on one side of the stadium. If that isn't enough, the area around the Rose Bowl is home to tony neighborhoods in the Arroyo Seco area of Pasadena. That makes for ideal tailgating, especially on the adjacent Brookside Golf Course and at Area H, a big grassy zone in front of the Rose Bowl. That's where the UCLA team gets dropped off—players walk through a throng of fans on their way to the locker room.

STRUCTURE The Rose Bowl is just that—a bowl. At one end is the famous neon sign that features a long-stemmed rose and the script "Rose Bowl"—the subject of countless photos over the years. The exterior is a striking white, giving the facility a clean look. A unique aspect about the interior is that fans must pass

through long portals to get to their seats. It can be a spooky experience when they're crowded. But once fans maneuver their way through the tunnel, the sunshine-bathed, bright green grass comes into view, making for an inspiring first impression.

FANS Yeah, fans in southern California can be laid back, but the UCLA denizens get into the game. One way they get fired up is by doing the legendary Eight Clap Cheer. It goes: "One, two, three, four, five, six, seven, eight ... U... rah, rah, rah, C ... rah, rah, rah, L ... rah, rah, rah, A ... rah, rah, rah ... U-C-L-A, fight, fight, fight!" The cheerleaders also will get one section of the stadium to say "U," another "C," another "L," and another "A" in what, naturally, is called the "UCLA Spell Out." If fans listen close enough, they might be able to hear the team sing the school fight song—"Mighty Bruin"—in the locker room after a win.

MAJOR RENOVATIONS
The Rose Bowl began as a horseshoe but was made into a bowl in 1929. The biggest makeover took place prior to the 1982 season. With UCLA moving in (the Bruins had played at the Los Angeles Coliseum from 1929-81) and 1984 Olympic soccer coming to town, the Rose Bowl overhauled its press box, built permanent concession stands and added chairbacks for more than 50,000 seats.

MILESTONE MOMENTS
• UCLA's first home game at the Rose Bowl was a 41-10 victory over Long

Beach State on September 11, 1982.
• In their first season as Rose Bowl tenants, the Bruins qualified for the Rose Bowl game, and they downed Michigan, 24-14, in the New Year's Day classic. UCLA finished with 10 wins for just the second time in school history.
• The first game played in the Rose Bowl facility was between Southern California and California on October 28, 1922. Cal won, 12-0.

FAST FACTS
• UCLA's home field from 1919-29 was Moore Field.
• On January 1, 1927, radio stations were linked for the first time for a coast-to-coast broadcast of the Stanford-Alabama Rose Bowl game. The clash ended in a 7-7 tie.
• On January 1, 1954, the Rose Bowl matchup between Michigan State and UCLA was the first color TV broadcast on a nationwide hookup.
• The Rose Bowl has played host to five Super Bowls, as well as men's and women's World Cup soccer and portions of two Olympic Games.

CAPACITY THROUGH THE YEARS

1922: 57,000	1972: 104,594
1929: 76,000	1992: 105,794
1932: 83,677	1994: 104,294
1949: 100,807	1996: 91,136

SATURDAY SHRINES

SIMPLY UNFORGETTABLE

January 1, 1934. When Columbia trotted onto the soggy Rose Bowl turf on the first day of 1934, the Lions did not enter to a roaring din from eager supporters. Instead, they heard chants of "We want Michigan!" Coach Lou Little's team was strong, but it was derided for playing a light schedule made up of Eastern teams and future Ivy League members.

Columbia's opponent was 8-1-1 Stanford, which was coached by Tiny Thornhill and boasted stars like Bobby Grayson, Horse Reynolds and Monk Moscrip. This was going to be a rout, plain and simple, and critics were actually rooting for a blowout, if only to give them fuel for the arrows they had launched at the Rose Bowl's organizers, who had turned away 7-0-1 Michigan, the Big Ten champions.

From the start, it appeared as if the Lions were in trouble. Stanford moved the ball at will, pushing the lighter Columbia line around and appearing ready to break loose at any moment. The problem was that Stanford couldn't score.

In the second quarter, with the score still 0-0, Columbia's Cliff Montgomery hit Tony Matal with a pass that took the ball to the Stanford 17. Al Barabas fumbled on the next play but recovered for a 1-yard loss. Then Montgomery called for the KF-79, a trick play that was one of Little's favorites. After the snap, Montgomery handed the ball to Barabas, then faked to another back and pretended to have the ball himself as he dashed around end. Stanford bought the fakes, and Barabas waltzed into the end zone, untouched. The point after made it 7-0, and that's how it remained.

X MAGIC MOMENTS
in the history of the Rose Bowl

I. HURRY UP AND WIN, *November 23, 1996.* Despite trailing USC by 17 points with less than 7 minutes to play, UCLA mounts a furious comeback to tie the game with 39 seconds left in regulation. The Bruins beat the Trojans, 48-41, in two overtimes. A 25-yard touchdown run by Skip Hicks to open the second overtime is the game-winner; UCLA preserves the win when Anthony Cobbs intercepts a fourth-down pass in the end zone.

II. THE HORSEMEN RIDE, *January 1, 1925.* Stanford's Ernie Nevers, who fractured both ankles earlier in the season, rushes for 114 yards—more than the combined yardage of the Four Horsemen—but Pop Warner's undefeated Stanford team turns the ball over eight times and falls to Knute Rockne and Notre Dame, 27-10. The Irish win the national championship.

III. ALMOST FAMOUS, *January 1, 1963.* No. 1 USC bolts out to a 42-14 lead and appears to be cruising to victory. But second-ranked Wisconsin, led by quarterback Ron Vander Kelen, scores 23 points in the fourth quarter. Vander Kelen finishes with 401 yards passing, but the Badgers' comeback falls short, and the Trojans win, 42-37.

IV. SMASHING THE BUCKEYES, *January 1, 1976.* Top-ranked Ohio State, led by Heisman Trophy winner Archie Griffin, comes to Pasadena expecting an easy time against a No. 11 UCLA team it beat, 41-20, earlier in the year. But John Sciarra, Wally Henry and Wendell Tyler confound OSU in a 23-10 UCLA victory.

V. DOWN TO THE WIRE, *November 21, 1992.* UCLA trails No. 15 USC, 31-17, entering the fourth quarter but fights back to go ahead, 38-31, with 3:08 left. The Trojans' Rob Johnson scores on a 1-yard quarterback sneak with 41 seconds left to put the Trojans within 1, but on the ensuing 2-point conversion attempt, Bruin Nkosi Littleton knocks down Johnson's pass to preserve a 38-37 UCLA win.

I. HURRY UP AND WIN

In the 1996 clash of heated rivals UCLA and USC, Bruins quarterback Cade McNown ran for two TDs and passed for 356 yards and another score in a two-overtime thriller.

VI. THE FOURTH, *January 20, 1980.* In a game that was supposed to be a blowout, the Pittsburgh Steelers juggernaut beats a stubborn Los Angeles Rams team, 31-19, behind two fourth-quarter touchdowns and an outstanding performance by Terry Bradshaw to win Super Bowl XIV, the Steelers' fourth Super Bowl win in six years.

VII. RAIDING THE TROPHY CASE, *January 9, 1977.* Raiders cornerback Willie Brown intercepts a pass from Vikings quarterback Fran Tarkenton and returns it 75 yards for a touchdown. Oakland gets coach John Madden a Super Bowl victory by pillaging Minnesota and the Vikings' Purple People Eaters defensive line, 32-14, making the Vikings the first team to lose four Super Bowl games.

VIII. LATER, HUSKERS, *September 10, 1988.* Nebraska arrives as the No. 2 team in the nation but leaves with a 41-28 loss to the No. 5 Bruins. In the teams' previous three meetings, UCLA was outscored by 80 points, but the 41 the Bruins scored were the most ever against a Tom Osborne-coached team.

IX. SIMPLY AMAZING, *January 25, 1987.* New York Giants quarterback Phil Simms completes 22 of 25 passes for 268 yards and three touchdowns in the Giants' 39-20 rout of John Elway and Denver. The Giants come back from a 10-9 halftime deficit to win their first NFL title in 30 years.

X. NAPOLEON'S WAR, *November 25, 1983.* The Army-Navy game, begun in 1890, never ventured farther west than Chicago until 1983, when the Cadets and Midshipmen came to Pasadena. Navy, powered by a 95-yard opening kickoff return and star tailback Napoleon McCallum's running, wins, 42-13.

WILLIAMS-BRICE STADIUM

SATURDAY SHRINES

SOUTH CAROLINA

Sitting in your seat during pregame at Williams-Brice, you'd swear the stadium had a heartbeat and was a living, breathing entity. South Carolina fans are ultra-passionate and love anything and everything that's Gamecocks-related.

The electricity builds in the parking lots in and around the South Carolina State Fairgrounds, which is home to Williams-Brice and about two miles from campus. Tailgating is taken to new heights by the Cockaboose Railroad, made up of a series of cabooses that have been converted into lavish digs that sit on tracks outside the stadium. Now that's living.

SETTING Get ready for perhaps the best entrance among all college teams. To juice up the crowd, the P.A. system begins with the theme from *2001: A Space Odyssey*, a tradition that started in 1983. The idea was spawned after an alum saw Elvis Presley enter a concert to that tune. With the band forming a tunnel and the music blaring, players burst onto the field on the right cue of the song amid a billow of smoke from the southwest corner of the stadium. The crowd erupts. It's time for South Carolina football.

STRUCTURE This is a massive facility that stretches high into the sky. At night from I-77, which runs past the stadium, the place resembles a monstrous spaceship. At one point in the mid-1980s, Williams-Brice started to sway, in particular the upper deck on the east side, because of the raucousness inside. Bumper stickers were produced that proclaimed: "If it ain't swaying, we ain't playing." Work was done to re-enforce the structure. Among the distinctive aspects of the stadium are the spiral walkways that dot each of the four corners of the facility, which features a deck on each side.

FANS The best way to describe them: rabid, loyal and patient (the Gamecocks have not captured a conference title since 1969 and have won only three bowl games in their history). But the fans have had many great players to watch, including 1980 Heisman Trophy winner George Rogers, Alex Hawkins and Sterling

SOUTH CAROLINA

Sharpe. Most fans are hard-working, blue-collar types who live and die with the Gamecocks. And they show their passion during the game. The most popular cheer is when half of the stadium yells "GAME!" and the other half screams "COCKS!"—all of which is orchestrated by the cheerleaders. And it gets loud.

MAJOR RENOVATIONS One of the biggest was a $13.5 million south end zone expansion, which was finished before the 1996 season. The year before, a $9.9 million project enhanced the west side of the stadium.

MILESTONE MOMENTS
• The first game was played September 23, 1934, and South Carolina topped Erskine, 25-0, in what then was called Carolina Stadium. The stadium was dedicated as Williams-Brice on September 9, 1972, with Virginia taking a 24-16 victory.
• The first night game was played November 3, 1950, a 13-13 tie with Marquette.

FAST FACTS
• In 1987, Pope John Paul II appeared at Williams-Brice Stadium.
• At halftime of a 1992 game vs. Tennessee, scenes for the movie *The Program* were filmed at the stadium.
• In 1972, the stadium was named for Thomas and Martha Williams Brice. Martha's family left a large sum of money to her nephews, who later donated it to the university. Husband Thomas was a Game-cocks football letterman in 1922 and 1923.

CAPACITY THROUGH THE YEARS

1934: 17,600	1982: 72,400
1970: 32,056	1996: 80,250
1972: 53,865	

The Cockaboose Railroad puts tailgating on the fast track at South Carolina.

X MAGIC MOMENTS

in the history of Williams-Brice Stadium

SIMPLY UNFORGETTABLE

September 23, 2000. Erik Kimrey was a walk-on backup quarterback; he spent the first two years as a Gamecock on the bench and got spot action in the first three games of 2000, his junior year. So this was not the quarterback fans wanted in the close games—or so they thought.

So forgive the USC community for fretting when Kimrey grabbed his helmet late in the fourth quarter of a tight game against No. 25 Mississippi State. Starter Phil Petty had suffered an ankle sprain and couldn't continue, meaning Carolina coach Lou Holtz had no choice. He looked to Kimrey, even though the Gamecocks trailed MSU, 19-13, on third down on the Bulldogs' 25. As Kimrey came over for final instructions before heading onto the field, he passed on a bit of information to Holtz. "Coach, I can throw the fade route," he said.

Holtz didn't need to hear that twice. "When a player tells me he can do something, I'm all for that," Holtz said.

So in went Kimrey to throw the fade—right into the hands of **Jermale Kelly** (right), who had beaten MSU defensive back Kendall Roberson. Kelly made into the end zone to tie the game, and Carolina took the lead with the extra point. USC then recovered a Mississippi State fumble and tacked on an insurance field goal. The Gamecocks won, and Kimrey was the improbable hero.

I. DOWN GO THE TROJANS, *October 1, 1983.* Led by the "Fire Ants Defense," South Carolina dumps Southern California, 38-14, in the battle of USCs. It's the first big win for new coach Joe Morrison.

II. TAMING THE 'DAWGS, *September 9, 2000.* After going 0-11 in his first season in Columbia, Lou Holtz serves notice that the Gamecocks' fortunes are changing when he leads Carolina to a 21-10 upset of ninth-ranked Georgia en route to an 8-4 season and an Outback Bowl victory.

III. FIRST TO 10, *November 10, 1984.* The Gamecocks stay undefeated by beating Florida State, 38-26, for their ninth win of the season. Two weeks later, they win at Clemson, making the 1984 USC team the first in school history to have 10 victories in a season.

IV. FIRST-TIME CHAMPS, *November 22, 1969.* South Carolina whips archrival Clemson, 27-13, to finish Atlantic Coast Conference play with a 6-0 record and capture its first ACC title.

V. TANGERINE BOUND, *November 22, 1975.* After stumbling to three straight losses, the Gamecocks beat Wake Forest and then club Clemson, 56-20, when senior quarterback Jeff Grantz passes for five touchdowns and runs for a sixth. The win earns South Carolina a Tangerine Bowl berth. It's USC's first postseason invitation in six seasons and only its third ever.

VI. AN SEC FIRST, *October 17, 1992.* After joining the Southeastern Conference, South Carolina loses its first four games. But the Gamecocks finally beat Mississippi State, 21-6, for their first SEC victory.

VII. EIGHT IS GREAT, *November 24, 1979.* With its 13-9 win over No. 13 Clemson, 19th-ranked South Carolina notches its first eight-win season since 1903.

VIII. GOING LONG, *October 12, 1985.* Sterling Sharpe's 104-yard kickoff return highlights South Carolina's 28-7 win over Duke. It remains the longest play in school history.

IX. ROLLING THE TIDE, *September 29, 2001.* No. 16 South Carolina wins a 37-36 come-from-behind thriller over Alabama for its first victory over the Crimson Tide. The Gamecocks were down, 36-24, with less than 10 minutes remaining in the game, but quarterback Phil Petty engineered a comeback, throwing for 107 yards in the final two drives. USC had been 0-9 previously against Bama.

X. LONG TIME COMING, *October 31, 1992.* South Carolina sneaks past No. 16 Tennessee, 24-23, for its first win over the Volunteers since 1903. The Vols' Mose Phillips caught a pass from Heath Shuler to pull within one point with less than 2 minutes left, but Hank Campbell stuffed Tennessee's attempt at the 2-point conversion. It remains just the second time in history the Gamecocks have beaten the Volunteers.

General Robert Neyland, the SEC and national titles, the checkerboard end zones, the smoke off the mountains—they're all part of the lore of Tennessee football.

And how about being named after thousands of volunteers Gen. Andrew Jackson corralled and led to battle in the War of 1812? Thus the name Volunteers—or Vols. That's history. So is Smokey, the famed blue tick coon hound who leads the Vols through the "T" at the beginning of the game and stays on the sideline as inspiration.

SETTING There's not a better view in college football. On one side of the stadium is the Tennessee River, where fans arrive by boat and tailgate hours before kickoff and hours after the game. On the other side is The Hill, the historic center of UT's old campus. Rising above it all are the Great Smoky Mountains, a perfect scenic backdrop for a fall Saturday afternoon. Former UT broadcaster George Mooney navigated his small runabout down the river in 1962, spawning what is now called the Volunteer Navy. It all comes together in a perfect game-day package moments before kickoff, when the Vols run through the big T formed by the Pride of the Southland Band.

STRUCTURE It's enormous. And it keeps getting big-ger, even though it trails Michigan Stadium and Penn State's Beaver Stadium in overall capacity: Neyland holds 104,079, Beaver Stadium 107,282 and Michigan Stadium 107,501. But Neyland's facility is unlike any in the nation. It rises straight up from the ground, towering over the playing field and intimidating opponents with its size. The stadium has undergone 16 renovations since the West stands were built in 1921 (those stands held 3,200 fans at the time). The latest addition was 78 executive suites completed in 2000. Also included: One of the nation's biggest video replay boards (44 X 28 feet).

FANS Ah, the Tennessee fan. Obsessed, maniacal and just a bit frightening. Step into Neyland Stadium and feel the orange experience. The volume booms from the opening introductions and continues with each play. Tennessee fans always have been passionate to the point of paranoia. How could they not be? Johnny Majors was beaten out by Paul Hornung for the Heisman Trophy in 1956, and Peyton Manning lost to Charles Woodson in 1997. As far as Vols fans are concerned, both were unforgivable blunders by Heisman voters. Better get used to "Rocky Top," the unofficial fight song of the Vols. If you don't know it, you will by the end of the day—from the constant crooning of 100,000-plus fans.

MAJOR RENOVATIONS The capacity has increased with great frequency from

Peyton Manning and the Volunteer Navy have meant smooth sailing for teams and fans.

TENNESSEE

the original 3,200 seats to the most recent expansion in 2000 when 78 executive suites were added. The north upper deck expansion in 1996 pushed the capacity past 100,000 and stirred the attendance race with Michigan Stadium and Penn State.

MILESTONE MOMENTS
- The first game at Shields-Watkins Field was played September 24, 1921. Tennessee overpowered Emory & Henry, 27-0.
- The stadium was named in honor of Volunteers coaching legend General Robert R. Neyland in 1962.
- The first night game was a September 16, 1972, game against Penn State. The Vols prevailed, 28-21.

FAST FACTS
- From October 3, 1925, to October 21, 1933, Tennessee went 55 home games in a row without a loss.
- From December 8, 1928, to October 21, 1933, the Vols won 30 consecutive games at home.

- Fans have torn down the goalposts at Neyland Stadium on eight occasions. The last time was on September 19, 1998, following a 20-17 overtime win vs. No. 2 Florida. It was the first OT game in Tennessee history.

CAPACITY THROUGH THE YEARS

Year	Capacity
1921:	3,200
1929:	17,860
1938:	29,390
1948:	45,390
1962:	51,227
1976:	79,250
1987:	91,110
1996:	102,544
2000:	104,079

X MAGIC MOMENTS

in the history of Neyland Stadium

SIMPLY UNFORGETTABLE

November 14, 1998. The Vols were a perfect 8-0 and ranked first in the nation. They had taken over No. 1 after a win over Alabama-Birmingham the week before. But anticipation was high as 10th-ranked Arkansas came to town. And the Hogs wasted no time proving just how tough they were; Arkansas jumped out to a 21-3 lead and was still on top, 24-22, with less than 2 minutes left in the game. The Hogs had held on to their lead despite a blocked field goal and a bad snap that had resulted in a safety. They appeared to be well on their way to unseating No. 1.

But then Arkansas QB Clint Stoerner, who would finish with 274 yards passing, was flushed from the pocket and stumbled. Instead of breaking his fall with his free hand, Stoerner tried to balance himself by leaning on the football. The ball squirted free, and Tennessee had new life.

Then sophomore tailback **Travis Henry** (right), filling in for the injured Jamal Lewis, ran the ball five times in the Vols' final drive—including into the end zone for the game-winning touchdown. Tennessee would go on to win the SEC East, polish off Mississippi State in the SEC title game and finish the year 13-0 after beating Florida State in the Fiesta Bowl. The Vols were the consensus national champions.

I. BROKEN JINX, *September 19, 1998.* The Volunteers listened to Steve Spurrier make fun of them for five long, ugly years, but Tennessee has the last laugh when quarterback Tee Martin leads the No. 6 Vols to a 20-17 overtime win over the second-ranked Gators. The Vols go on to an undefeated season and win the national championship.

II. STEMMING THE TIDE, *October 16, 1982.* After losing 11 straight meetings with Alabama, unranked Tennessee intercepts a pass in the end zone with 17 seconds left to beat the No. 2 Crimson Tide, 35-28, taking some of the sting out of what would be only a six-win season.

III. MAKING A STATEMENT, *September 28, 1985.* Unranked Tennessee knocks off No. 1 Auburn, 38-20, and holds eventual Heisman winner Bo Jackson to 80 yards rushing. The Vols leap into the AP top 20 and set the stage for an SEC title.

IV. TAMING THE TIGERS, *November 7, 1959.* Six weeks after the Vols defeated No. 3 Auburn, they hand top-ranked LSU a 14-13 defeat. The Vols stuff future Heisman winner Billy Cannon's 2-point conversion attempt and end the Tigers' winning streak at 19 games.

V. FIRST TO 11, *December 5, 1970.* The fifth-ranked Vols handle UCLA, 28-17, for win No. 10 of the season under first-year coach Bill Battle. When UT beats Air Force in the Sugar Bowl, Battle becomes the nation's first first-year coach to win 11 games.

VI. BACK ON TOP, *December 2, 1967.* The Vols clinch their first SEC championship since 1956 with a 41-14 win over Vanderbilt. After stumbling in the opener against UCLA, Tennessee rips through the SEC and earns an Orange Bowl berth.

VII. BRIGHT LIGHTS, *September 16, 1972.* The Volunteers make the first night game at Neyland Stadium a memorable one when they knock off sixth-ranked Penn State, 28-21, and climb to No. 5 in the rankings.

VIII. A DAY OF FIRSTS, *September 14, 1968.* Tennessee makes its debut on the new Tartan Turf at Neyland Stadium with a thrilling, come-from-behind 17-17 tie with Georgia, and the Vols' Lester McClain becomes the first black player to compete in a Southeastern Conference game.

IX. DOWN GO THE IRISH, *November 10, 1979.* Notre Dame comes to Knoxville for the first time, and the unranked Volunteers beat the No. 13 Irish, 40-18.

X. NO. 1 AGAIN, *November 7, 1998.* Alabama-Birmingham doesn't put up much of a fight in a 37-13 UT victory, but the triumph lifts the Volunteers to the top spot of the AP rankings, and Tennessee goes on to win the national title.

It's intimidating, aesthetically pleasing and loud. But most of all—it's big. But what did you expect? This is Texas, after all. Royal-Texas Memorial Stadium is one of the crown jewels of the college football realm.

Who's who of the sport's greats have rumbled up and down the turf of this Saturday afternoon cathedral, headed by Heisman winners Earl Campbell and Ricky Williams. And the sideshows inside the stadium are unmatched. There's the sound of Smokey the Cannon being shot after the Longhorns score. Adding to the cacophony is the band, known as the Showband of the Southwest. Part of the band is Big Bertha, which the school touts as the world's largest bass drum. And then there's Bevo, the school's longhorn mascot, who seems unmoved by the goings on, unlike the thousands of others in this pulsating stadium.

SETTING Austin is one of the most beautiful areas of Texas, with gentle rolling hills doting the landscape. Adding to the game-day environment is Waller Creek, which flows next to the stadium. Barbecue simmers from myriad cookers around the stadium, as tailgaters try to outdo each other. But inside is where the real action is. The players' entrance gets fans jacked up. On the big screen, digital images of Longhorns running through the streets of Austin are projected. As the animated Longhorns enter the stadium, they morph into images of Campbell and Williams. That's the cue for the Longhorns to enter the field, amid plumes of smoke.

STRUCTURE Royal-Texas Memorial Stadium has seen many changes over the

years and has grown into one of the most imposing facilities in the nation. According to a 1926 Texas football program: "Memorial Stadium is built of everlasting concrete, defying age, fire and the elements. It will still be sound and strong when this generation's great, great, grandchildren are out there winning for Texas." The trademark arches at the bowl end of the double-decker stadium are made of steel and mortar.

FANS Before Mack Brown arrived, Texas had suffered five losing seasons in six years, and fans were known to arrive late and leave early. But he has changed that, turning this into one of the most hostile environments in the country. Fans decked in burnt orange revel in singing "The Eyes of Texas," the school's alma mater. After that, the crowd will break into "Texas Fight," which is better known as "Taps." And at any point in time during a song, you'll likely see some fan jutting a hand in the air and making the famous Hook 'em Horns sign. If Texas wins, the school's famous 27-story UT Tower is bathed in orange light. Win or lose, after games fans flock to Sixth Street and the Warehouse District, two of the nation's hottest music scenes.

MAJOR RENOVATIONS The facility received a big overhaul from 1967-72, as artificial turf, aluminum seats and a track were installed. Also, a 15,900-seat upper deck was built. In 1926, a north end

TEXAS

horseshoe with 13 arches was added to increase capacity by 27,000. The field was lowered six feet and a track was eliminated following sweeping changes completed in 1999.

MILESTONE MOMENTS
• The first game was played on November 8, 1924, when Baylor topped Texas, 28-10.
• The Longhorns first played under the lights at home on September 17, 1955, with Texas Tech taking a 20-14 decision.
• Artificial turf was added for the 1969 season. The school returned to grass in 1996.

FAST FACTS
• At one end of the stadium is the Louis Jordan flag pole, which is dedicated to a three-sport former Texas star who was the first Texas officer killed in World War I.
• Before entering the field, players touch a pair of longhorns that are adorned with the phrase "Don't Mess With Texas." As they approach the scoreboard, they touch a photo of Freddie Steinmark, a starting safety in 1968-69 who died of cancer.
• The university honored former coach Darrell Royal, who led the school to three national titles and 11 Southwest Conference banners in 20 seasons, by adding his name to the stadium in 1996.

CAPACITY THROUGH THE YEARS

Year	Capacity
1924:	13,500
1926:	40,500
1948:	60,130
1971:	77,809
1998:	79,471
1999:	80,082

X MAGIC MOMENTS
in the history of Memorial Stadium

SIMPLY UNFORGETTABLE

November 27, 1998. They thought it was big in Austin when **Ricky Williams** (below) announced he would return for his senior season rather than head to the NFL. Nobody thought Williams would be back for the '98 season, not after he led the nation in rushing and was deemed a certain top-10 draft pick. But he surprised the Burnt Orange Nation by coming back and authoring a tremendous encore.

By the time Williams (right) was finished, he was the top rusher in NCAA history, a Heisman Trophy winner and a Longhorn icon. His senior season was notable, right down to the end, when he broke Tony Dorsett's 22-year-old all-time collegiate rushing record. Williams finished the year with 2,124 yards and left Texas with 21 NCAA marks and 46 UT records.

It all came to a head during Texas' annual day-after-Thanksgiving shootout with Texas A&M. With 1:13 remaining in the first quarter, Williams needed just 11 yards to break Dorsett's record. He gained a lot more than that.

With Dorsett looking on from the sideline, Williams took a handoff from Major Applewhite and blasted through a hole on the left side. He sprinted down the sideline, set up a block at the 12-yard line and then barreled through an Aggie defender at the goal line to complete a dramatic 60-yard run. Later that day, he surpassed Napoleon McCallum's NCAA career mark for all-purpose yards. More important, he was part of unranked Texas' 26-24 win over the sixth-ranked Aggies.

I. NOBLE NOBLE, *November 28, 1940.* Noble Doss' "impossible" over-the-shoulder catch in the first quarter sets up Pete Layden's 1-yard TD run. It is the only touchdown of the game, and Texas edges Texas A&M, 7-0, snaps the Aggies' 19-game winning streak and prevents A&M from winning back-to-back national titles.

II. LAST-MINUTE MAGIC, *October 3, 1970.* With just 20 seconds left and facing a third-and-19 from the UCLA 45, quarterback Eddie Phillips hits Cotton Speyrer on a crossing pattern, and Speyrer runs 20 yards for a touchdown that gives UT a 20-17 win over the Bruins and extends the team's unbeaten streak to 23 games.

III. CRAIN'S MUTINY, *October 21, 1939.* With 20 seconds remaining in the game, Jack Crain turns a short pass from quarterback R.B. Patrick into a dramatic 67-yard touchdown to bring Texas back from a 13-7 deficit against Arkansas. After the delirious fans who storm the field are cleared away, Crain drills the extra point to give the Longhorns a 14-13 win.

IV. STANDING TALL, *October 20, 1962.* In a meeting of undefeated teams, No. 7 Arkansas scores on a field goal early in the game and carries that advantage into the third quarter. Longhorns Johnny Treadwell and Pat Culpepper drill Arkansas fullback Danny Brabham on the Texas 3-yard line and force a fumble that the Longhorns recover. Texas then mounts a 90-yard drive that ends with a touchdown, and the Longhorns win, 7-3, and preserve their No. 1 ranking.

V. TO DOAK, *October 3, 1998.* With a heavy heart after the death of his friend, SMU legend Doak Walker, future Heisman

VIII. BIG COMEBACK

winner Ricky Williams lights up Iowa State for 350 yards and five touchdowns in a 54-33 Texas win. Williams moves past Anthony Thompson on the NCAA career touchdowns list. Williams also set NCAA records for non-kicker scoring and rushing yards in consecutive games.

VI. STAYING NO. 1, *November 9, 1963.* Duke Carlisle's last-minute leaping end-zone interception of what appeared to be a sure TD pass preserves Texas' 7-0 win over Baylor and keeps the Longhorns on their run to the national championship.

VII. BIG KICK, *October 21, 1995.* No Texas Longhorn had ever won a game with a last-second kick until Phil Dawson's 50-yard field goal on the final play gives the No. 16 Longhorns a 17-16 victory over No. 14 Virginia. The final scoring drive includes two fourth-down conversions.

VIII. BIG COMEBACK, *October 23, 1999.* No. 18 Texas overcomes a 13-3 halftime deficit against third-ranked Nebraska and gives the Huskers their only loss of the season, 24-20. A fourth-quarter TD pass from **Major Applewhite** (top) to Mike Jones caps the comeback.

IX. TAMING THE MUSTANGS, *November 4, 1950.* No. 7 Texas holds SMU All-American running back Kyle Rote to minus-3 yards rushing on seven carries and upsets top-ranked Southern Methodist, 23-20.

X. RUN-AND-SHOOT SHOT DOWN, *November 10, 1990.* After having given up 173 points in three consecutive losses to Houston and its powerful run-and-shoot attack, unranked Texas stifles the No. 3 Cougars, picking off four passes in a 45-24 win. Meanwhile, the UT attack piles up 626 yards of offense.

KYLE FIELD

TEXAS A&M

You can see it from a distance, standing tall on the Texas plain, seemingly stretching a mile into the sky: Kyle Field. There has been plenty of top-notch football played here—and it has been contested in one of the most intense atmospheres in the college game.

Kyle Field was home to a national champion in 1939, and the likes of Jack Pardee, John Kimbrough, Edd Hargett, John David Crow, Kevin Murray and Bucky Richardson, among others, have made Kyle Field a great home for a proud, tradition-rich program. It's enough to make any diehard Aggie fan yell, "Gig 'em!"

SETTING This is a true college town in that the university defines College Station. One of the first things you see upon entering this town in east-central Texas is a cow pasture, but fans and alums are proud of the school's agricultural background. In fact, the lack of attractions is one reason Aggie football is so popular. The play of team often shapes the mood of the area.

STRUCTURE What Kyle Field lacks in architectural splendor, it makes up for in size. It's a triple-decked stadium, and it bears the phrase "Welcome to Aggieland Home of the 12th Man" on the facades of the second and third decks. The facility added another dimension in 1999 with the opening of the Bernard C. Richardson Zone— better known as the Zone—a huge north end zone seating section that has become a wall of noise on Saturday afternoons. Visitors to Kyle Field might be surprised to find a mini-cemetery just outside the stadium. The graves are the final resting places for Reveille, the school's collie mascot.

FANS One word: Insane. Among the traditions are Silver Taps, the 12th man, the Elephant Walk, Aggie Muster, Saw Varsity's Horns Off, Farmers Fight, Midnight Yell Practice, the Spirit of Aggieland and the Fightin' Texas Aggie Band. Yell Leaders decked out in white lead the throng in cheers while Reveille stands watch over the field. At midnight on the nights before games, as many as 20,000 students turn out at Kyle Field to practice yells. On game days, the students stand the entire game, demonstrating, in true 12th-man fashion, that they are ready to enter the game at any time.

MAJOR RENOVATIONS In 1999, the school opened the Bernard C. Richardson Zone, which cost $32.9 million and increased capacity to its current level. Long-term expansion plans could increase capacity to as much as 115,000, but "long term" means just that—20 or so years.

Yell leaders, cadets and other tradition-minded Aggies polish up their acts.

TEXAS A&M

MILESTONE MOMENTS

• The first game was played October 7, 1905, as the Aggies beat Houston YMCA, 29-0.

• The first game on artificial turf was played in 1970 against Wichita State. Texas A&M switched back to grass for the 1996 season.

FAST FACTS

• Kyle Field is named for E.J. Kyle, a professor and president of the General Athletic Association.

• One of the best spectacles is the entrance of A&M's Corps of Cadets. Only seniors are allowed to wear boots.

• When the Aggies score, dates celebrate by kissing.

• From 1989-95, Texas A&M had a 35-game unbeaten streak at Kyle Field. The Aggie won 24 straight from 1996-2000.

CAPACITY THROUGH THE YEARS

1905: 600	1967: 48,000
1915: 6,800	1980: 70,016
1923: 8,500	1982: 72,387
1929: 32,890	1999: 82,600

SIMPLY UNFORGETTABLE

November 26, 1999. It had been one of the most colorful traditions in all of college football, a symbol of the spirit at Texas A&M and the support the Aggies had from students and fans. The annual bonfire before the season-ending game with Texas had it all: excitement, tradition and spectacle. In November 1999, however, it also had tragedy.

The week before the big game, 12 Aggies who were constructing the massive pyramid of wood to be burned at the bonfire were killed when the structure collapsed on them. To have young people killed taking part in a strong university tradition shook the school to its core. Some wondered whether the game with the Longhorns should be played. Others were concerned about how the A&M community would respond.

The night before the game, 65,000 people crowded into Kyle Field. On most occasions, they would have been participating in a pep rally—called "Yell Practice" at College Station. But this was different. A candlelight vigil was held, honoring the fallen heroes and creating an atmosphere so emotionally charged that few imagined the Aggies could have been defeated by anyone the next day.

No. 5 Texas couldn't do it. The next morning, in front of the largest crowd (86,128) ever to see a football game in Texas, the Aggies unleashed running back Ja'Mar Toombs on the Longhorns. Toombs carried the ball 37 times and gained 126 yards. He scored two touchdowns and was the clear difference in a 20-16 win. The Aggies may have suffered a crushing blow earlier in the week, but the A&M family had rallied together to mourn the losses and support one another. It was bittersweet and unforgettable.

X MAGIC MOMENTS
in the history of Kyle Field

I. THE FIRST BIGGIE, *November 19, 1915.* After being inspired by letters written by a former coach, the "Farmers" use a Rip Collins touchdown to beat Texas, 13-0, in the Longhorns' first visit to Kyle Field. It was Texas A&M's first Southwest Conference victory.

II. BRINGING DOWN NO. 1, *November 9, 2002.* Oklahoma rides into College Station undefeated and ranked No. 1, but true freshman quarterback Reggie McNeal comes off the bench and throws four TD passes in a 30-26 upset win, the only time the Aggies have beaten an AP top-ranked team.

III. TEN IS ENOUGH, *November 23, 1967.* The Aggies enter the game having lost 10 in a row to Texas, but quarterback Edd Hargett completes an 80-yard TD pass to Bob Long in the fourth quarter, and A&M comes from behind to beat the Longhorns, 10-7.

IV. ALL THE WAY BACK, *October 18, 1986.* After falling behind, 17-0, to No. 20 Baylor, the 11th-ranked Aggies mount a furious comeback and get a rushing TD and three scoring passes from quarterback Kevin Murray to win, 31-30, in a battle of ranked teams.

V. BACK TO DALLAS, *November 28, 1985.* On coach Jackie Sherrill's 42nd birthday, the Aggies win the Southwest Conference title and return to the Cotton Bowl for the first time in 18 years by whipping Texas, 42-10, behind three Kevin Murray TD passes and a defense that forces six Longhorn turnovers.

VI. BEATING THE CLOCK, *October 3, 1992.* After Aggies kicker Terry Venetoulias misses an extra point that puts No. 5 A&M in danger, he nails a 21-yard field goal as time expires to beat Texas Tech, 19-17. The Aggies go on to a 12-0 regular season.

VII. NO SUGAR FOR TEXAS, *December 1, 1979.* Texas comes to Kyle Field needing one win to clinch a Sugar Bowl berth and leaves still looking for the triumph. The Aggies spank the Longhorns, 13-7, to finish 6-5 and keep UT out of New Orleans.

VIII. ALMOST PERFECT, *November 28, 1975.* A&M runs its record to 10-0 with a 20-10 win over Texas. It's the Aggies' first win against the Longhorns in eight years. But the Aggies are blown out the next week at Arkansas and are shut out of the Cotton Bowl.

IX. SWEET REVENGE, *September 10, 1994.* The year before, Oklahoma had romped to a 30-point victory in Norman. This time, the Aggies get 17 fourth-quarter points to blow open a close game and earn a 36-14 win over the Sooners.

X. SLOCUM'S FIRST, *September 2, 1989.* The Aggies start R.C. Slocum's head-coaching tenure in style by whipping seventh-ranked LSU, 28-16. Larry Horton returns the opening kickoff 92 yards for a touchdown to set the tone for the win.

II. BRINGING DOWN NO. 1

COLISEUM

When you talk about the fabric of American sports venues, huge events and big stars weave the tapestry that is the Los Angeles Memorial Coliseum.

This place helped sports west of the Mississippi gain a foothold in the national limelight. And it has as much history as any football stadium in the nation. The star power has included USC Heisman winners Mike Garrett, O.J. Simpson, Charles White, Marcus Allen, Carson Palmer and Matt Leinart. And that's just scratching the surface for a program that has won 11 national crowns. Indeed, there are few things better than a balmy Saturday afternoon in the Coliseum watching the Trojans march down the field with the USC Song Girls and Yell Leaders cheering them forward.

SETTING The Coliseum sits on 17 acres in Exposition Park, which also features the L.A. Sports Arena, gardens and museums. It's near campus and about three miles southwest of downtown Los Angeles. The city's skyline is part of the view from the Coliseum's press box. On the field, Traveler, USC's mascot—a majestic white horse—storms up and down the sideline. It's said that Simpson was inspired to come to USC after seeing the horse on TV during a Trojans game. Adding to the atmosphere is the Spirit of Troy, the Trojan Marching Band (with its famous gladiator helmets and stirring processional march "Conquest," a salute to every USC score and victory).

STRUCTURE The signature view of this one-of-a-kind venue is from the front, where a grand wall features a symmetrical array of arches in a style that evokes the feel of the Roman Colosseum. Above the large central arch sits a flame that was lit during the Olympic Games of 1932 and 1984; below the flame is lettering that says "Los Angeles Memorial Coliseum," along with the Olympic rings. Inside, this is a wide, sweeping bowl that has a gentle pitch to its seats, pushing fans away from the action. Still, this was a place built for football and it has a clean look.

FANS In a town with marquee professional sports teams (except for the NFL, that is), the Trojans' fan base is a mix of intensely loyal locals and alumni. The tailgating is on par with any Midwest or Southeast venue, with fans circling the perimeter of

USC

the Coliseum and setting up fancy spreads replete with linen tablecloths and superb wine. This isn't your usual hamburger and hot dog crowd. With typically good weather, few tents or RVs are needed, as fans simply back up, set up their tables and enjoy pregame festivities.

MAJOR RENOVATIONS
Before the 1993 season, the Coliseum had a $15 million makeover that saw the stadium surface lowered 11 feet and the track that circled the field removed, among other things. A year later, an earthquake hit, forcing the Coliseum to make repairs that cost $93 million.

MILESTONE MOMENTS
• USC has called the Coliseum home since the stadium was opened in 1923, with the Trojans topping Pomona College, 23-7, on October 6 of that year.
• The Trojans' first night game in the Coliseum was October 23, 1944, and USC beat Washington, 38-7.
• USC "Super Fan" Giles Pellerin was watching his 797th consecutive Trojans game on November 21, 1998, when the 91-year-old fell ill, left the game and died of a heart attack.

FAST FACTS
• The Coliseum has a present full capacity of 92,000 (almost all are chairback seats).

However, for most USC games, a retractable fabric covers many seats, putting capacity at about 68,000.
• In addition to housing the 1932 Olympic Games, the track events of the 1984 Olympics took place at the Coliseum.
• The Coliseum has played host to such luminaries as Pope John Paul II, Bruce Springsteen, Billy Graham and John F. Kennedy (for his acceptance speech at the Democratic National Convention in 1960).
• The facility has been the site of two Super Bowls (I and VII), in addition to being home of the Los Angeles Rams (1946-79), Los Angeles Raiders (1982-94), Los Angeles Dons (1946-49), Los Angeles Chargers (1960), UCLA (1929-81) and Los Angeles Dodgers baseball (1958-61), with the World Series being played there in 1959. A USFL team (Express, 1983-85) and an XFL team (Xtreme, 2001) also called the Coliseum home.

CAPACITY THROUGH THE YEARS

Year	Capacity
1923:	75,000
1932:	101,000
1966:	92,800
1993:	68,000/92,000*

*Full capacity

X MAGIC MOMENTS
in the history of Los Angeles Memorial Coliseum

I. **THE JUICE GETS LOOSE,** *November 18, 1967.* With fourth-ranked Southern California trailing No. 1 UCLA, 20-14, early in the fourth quarter, Trojans tailback O.J. Simpson bolts 64 yards through the heart of the Bruins defense to give USC a 21-20 victory and a Rose Bowl berth. The Trojans go on to win the national championship.

II. **MAGICAL ASCENT HALTED,** *November 28, 1964.* Notre Dame enters its season-ending clash with USC undefeated, ranked No. 1 and, after a 2-7 season in 1963, on the verge of one of college football's most astounding turnarounds. A win would make the Irish national champions, but Craig Fertig hits Rod Sherman with a 15-yard touchdown pass with just 1:33 to play, bringing USC back from a 17-0 halftime deficit to a 20-17 victory.

III. **SOONER OR LATER,** *September 26, 1981.* Top-ranked USC plays host to No. 2 Oklahoma and ekes out a 28-24 victory when John Mazur connects with Fred Cornwell on a 7-yard touchdown pass with 2 seconds left. The catch is only the second of Cornwell's career.

IV. **THE BIRTH OF A GIANT,** *January 15, 1967.* Seven months after the rival National Football League and American Football League agree to merge, the leagues meet in the first NFL-AFL World Championship Game, later dubbed Super Bowl I. Vince Lombardi's Green Bay Packers of the NFL beat Hank Stram and the AFL's Kansas City Chiefs, 35-10. The game was more than 30,000 fans short of selling out.

V. **AIR JORDAN,** *November 25, 1978.* Less than a minute after Notre Dame, led by quarterback Joe Montana, takes a 25-24 lead over the Trojans, USC kicker Frank Jordan drills a 37-yard field goal with 2 seconds remaining, giving the Trojans a 27-25 win.

VI. **SWEET REVENGE,** *October 9, 2004.* One year after California spoiled USC's perfect season with a three-overtime win in Berkeley, the No. 1 Trojans beat the Bears, 23-17, in what would be Cal's only loss in the regular season. USC stays undefeated and goes on to win the Orange Bowl and the national championship.

VII. **JONESTOWN,** *November 22, 1969.* Jimmy Jones hits Sam Dickerson with a 32-yard touchdown pass with 1:32 left, giving the fifth-ranked Trojans a 14-12 win over No. 6 UCLA and propelling USC into the Rose Bowl.

VIII. **NEVER SAY DIE,** *October 24, 1964.* Down 21-20 to California, quarterback Craig Fertig leads the Trojans on a 95-yard scoring drive that culminates with a 22-yard touchdown pass to Rod Sherman with 50 seconds remaining. USC beats the Bears, 26-21.

IX. **TWO TIMES A HERO,** *October 17, 1992.* Estrus Crayton scores twice in the final 5:45 to help Southern California rally and beat California, 27-24. Brian Williams intercepts a Bears pass with 2:19 remaining to preserve the win.

X. **DOWN BUT NOT OUT,** *November 21, 1987.* No. 5 UCLA has a 13-0 third-quarter lead, but unranked USC storms back to capture a 17-13 victory and the Pac-10's Rose Bowl berth. **Rodney Peete's** (bottom left) 33-yard fourth-quarter touchdown pass to Erik Affholter provides the winning margin.

SIMPLY UNFORGETTABLE

November 30, 1974. Fifth-ranked Notre Dame bolted to a 24-0 lead in the first half of this regular-season finale and appeared ready to replicate the 51-0 rout the Irish handed the Trojans at the Coliseum in 1966. The Irish moved easily through the USC defense and stifled the Trojans' attack with their own defensive unit, which was ranked first in the nation. When Southern California scored on a 7-yard touchdown pass to Anthony Davis with 10 seconds remaining in the half, few in the stadium thought much of it.

After spending the first half kicking short and away from Davis, the Irish sent the opening kick of the second half deep. Davis bolted up the sideline on a 102-yard return that made the score 24-13 and signaled the eruption of the Trojans offense. USC scored 35 points in the third quarter; Davis had a pair of short touchdown runs, and quarterback Pat Haden threw two TD passes. After Haden fired a 16-yard scoring strike and Charles Phillips returned an interception 58 yards for a TD to open the fourth quarter, the carnage was over: USC 55, Notre Dame 24. The Trojans scored all of their points in a 17-minute span.

X. DOWN BUT NOT OUT

SATURDAY SHRINES

LANE STADIUM

VIRGINIA TECH

This is what college football is all about in a small city (population: 40,000) tucked in the hills of western Virginia. The stadium sits on a little plateau between the Blue Ridge and Allegheny Mountains.

It is mountainous all around Blacksburg in what's an idyllic setting. The stadium has grown as rapidly as the program. Hokies fans love the night games so they can tailgate all day. It has become an event. Fans discuss plans on the Internet leading up to the game.

SETTING Don't let the tranquil backdrop fool you. This has developed into an intense football environment over the past decade. It all begins with a first-rate tailgate setting. There are plenty of grassy areas adjacent to the stadium to accommodate the army of tailgaters who grill everything from venison to brats to hot dogs. The venue is most spectacular in October, when the leaves start turning. Adding to the setting is the Corps of Cadets, which marches across the field to its seats before games, a practice that dates to Virginia Tech's days as a military school. Interestingly, Tech is one of the few schools that has two bands. In addition to the Corps of Cadets, there's a larger student band—the Marching Virginians. At the end of the third quarter, the tuba players line up along the north goal line and play the "Hokie Pokey," with the fans getting into the action.

STRUCTURE This is a single-level, concrete-and-steel facility that has changed markedly over the years. With the addition of a south end zone project in 2003, the volume in the stadium has a difficult time escaping, making the venue even louder than before. Work is being done on the west side of the stadium, where the structure will feature four castle-like turrets. They will resemble the ones on Burris Hall, which is a signature building on campus. And the new work will feature more Hokie stone, a limestone that is quarried just off campus and is a dominant part of the campus architecture. In fact, there's a piece of Hokie stone in the tunnel that leads to the field—the players touch it as they pass by.

FANS This is a very loud and proud group that packs a passionate punch. To get ready for games, many fans flock to the Hokie House to get something to eat. Many also like to be on hand when the team arrives, with players passing through throngs of fans on their way to the locker room about two hours before kickoff. Perhaps the most energetic time is when the team enters the field. Fans bounce up and down as Metallica's "Enter Sandman" is blared over the P.A. system. At

Perhaps the most energetic time is when the team enters the field. Fans bounce up and down as Metallica's "Enter Sandman" is blared over the P.A. system.

VIRGINIA TECH

just the right time in the song, the players sprint onto the field. Unsuspecting fans can be startled when a cannon called Skipper is shot after Tech scores.

MAJOR RENOVATIONS This place is ever-evolving. A recent $1.9 million facelift has been among the biggest projects. A major change was the expansion of the west side, a new press box with lights, luxury seating, a ticket office and hall of fame, among other things.

MILESTONE MOMENTS
• The first game was played October 2, 1965, a 9-7 Virginia Tech triumph over William & Mary. At the time, the stadium construction wasn't complete; only the west stands and center section of the east stands were open.
• The dedication game took place on October 23, 1965, a 22-14 Hokies win against Virginia.
• The first night game was played on Thanksgiving 1982. Tech won the November 25 game, topping Virginia, 21-14.

FAST FACTS
• The facility is named for Edward Lane, an alum who led an educational foundation project that raised more than $3 million for construction of the stadium. In 1992, the field was dedicated Worsham

Field in honor of two longtime Virginia Tech supporters.
• The Hokies won a school-record 16 home games in a row from 1999-2001.
• There are plaques in the stadium honoring the retired jerseys of Tech greats Bruce Smith, Carroll Dale, Frank Loria, Jim Pyne, Frank Beamer, Michael Vick and Cornell Brown.
• Prior to Lane Stadium, Tech played its games at Miles Stadium, which had a capacity of 17,000.

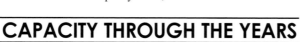

CAPACITY THROUGH THE YEARS

1965: 40,000	1995: 50,000
1966: 30,100	1999: 52,000
1967: 35,000	2000: 55,075
1975: 40,000	2001: 51,220
1981: 52,500	2002: 65,115
1984: 51,000	

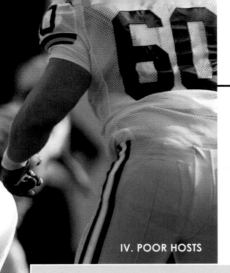

IV. POOR HOSTS

X MAGIC MOMENTS
in the history of Lane Stadium

SIMPLY UNFORGETTABLE

Beamer Ball. It would have been hard for anyone to imagine that a Virginia Tech defensive back during the 1960s would become one of the nation's most successful coaches and the architect of a remarkable progression from regional concern to national powerhouse, but that's just what happened with Frank Beamer. A starter on VT's 1966 and '68 Liberty Bowl teams, Beamer took over in Blacksburg in 1987, with the Hokies a successful Southern program but hardly on the radar screens across America.

Beamer had played under Jerry Claiborne at Tech, so there was no doubt he understood how to play strangling defense. And that was his trademark from the start of his coaching career. Virginia Tech would score, but it would shut you down first. Although the Hokies started slowly, posting losing records in Beamer's first two seasons and making no substantial waves through 1992, things started to cook in 1993. That year, the Hokies were 9-3, including an Independence Bowl win over Indiana.

The Hokies had joined the Big East Conference as a charter member in 1991, but Tech didn't see big dividends from the alliance until 1995. It beat Texas, 28-10, in the Sugar Bowl that year to complete a 10-2 season. All of a sudden, the college football world was raving about the team that specialized in special teams. During the 1990s, the Hokies blocked 63 kicks, tops in Division I. The sight of the fired-up Hokies itching to charge the punter was a frightening one for opposing special-teams coaches. And Beamer put it all together, taking on the kicking-game chores himself.

By 1999, Virginia Tech had arrived. Thanks in large part to quarterback Michael Vick, the Hokies went 11-0 that season and made it to the Sugar Bowl to play Florida State for the national title. Although the Seminoles prevailed, Beamer's transformation of the program was complete.

I. **TASTING SUGAR**, *November 26, 1999.* Behind 366 yards of offense from redshirt freshman quarterback Michael Vick, the Hokies beat Boston College, 38-14, to finish the regular season 11-0. The triumph sends Virginia Tech to the Sugar Bowl to play Florida State for the national championship.

II. **SNAPPING THE STREAK**, *November 1, 2003.* The No. 10 Hokies force four Miami turnovers and roll to a 31-7 prime-time victory over the second-ranked Hurricanes, snapping Miami's 39-game regular-season winning streak. Miami is the highest-ranked opponent Virginia Tech has beaten.

III. **BIG DEBUT**, *September 4, 1999.* Michael Vick bursts upon the Virginia Tech scene with three touchdown runs, including a 54-yard highlight-reel performance, as the Hokies beat James Madison, 47-0.

IV. **POOR HOSTS**, *September 1, 2002.* After enduring years of criticism for playing a weak nonconference schedule, the No. 16 Hokies play host to 14th-ranked LSU and beat the Tigers, 26-8. Virginia Tech retires Michael Vick's jersey at halftime.

V. **STROCK II**, *October 14, 1972.* Dave Strock, brother of famed Hokie quarterback Don Strock, kicks a field goal with 12 seconds remaining to give Virginia Tech a thrilling 34-32 upset victory over 19th-ranked Oklahoma State.

By 1999, electrifying Michael Vick had arrived—and so had Hokies football.

VI. **BRINGING IT BACK**, *October 29, 1966.* Safety Frank Loria, Tech's first consensus All-American, returns a punt 80 yards for a score to key an exciting 23-21 win over Florida State. It's one of three punts he returns for touchdowns during the season.

VII. **FALLING FROM THE TOP**, *November 24, 1990.* Beating Virginia is always a treat for the Hokies, but bumping off the top-ranked Cavaliers, who had been No. 1 for several weeks, in the season finale is historic. Vaughn Hebron rushes for 142 yards to lead VT to a 38-13 win while a state-record 54,157 fans witness the upset.

VIII. **THE FIRST**, *September 23, 1995.* Miami is reeling from the effects of probation, but the Hurricanes still are formidable and enter the game never having lost to VT. Miami leaves the contest, however, with a 13-7 defeat—Virginia Tech's first win of the season. The Hokies bat down a fourth-down pass with 17 seconds remaining to secure the victory.

IX. **WHITEWASH**, *October 18, 1980.* The Hokies' road to the Peach Bowl is paved with a 30-0 win over Virginia, in front of the first crowd of more than 50,000 in the state of Virginia's history.

X. **STYLISH START**, *September 18, 2004.* Virginia Tech falls behind early, but Bryan Randall throws for a touchdown and runs for another to give the Hokies a 41-17 win over Duke in Virginia Tech's first Atlantic Coast Conference game.

SATURDAY
SHRINES

HUSKY STADIUM

When it comes to combining aesthetic beauty and athletic excellence, few—if any—schools can match Washington. The lush green environs of Lake Washington's Union Bay make this site a frequent fan pick as the most attractive college football venue in the nation.

And the tradition here is nothing to sneeze at. Reaching back to 1920, Husky Stadium is younger than only four Division I-A venues in the nation, and a fair number of stars have played on its field. Noted coach Don James lead U-Dub to a share of the 1991 national title, led by defensive tackle Steve Emtman. And many standout quarterbacks have shown off their arms in the Pacific Northwest's biggest stadium, including Sonny Sixkiller, Warren Moon, Damon and Brock Huard, Billy Joe Hobert, Cody Pickett, Chris Chandler, Mark Brunell, Cary Conklin, Marques Tuiasosopo and Don Heinrich.

SETTING Fans can see Lake Washington from their seats. And myriad boats are docked nearby, as about 5,000 fans reach the stadium via the water on game days. Members of the Washington rowing team shuttle fans from moorings to the dock. The peaks of Mount Rainier and the Olympic Mountain Range as well as the Seattle skyline all tower above the horizon and are within view from the north upper deck. During games, it's not uncommon for fans to see seaplanes taking off and landing on Lake Washington. Fans like to make sure they get to their seats early to watch the team enter the field via a tunnel in the northwest corner of the stadium.

STRUCTURE The stadium has a bigger-than-life feel, especially when standing next to it. And it's set up for the fans, as almost 70 percent of the seats are between the end zones. Husky Stadium is shaped like a horseshoe and has an upper deck on each side. A large overhang to protect fans from the famous Seattle rain stretches across each side of the stadium. Before the place was built, planners wanted to limit the glare of the sun inside the stadium. To do that, the astronomy department took measurements to "establish the longitudinal axis" of the stadium. Planners also wanted to make sure to maximize the views of the lake and surrounding mountains.

FANS It's a sea of purple on Saturdays, and the stadium gets unusually loud for an open-air stadium. During a 1992 night game with Nebraska, ESPN measured the crowd noise at 135 decibels. To get fans in a yelling mood, the Husky Marching Band performs a "Band Jam" before each game in the Dempsey Indoor Facility. There isn't a lot of green space for tailgating, but fans make the most of their resources by conducting pregame cookouts and other rituals on their watercraft. The Washington mascot is Whitepaws Arlut Spirit of Goldust, an Alaskan Malamute, who also answers to simply "Spirit." The first actual dog to lead the team onto the field was

named Frosty I, and. yes, his successor was Frosty II. Fans also can visit a life-size bronze statue of a husky named "Husky Spirit," which rests between Husky Stadium and the Bank of America Arena.

MAJOR RENOVATIONS The structure has undergone many changes over the years, the most notable taking place in 1987 when 13,500 seats and a glass-enclosed reception area with a field view from goal line to goal line were added in a $13 million project.

MILESTONE MOMENTS
• The first game in Husky Stadium was November 27, 1920. Dartmouth topped Washington, 28-7.
• A moat surrounds the field to help drainage. But it also can help the team's spirit, as it did on October 31, 1992, when the Stanford Cardinal tree fell in the moat before the game. The Huskies won the game, 41-7.

FAST FACTS
• Between the third and fourth quarters, a former Washington standout is introduced to fans. Highlights of the legend are beamed on a video board.
• Washington claims the wave was started at Husky Stadium on October 31, 1981, by cheerleader Robb Weller (who once co-hosted *Entertainment Tonight*). The wave started during the third quarter of a game vs. John Elway-led Stanford, when the Huskies tallied 28 points en route to a 42-31 victory.

• If you go to a game, make sure you tune to Sportsradio KJR 950 AM. When the Huskies score, listen to venerable announcer Bob Rondeau's signature shout of "Touchdown, Washington!"

CAPACITY THROUGH THE YEARS

1920:	30,000	1968:	59,000
1936:	40,000	1987:	72,500
1950:	55,000		

X MAGIC MOMENTS
in the history of Husky Stadium

SIMPLY UNFORGETTABLE

September 17, 1983. Washington already had established a rivalry with Michigan when the Wolverines came to Seattle for the third time in history. In the 1978 Rose Bowl, Warren Moon and Spider Gaines led the Huskies to a 27-20 victory over the Wolverines, a favor UM returned in the '81 Rose Bowl with a 23-6 win.

So, there was history. And after 60 minutes of football, there was legend. Michigan came to Husky Stadium ranked eighth in the country, down two spots from the previous week's ranking, thanks to a tight 20-17 season-opening win over Washington State in Ann Arbor. The Huskies were ranked 16th, up two places from the preseason poll after dealing Northwestern a 34-0 defeat.

The Michigan team was your typical Bo Schembechler squad. The Wolverines ran the ball well and passed mainly when they had to. That formula served them quite well, as they took a 24-10 lead into the fourth period. It appeared the trip West was going to be a successful one.

Then the Huskies' Walt Hunt scored on a 3-yard touchdown run with 9:06 left, narrowing the Wolverines' lead to 24-17. As the seconds ticked off the clock, Steve Pelluer led another drive. The senior quarterback completed nine straight passes against a suddenly vulnerable Michigan defense that would allow only two other teams to score more than 20 points all season. He hit Mark Pattison with a 7-yard scoring pass with only 34 seconds to play and then threw a 2-point conversion pass to tight end Larry Michael for Washington's winning margin in a 25-24 victory.

I. NOT YET, *September 9, 2000.* Fourth-ranked Miami is shut down by Marques Tuiasosopo and the 15th-ranked Huskies, 34-29. It's the last loss the Hurricanes will incur until their Fiesta Bowl loss to Ohio State in 2003, as they begin a 34-game winning streak the next week.

II. MOON OVER WAZZOU, *November 22, 1975.* In the game that will establish him as the Huskies' top man, sophomore quarterback Warren Moon leads Washington to a come-from-behind 28-27 win over Washington State. Washington State led, 27-14, with 3:01 left to play. On fourth-and-1 on the Husky 15, Cougars quarterback John Hopkins threw an interception, and the Huskies went on to win in Don James' first season as UW's head coach.

III. BEAR-LY SURVIVING, *November 12, 1988.* John McCallum kicks a 25-yard field goal with 2 seconds left to give Washington a 28-27 win over California. The kick caps a furious rally in which Washington scores 25 second-half points. Two touchdown runs by Greg Lewis are keys in the rally. With the victory, the Huskies' Don James becomes the winningest coach in Pac-10 history.

IV. PERFECTION, *November 23, 1991.* Washington caps a perfect regular season with a 56-21 rout of Washington State. The win clinches a Rose Bowl berth and sets the stage for the Huskies' first national title, which comes after a win over Michigan in Pasadena. Washington shares the national title with Miami.

V. PASADENA BOUND, *November 21, 1981.* With a Rose Bowl invitation hanging in the balance, No. 17 Washington

I. NOT YET

upsets 14th-ranked Washington State, 23-10, to clinch the Huskies' second consecutive trip to Pasadena.

VI. STILL KICKING, *November 18, 1995.* The Huskies are down, 22-15, in the fourth quarter but fight back for a 33-30 win over Washington State. John Wales kicks a 21-yard field goal with 1:02 left for the final margin of victory, and Rashaan Shehee runs for 212 yards and three touchdowns. The win gives Washington a co-Pac-10 championship.

VII. AN ALL-AMERICAN GAME, *November 7, 1925.* In a much-anticipated matchup of two All-Americans—Ernie Nevers of Stanford and George Wilson of Washington—the Huskies keep Nevers and Pop Warner's Stanford team in check and earn a 13-0 victory en route to a Rose Bowl berth.

VIII. THE FINISHING TOUCH, *November 26, 1936.* After opening the season with a loss to Minnesota, the Huskies are unbeaten in their next eight games, including a regular season-ending 40-0 thrashing of Washington State that lands UW a Rose Bowl invitation.

IX. SMELLING THE ROSES, *December 1, 1923.* Two weeks after a 9-0 loss to California spoiled their hopes for an undefeated season, the Huskies whip Oregon, 26-7, to finish the regular campaign 10-1 and earn a trip to Pasadena for their first Rose Bowl appearance.

X. SONNY DAY, *September 19, 1970.* The Huskies start the season with a 42-16 win over Michigan State that features a strong performance by sophomore quarterback Sonny Sixkiller, who would become one of the school's most legendary performers.

SATURDAY SHRINES

MOUNTAINEER FIELD

WEST VIRGINIA

WEST VIRGINIA MOUNTAINEERS

Talk of intense environments and crazy fans often brings to mind visions of SEC schools. But overlooking Mountaineer Field at Milan Puskar Stadium would be a mistake.

Game day in Morgantown is bedlam. And the night games can be even wilder in this town tucked in just a few miles south of the Pennsylvania border. In 1988, esteemed coach Don Nehlen whipped the loyal fan base into a frenzy by taking the Mountaineers to the brink of a national title on the strength of Major Harris' arm. Nehlen also led West Virginia to an 11-0 regular season in 1993, cementing the bar at a high level. That's why the Mountaineers protect their turf with fever and fervor, making their home field positively electric.

SETTING Hills surround this beautiful college town, so bring your hiking boots. And sounds as well as sights are delightful here—the school takes great pride in its marching band, which is dubbed The Pride of West Virginia. The band pregame show, which hasn't changed since 1972, has become legendary. The band's signature is when it forms an outline of the state, marching down one side of the field, flipping the formation and marching back the other way. Fans also enjoy the pregame ritual of the band's performance of "Simple Gifts." During the tune, the band marches inward and forms a tight circle and gets

quiet. Then, the band turns, begins marching outward, blaring the song. If West Virginia wins, the team serenades the crowd with a rendition of "Country Roads."

The area around the stadium has been a work in progress. There was nothing near the facility when it was built. It used to be the university golf course. But flat land on which to build is at a premium in Morgantown. A new hospital has been added at one end of the parking lot. Now, the stadium area is the focal point of Morgantown. The law school is on a hill and looks down at the stadium.

STRUCTURE This isn't a massive facility, but it has a subtle stateliness about it. Located in a small valley, the stadium opened in 1980, making it one of the newer venues in the nation. Mountaineer Field has two decks on each side and steadily has undergone changes to become a bowl. At one end, the football offices, a weight room and locker room are located underneath the stands. The other end houses suites for the high rollers. When the stadium is full—which usually is the case—it becomes the biggest "city" in the state, surpassing Charleston and Huntington. The sta-

Coach Don Nehlen whipped the loyal fan base into a frenzy by taking the Mountaineers to the brink of a national title.

WEST VIRGINIA

dium was built just for football, with both sides curved toward the middle. Helping make this one of the nation's most hostile settings is the fact the fans are right on top of the action.

FANS This loyal fandom arrives from all corners of the state to cheer on the beloved Mountaineers. Most of the intense tailgating takes place in what locals call the "hospital" lots, which are between the stadium and hospital. Also, many fans have forged long-standing agreements to park in people's yards. In the end, it's a wall-to-wall buffet of RVs and cars. In fact, there are a lot of natives who tailgate and never go to the game. Few stadiums feature as wide a range of cuisine as Mountaineer Field, with the menu ranging from Italian to wild game. The crowd gets especially fired up when the team hits the field and the Mountaineer mascot shoots his gun, which also is fired whenever West Virginia scores.

MAJOR RENOVATIONS There haven't been any major overhauls for a stadium that has held its age well. In 1985, 7,500 seats were added to the south end zone; in 1986, 6,000 seats were added to the north end zone. Those additions helped the stadium retain sound, making it even louder than before.

MILESTONE MOMENTS
• The first game was on September 6, 1980, a 41-27 win over Cincinnati. It was Don Nehlen's debut as coach.
• The first night game was on October 20, 1984, a 21-20 Homecoming victory over Doug Flutie-led Boston College.

FAST FACTS
• Fans can get to games traveling on the PRT—that's Personal Rapid Transit. A government experimental project, it is a small train that was built in the 1970s. A lot of subway and public transit systems across the nation are based on it. The idea was to build a small-scale system to see how climate and other factors impacted on how it ran.

• Prior to moving into Mountaineer Field, West Virginia played at the downtown campus from 1924-79. That structure also was called Mountaineer Field.
• In 2004, the name of the current stadium was renamed Mountaineer Field at Milan Puskar Stadium in honor of Morgantown businessman and philanthropist Milan "Mike" Puskar.

CAPACITY THROUGH THE YEARS

1980:	50,000
1985:	57,500
1986:	63,500

X MAGIC MOMENTS

in the history of Mountaineer Field

SIMPLY UNFORGETTABLE

1988. This one came out of nowhere. West Virginia had been successful before, but it had never had a perfect regular season in nearly 100 years of football.

West Virginia had been a combined 10-13 the previous two years and was struggling with its consistency. The 1986 outfit had a stout defense but didn't score well; the '87 team could pile up the points, but it couldn't stop anybody. The Mountaineers began the 1988 season ranked 18th—not exactly the stuff of national title contenders.

That was before West Virginia hit its first three opponents with a total of 162 points. Thanks to Major Harris, a dangerous multiple-threat quarterback who ran the varied WVU attack to perfection, the Mountaineers could score at will. Harris was a solid passer and an elusive runner who could torment defenses on the option or from the pocket. He was surrounded by a solid, deep core of players who had grown tired of being mediocre.

By the end of October—West Virginia finished the month by pounding longtime headache Penn State, 51-30—the team was an official phenomenon. The Mountaineers went on to finish 11-0 and headed to the Fiesta Bowl to meet No. 1 Notre Dame for the national championship.

The Mountaineers fell to the Fighting Irish and their own multi-threat quarterback, Tony Rice, 34-21, but the Mountaineers had authored a season to remember and enough thrills (and points) to last for generations.

I. AT LAST, *October 27, 1984.* After 29 years of losses (and one tie) to the Nittany Lions, West Virginia finally beats Penn State, 17-14. The Mountaineers hold Penn State to just two first downs and 92 yards of offense in the second half and secure the victory when defensive back Larry Holley intercepted a Nittany Lions pass with 2:25 left in the game.

II. HOKIE HUNTING, *October 22, 2003.* The unranked Mountaineers beat No. 3 Virginia Tech, 28-7, and the Hokies become the highest-ranked opponent West Virginia has beaten. Rasheed Marshall runs for one touchdown and throws for another—a 93-yard pass to Travis Garvin—and the Mountaineers defense forces four Virginia Tech turnovers.

III. SUGAR, SUGAR, *November 20, 1993.* West Virginia takes a big step toward a Sugar Bowl berth with a stunning 17-14 upset of fourth-ranked Miami. The Mountaineers finish the regular season 11-0 and head to New Orleans ranked third.

IV. PERFECTION, *November 19, 1988.* No. 4 West Virginia capitalizes on five Orange turnovers and beats fourth-ranked Syracuse, 31-9, to finish the regular season 11-0 and earn a Fiesta Bowl berth and a shot at the national championship. It is the Mountaineers' first undefeated, untied regular season in 96 years.

V. BROKEN WINGS, *October 20, 1984.* Before a delighted Homecoming crowd, West Virginia sneaks

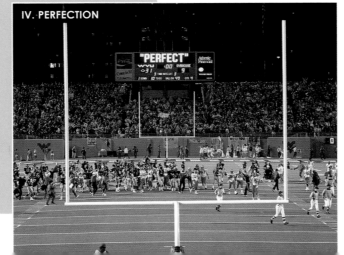

IV. PERFECTION

past undefeated No. 4 Boston College and eventual Heisman winner Doug Flutie, 21-20. The Eagles lead at halftime, 20-6, but West Virginia fights back, and junior tailback John Gay scores on a 5-yard sweep with less than 5 minutes remaining to put the Mountaineers ahead for good.

VI. FINE FINISH, *November 29, 2003.* After staggering out of the blocks with a 1-4 record, West Virginia regroups and rolls to a 6-1 mark in Big East play that includes a 45-28 win over Temple. West Virginia manages just 299 yards of total offense but scores on a punt return and fumble recovery. The victory gives the Mountaineers a share of the conference title.

VII. GRAND SENDOFF, *November 18, 2000.* In **Don Nehlen**'s final home game as coach of the Mountaineers, WVU dumps East Carolina, 42-24, en route to a Music City Bowl berth against Mississippi. Nehlen finishes his 21-year stint in Morgantown with 149 wins.

VIII. STREAKING, *November 15, 2003.* In the midst of a seven-game winning streak that leads to a share of the Big East title, unranked West Virginia beats No. 16 Pittsburgh, 52-31. The game is tied, 24-24, at the half, but Quincy Wilson scores three of his four touchdowns to key a second-half explosion.

IX. LIGHTING UP THE SCOREBOARD, *November 3, 2001.* Coach Rich Rodriguez's first Big East victory is a whopper—80-7 over Rutgers. Avon Cobourne runs for four touchdowns as West Virginia amasses 446 yards on the ground. The score at halftime: Mountaineers 59, Scarlet Knights 0.

X. ORANGE CRUSHED, *November 7, 1998.* After losing two in a row, West Virginia upsets No. 15 Syracuse, 35-28, and knocks the Orange out of sole possession of first place in the Big East. The victory begins a four-game winning streak to end the regular season, a run of success that brings an invitation to the Insight.com Bowl.

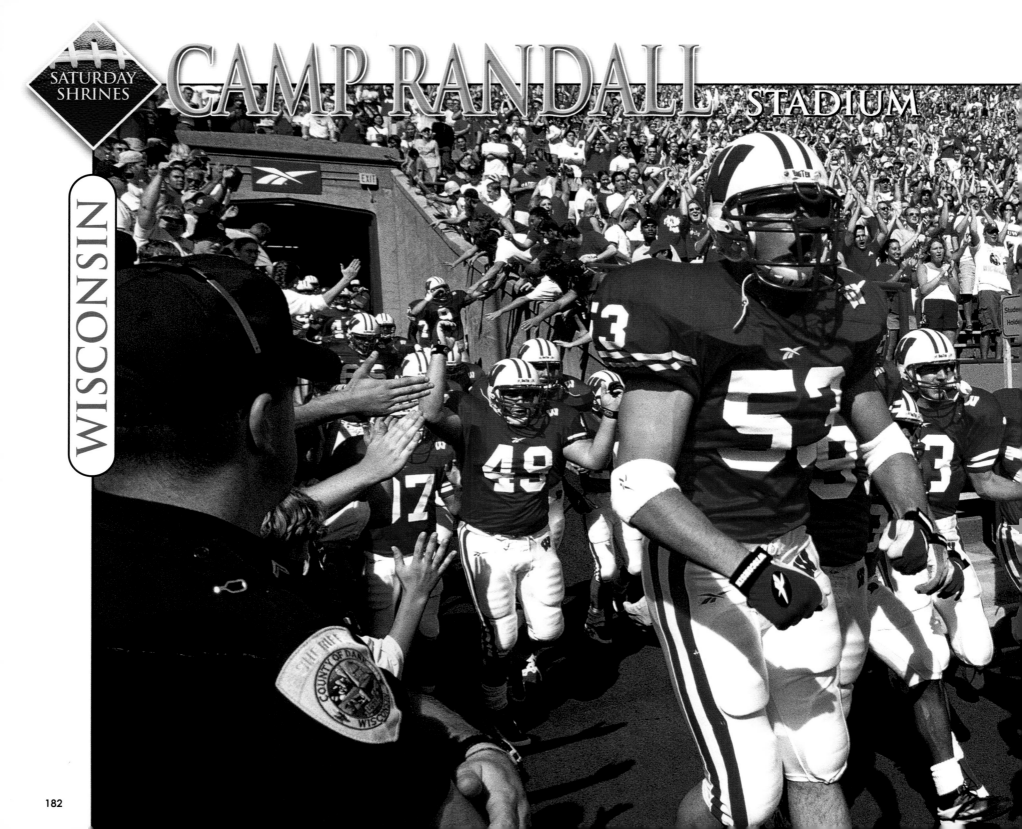

I t's 1 p.m. on a late-October day inside Camp Randall Stadium. Kickoff is looming. The sun is shining, the leaves are falling and your coat is zipped to the top with your hands jammed in your pockets. Now, close your eyes and let your imagination run wild.

There goes Ron Dayne, rumbling down the sideline. There's Ron Vander Kelen heaving a pass deep. And if you listen close enough, you still might hear the echoes of star offensive tackle Dennis Lick leveling someone. But before Camp Randall's grounds became a football stadium in 1917, the land was used to train troops in the late-1800s. Thus, the naming of the stadium—Alexander W. Randall was the state's first governor to serve during a war, and a veterans group requested at one time that the site always be referred to as a "camp" and not a "field." The state fair also was on the site before any pigskin flew here.

SETTING Ever been to a neighborhood block party? That's what Wisconsin's Camp Randall Stadium is like on fall Saturdays. The stadium is tucked amid myriad dorms and is within walking distance through the heart of campus past Bascom Hill from State Street, a strip lined with bars, shops and restaurants. The

tailgating starts early and ends late, with fans being warmed by stocking caps and some of their enthusiasm fueled by beer. Many hang out at the "Terrace" behind the union. The fun continues after the game during the band's Fifth Quarter, a celebration that's highlighted by the "Bud Song" and "On Wisconsin." Adding to the Camp Randall setting is a view of the state capitol, as well as lakes Monona and Mendota.

STRUCTURE Camp Randall, a concrete and steel monument, is noted for its horseshoe design and double-deck structure. The south end zone contains the ancient Wisconsin Field House, which was home to Badgers basketball in pre-Kohl Center days. On the facade of the second deck of the stadium is a tribute to the two greatest Badgers: Heisman Trophy winners Dayne and Alan Ameche.

FANS Few fans know how to tune up for a game like the ones who inhabit Madison,

WISCONSIN

also known as Mad City. Everyone dons red and white, with many also sporting the famous cheese hat. Smoke plumes billow about the stadium, as—what else?—bratwurst sizzles on grills. From Eau Claire to Kenosha, Bucky Badger's followers come out for game day. And the boisterous fans don't make it easy on opponents, who must pass the student section as they walk onto the field.

MAJOR RENOVATIONS
A recent $107 million project has boosted capacity to 80,000. The concourses were widened, FieldTurf was installed and video replay boards were put up.

MILESTONE MOMENTS
• The stadium was dedicated on November 3, 1917, with the Badgers edging Minnesota, 10-7. The first game on the field also was a victory—Wisconsin blanked Beloit, 34-0, on October 6, 1917.
• The first night game was played on December 11, 1982. The Badgers won over Kansas State, 14-3.

FAST FACTS
• Camp Randall is the fourth-oldest college-owned Division I-A stadium in the nation, behind Georgia Tech, Mississippi State and Cincinnati.
• The tradition of Bucky Badger began in 1949, when a student wore the get-up for the Homecoming game. The sidelines

haven't been safe since.
• You'll likely depart Camp Randall with the strains of "On Wisconsin" running through your head. How catchy of a tune is it? Hundreds of schools in the U.S. educational system have adopted the song, tailoring the lyrics to their teams.

CAPACITY THROUGH THE YEARS

1917:	10,000	1958:	63,710
1924:	33,000	1965:	75,935
1940:	45,000	1994:	76,129
1952:	51,000	2005:	80,000

X MAGIC MOMENTS

in the history of Camp Randall Stadium

I. A TRUE FORCE IN THE BIG TEN, *October 30, 1993*. A 13-10 victory over Michigan solidifies the Badgers as a legitimate Big Ten force and helps propel the school to its first Rose Bowl since the 1962 season. The game creates such a frenzy that students in the northeast corner of the stadium surge toward the field and cause a fence to collapse. No one is killed, but many fans are severely injured. Players carry ailing students to medical attention.

II. NO. 1 AND DONE, *September 12, 1981*. Mighty Michigan invades Camp Randall for the season opener, ranked No 1 and boasting a 14-game winning streak against the Badgers. But Dave McClain's team pulls a colossal 21-14 upset that isn't secure until a late defensive stand.

III. NO. 1, AT LAST, *October 4, 1952*. Wisconsin thumps Illinois, 20-6, to rise to the top of the AP rankings for the first—and only—time in school history. Alas, the good times are short-lived as the Badgers lose the following week at Ohio State and fall to 12th.

IV. SHOWDOWN SATURDAY, *October 31, 1942*. Top-ranked Ohio State is no match for the sixth-rated Badgers, who lay a 16-6 hurting on the Buckeyes and vault to second in the AP poll.

V. A.D. ALL DAY, *November 23, 2002*. Anthony Davis explodes for 301 yards rushing and five touchdowns in Wisconsin's 49-31 win over Minnesota in the Badgers' 13th regular-season game of the year, their most ever in one season.

VI. KNOCKED OFF, *November 10, 1962*. Northwestern may be No. 1 in the nation under coach Ara Parseghian, but the Badgers bump off their Homecoming guests, 37-6, en route to a Big Ten title and the Rose Bowl.

VII. PASADENA, HERE WE COME

VII. PASADENA, HERE WE COME, *November 21, 1998*. One week after suffering a crushing loss to Michigan in Ann Arbor, **Ron Dayne** (left) and Wisconsin rebound in style, drubbing Penn State, 24-3, to earn the first of two straight Rose Bowl berths.

VIII. CATCHING ON, *November 15, 2003*. There's a bright spot in the middle of a tough season-ending stretch, during which Wisconsin loses five of six games. Lee Evans piles up 258 receiving yards and scores five touchdowns in a 56-21 rout of Michigan State.

IX. RUNNING WILD, *November 23, 1974*. Billy Marek rushes for a then-school-record 304 yards as Wisconsin blasts Minnesota, 49-14.

X. STREAKBUSTERS, *October 11, 2003*. Lee Evans catches a 79-yard scoring pass from backup quarterback Matt Schabert to give the Badgers a stunning 17-10 win over third-ranked Ohio State, stopping the defending national champion's 19-game winning streak.

SIMPLY UNFORGETTABLE

November 13, 1999. From the moment he arrived on campus as a burly 255-pound man-child, Ron Dayne had a special place in the hearts of the Wisconsin faithful. Here was a back who could barrel through tacklers and then run away from the rest of the field. He created excitement every time he carried the ball and left Madison as the most honored player in Wisconsin history.

It all came to a fitting conclusion on the second Saturday of November in Dayne's senior year. The Badgers were playing for a spot in the Rose Bowl, yes, but the fans had come to see Dayne, who was on the verge of becoming college football's all-time leading rusher.

The regular-season finale against Iowa featured little drama. The Badgers pulled away early and won, 41-3. All that was left was the waiting. As the game rolled on, there would be little doubt. Finally, on a 31-yard burst through the overmatched Hawkeyes, Dayne broke the record of 6,279 held by Texas' Ricky Williams. By game's end, he had amassed 216 yards in the game and and 6,397 in his career. Less than a month later, Dayne won the Heisman Trophy (in a landslide), the Maxwell Award and the Doak Walker Award.

Dayne's final resume was amazing. He rushed for 2,000 or more yards twice (counting bowl games). When he wrapped up his career, he was one of just four players to gain at least 1,000 yards in four consecutive seasons. And Dayne out-rushed opposing teams in 29 of his 43 career starts. His was an amazing run.

SATURDAY
SHRINES

YALE

Yale-Harvard games are fiercely fought (left) and full of high jinks (Yale students, top, take a Crimson flag). The bowl (above) wasn't so raucous for a Princeton game.

This is a true American classic that has stood the test of time. Located about 95 miles from Manhattan, the Yale Bowl has served as home for two Heisman winners: Larry Kelley and

Clint Frank, the second and third recipients of the award. More recently, Carmen Cozza, who coached the likes of Calvin Hill, Dick Jauron and Gary Fencik, took Yale to great heights by winning 10 Ivy League crowns from 1965-96 en route to being enshrined in the College Football Hall of Fame.

STRUCTURE The Yale Bowl, about three miles from campus and five miles from Long Island Sound, is a concrete-and-steel facility that was the first enclosed stadium in the country. Its long portals were constructed before excavation began. The Rose Bowl's look was inspired by the Yale Bowl; in fact, one of the members of the Rose Bowl committee at the time of its construction was a Yale grad. Because of the bowl configuration and the fact all of the seats point toward the field, there are many good sightlines.

SETTING The area around the Yale Bowl is flat. There's a lot of parking around the facility for tailgaters, with fans coming from all over New England for the games. In fact, some folks fly their planes to New Haven. Money obviously is not a problem when it comes to getting here. Many credit Yale with inventing tailgating, with the fare ranging from hot dogs and hamburgers to brie and pate. How fancy can it get? One tailgater was known to bring his own chef to games.

FANS When alums are back, they like to go to Mory's, which is on campus. You have to be a member or present student to get in. Mory's started as the Yale drinking club. The Yale fan base can get raucous. During games, fans and alums revel in singing the fight song, "Down the Field," which is considered one of the best fight songs in the country. While walking through the portals to their seats, fans belt out another famous ditty called "Boola, Boola"; the tradition began at the 1900 Harvard game.

MAJOR RENOVATIONS This structure isn't easy to remodel. Basically, the Yale Bowl is the same as it was when it opened in 1914. However, the stadium currently is being refur-

YALE

bished. Among the changes will be plaques that chronicle the history of Yale football, an upgraded press box, a new scoreboard and improved seating. It's an ongoing renovation project that will cost $27 million.

MILESTONE MOMENTS
• The first game was played on November 21, 1914. Yale lost to Harvard, 36-0.
• The Yale Bowl has played host to crowds of 70,000 or more on 20 occasions, most recently for a November 19, 1983, Yale-Harvard clash, which was the 100th meeting between the universities. Yale lost, 16-7.
• The biggest crowd to see a game at the Yale Bowl was when 80,000 showed up for the Yale-Army meeting on November 3, 1923. Yale won, 31-10.

FAST FACTS
• In 1973 and '74, the NFL's New York Giants played home games at the Yale Bowl while Yankee Stadium was being renovated.
• The Bulldogs' previous home was 33,000-seat Yale Field, which opened in 1884.
• Many concerts have taken place in the Yale Bowl, featuring the likes of the Eagles and Simon & Garfunkel.

CAPACITY THROUGH THE YEARS

1914: 60,617	1974: 70,874
1916: 70,869	1984: 70,896
1943: 70,608	1994: 64,269

X MAGIC MOMENTS
in the history of Yale Bowl

SIMPLY UNFORGETTABLE

October 26, 1929. Mighty Army was a 2-to-1 favorite, and the oddsmakers might have been giving Yale the benefit of the doubt. The Cadets, led by two-time All-American Chris "Red" Cagle, were an impressive squad with a 3-0-1 record. Coach Mal Stevens' Yale team had a 2-1 mark entering the game, having lost a 15-0 decision to Georgia between wins over weak Vermont and Brown.

Just into the second quarter, Army was having its way with the Yalies. Cagle had returned an interception 45 yards for a touchdown. Then, Army's John Murrell got loose for a 35-yard touchdown run. Army led, 13-0, and it appeared the rout was on.

Then Stevens sent in quarterback Albie Booth—all 5-6, 144 pounds of him. The sophomore looked like a kid, especially among the giant Army players. But Booth, who had been nicknamed "Little Boy Blue," fit right in. In fact, he started a tremendous Yale comeback. First, he scored on a 32-yard run and drop-kicked the extra point, narrowing the gap to 13-7. Then, Booth went 35 yards for a score and again drop-kicked the extra point. Yale 14, Army 13. The overflow Yale Bowl crowd was going crazy.

The Cadets couldn't mount a charge, so they punted. To Booth. He took the ball on his own 35 and avoided a collection of Army tacklers. He bobbed. He danced. He finally broke loose on a 65-yard touchdown run. Army was finished.

But the legend of Little Boy Blue would live on forever at Yale.

I. THE BIG BLUE TEAM,
November 12, 1960. Jordan Olivar's 7-0 Yale Bulldogs play host to Princeton and beat the Tigers, 43-22, clinching at least a share of the Ivy title. One week later, the team mauls Harvard in Cambridge, 39-6, to stay perfect and win the league title outright.

II. THE CATCH,
November 20, 1999. Trailing Harvard, 21-17, with just 29 seconds left, Joe Walland, despite having been in the hospital the day before with tonsilitis, hits Eric Johnson with a touchdown pass to clinch the Ivy title with a 24-21 win. The title is the Bulldogs' first since 1989.

III. B.D., *November 25, 1967.* Brian Dowling keeps alive his unbeaten streak as a starting quarterback by throwing a touchdown pass with 2:16 left in the game to give Yale a 24-20 triumph over Harvard and coach Carm Cozza's first Ivy League title.

IV. THE FIRST, *November 17, 1956.* Yale beats Princeton, 42-20, to clinch at least a share of the first official Ivy League championship. The Bulldogs win it outright the next week, when they defeat Harvard, 42-14.

V. SALVAGING A SEASON, *November 21, 1981.* One week after being upset, 35-31, by Princeton and having their hopes for an unbeaten season ruined, the Bulldogs turn around and claim a share of the Ivy crown by beating Harvard, 28-0.

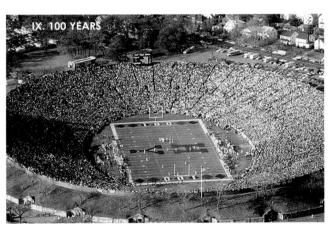
IX: 100 YEARS

VI. A NOT-SO-SWEET HOME, *November 10, 1974.* When their Yankee Stadium home undergoes major renovations, the New York Giants are exiled to the Yale Bowl. In just the second regular-season Giants-Jets matchup in history, creaky-kneed Jets quarterback Joe Namath staggers into the end zone for a game-tying touchdown and then leads the winning drive in a 26-20 overtime win that spawns a season-ending six-game winning streak for the Jets.

VII. FIRST TO 800, *September 16, 2000.* The Bulldogs defeat Dayton, 42-6, to become the first school in football history to win 800 games.

VIII. BIG CROWD, BIG WIN, *November 3, 1923.* A Yale Bowl-record crowd of 80,000 watches Thomas A.D. "Tad" Jones' team take a major step toward an unbeaten season by walloping Army, 31-10. The Bulldogs finish the year 8-0.

IX. 100 YEARS, *November 19, 1983.* It's the 100th meeting in the Harvard-Yale series, and though the Crimson wins, 16-7, it's a memorable day for the Ivy League and two of college football's most storied programs.

X. FINALLY, *November 22, 1969.* One year after a heartbreaking tie at Harvard, the Bulldogs appear headed for more trouble when they botch scoring chances in the first half. But an 80-yard drive yields a third-quarter touchdown, and Yale earns a share of the Ivy title with a 7-0 win.

the

AIR FORCE · BOISE STATE · FRESNO STATE · HAWAII · KANSAS · KANSAS STATE · MARYLAND · MICHIGAN STATE

TRADITIONS

MISSISSIPPI · MISSOURI · NAVY · NORTH CAROLINA · N.C. STATE · SYRACUSE · VIRGINIA

CONTINUE...

FALCON STADIUM

AIR FORCE

TOP 5 MOMENTS

1. THE OPTION QUARTERBACK TRADITION One can't talk about Air Force football without mentioning the performance of its quarterbacks since the school adopted the option in 1981. Since then, the academy has had five players rush and throw for 1,000 yards in a season.

2. THE FISHER DeBERRY ERA, *1984-present.* Air Force has had its most consistent string of success since Fisher DeBerry became the Falcons' coach in 1984. The Falcons have gone to 12 bowl games under DeBerry, had 17 winning seasons and won three conference championships.

3. HERE COME THE IRISH, *October 19, 2002.* It's a huge game on the national stage for 6-0 and 18th-ranked Air Force, which takes on a Notre Dame team also boasting a perfect record. The No. 7 Fighting Irish limit the Falcons to 104 yards rushing—AFA was leading the nation with 339 yards per game on the ground—and win the stirring night game, 21-14.

4. DEE DOWIS' CAREER, *1986-89.* For a school that has had so many great option quarterbacks, Dee Dowis stands out. He holds the academy career rushing record (3,612 yards) and single-game rushing record (249 yards against San Diego State in 1989). Dowis finished his career in style, earning WAC Offensive Player of the Year honors in '89 and leading the Falcons to the Liberty Bowl.

5. BEAU MORGAN'S 1996 SEASON Beau Morgan sets the NCAA quarterback record for rushing yards in a season with 1,494. His 1,210 passing yards places him in the 1,000/1,000 club for an NCAA-record second time.

SETTING Trained by the Air Force Academy to fly high, Air Force football players should be right at home at Falcon Stadium, which is about 7,300 feet above sea level. The stadium rests in a valley at the base of the Rampart Range of the Rocky Mountains. Falcon Stadium is on the eastern side of the academy campus, north of the airfield. The stadium is easy to reach because of its proximity to I-25, though there are more restrictions on entry nowadays because of security concerns. Parking lots border the stadium to the east, west and south, making the fans' commute from their cars to the stadium a short one. Because these parking lots are regularly patrolled by military personnel, fans don't have to worry about the safety of their tailgating gear while they watch the game. The stadium is mostly secluded, though the academy Officer's Club and golf course sit just across Academy Drive east of the stadium.

STRUCTURE Falcon Stadium was built in 1962 but has undergone radical changes in the past 10 years. The renovations began in 1996 with the installation of a Fairtron scoreboard and continued the next year with a complete replacement of the playing field. The surface and drainage systems were removed and replaced with state-of-the-art irrigation and turf. A permanent lighting system, added in 2002, was the most recent addition. Falcon Stadium, which cost $3.5 million to build, seats 52,480. In 1991, nine skyboxes were installed, providing 450 indoor seats, and the press box was remodeled. The athletic department uses the press box as a banquet and meeting room.

FANS There are many ways for Air Force fans to entertain themselves or to be entertained. Tailgating is always an option. Also for each game, Air Force parachutists drop in with the game ball, the coin for the coin toss and the U.S. flag. Another tradition is the cadet wing's march onto the field in formation for the national anthem. And, of course, the most famous pregame sight is the Air Force aircraft fly-by. Tailgating is permitted at any of the stadium parking lots, and *USA Today* recognized Air Force as one of the top tailgating spots in a 2000 article. The only downside is that the academy's entrance gates don't open until four hours before kickoff, limiting the amount of quality tailgating time. Rocky Mountain trout, served pan-fried, is an Air Force tailgating specialty.

FAST FACTS
• The F-16 is the most common aircraft for the fly-bys before each home game, but sometimes the aircraft are a little harder to see—occasionally, a stealth bomber or fighter will make an appearance.
• The new irrigation system has 1.5 miles of drainage pipes and 27 miles of heating cables underneath the field, and 10 miles of electrical wiring to control the irrigation and heating systems.
• The grass on the field, planted in 1997, is a specially mixed combination of Kentucky bluegrass and rye. It took almost 350 pounds of seed to plant the field.

BOISE STATE

SETTING Boise State's Bronco Stadium rests on the northeastern edge of campus, south of the Boise River and the downtown area, which can be seen through the north end of the structure. The stadium complex includes the Simplot Center for Athletic Excellence, where all Boise State athletes train; the Idaho Sports Medicine Institute, a private orthopedic office that houses the team's doctors; the Allen Noble Hall of Fame; and the Bronco Football Complex, the football staff's office. Also nearby is historic Opaline School, which is east of the stadium. After commencement, graduating students sound an old bell outside the school, passing the torch to the next graduating class.

STRUCTURE There is one thing about Bronco Stadium that sticks out more than any other, one thing that no other university has: a blue playing surface. Bronco Stadium had regular green AstroTurf when it opened in 1970, but the blue turf was installed in 1986. The current field, a new AstroPlay surface, was installed before the 2002 season. A $10 million renovation of Bronco Stadium, completed before the 1997 season, created the Broncos' Hall of Fame and added seats in the southwest and southeast corners to bring the capacity from 22,600 to 30,000. The stadium is shaped like a horseshoe, with the open end facing north toward the river. The track and field team also calls Bronco Stadium home during the outdoor season, when it uses Ed Jacoby Track, which runs around the football field.

FANS Tailgating is a big event around Bronco Stadium before kickoff, and fans have many options. Those who think it's a hassle to bring food, a grill and beverages along can purchase food, drinks and tailgating spaces complete with tents and chairs from Broncoville, a tailgating service operated through the university. The alumni association also plays host to a tailgate event called Bronco Bash at the Alumni Center, which is south of the stadium and across University Drive. The Boise State Student Alumni Association shows its enthusiasm for football by driving the Spirit Cart, a blue and orange golf cart decorated with balloons and signs, around the track after each Boise State score.

FAST FACTS • The MPC Computers Bowl (formerly known as the Humanitarian Bowl) is played at Bronco Stadium.• The playing surface at Bronco Stadium is named after legendary Boise football coach Lyle Smith.

TOP 5 MOMENTS

1. PUTTING BOISE STATE FOOTBALL ON THE MAP, *1947-67*. When Lyle Smith took over as the Broncos' football coach in 1947, Boise State was a junior college with a lightly regarded football program. When Smith retired 20 years later with six undefeated seasons, an .800 winning percentage and one national junior college championship, the school was about to become a four-year university with a strong football tradition.

2. CLIMBING THE COLLEGE FOOTBALL LADDER, *2004*. Boise State completes its first undefeated regular season as a four-year school, going 11-0 and winning the WAC for the third consecutive season. Along the way, the Broncos defeat a Pacific-10 team (Oregon State) for the first time, are ranked as high as No. 10 in both major polls and set a WAC record with their 26th straight conference victory. The only downside: The season ends with a 44-40 loss to Louisville in the Liberty Bowl.

3. RYAN DINWIDDIE TAKES FRESNO STATE BEHIND THE TOOL SHED, *October 18, 2002*. Quarterback Ryan Dinwiddie completes 19 of 22 passes for 406 yards and five touchdowns as the Broncos torch WAC rival Fresno State, 67-21.

4. BOISE STATE DRIVES TO CHAMPIONSHIP, *1980*. After years of success in the junior college and Division II ranks, the Broncos capture the I-AA national title in 1980. Season highlights include a Big Sky Conference championship (the school's fifth), a road win against Utah (a Division I-A school) and a playoff upset of perennial powerhouse Grambling.

5. BOISE STATE MAKES FIRST DIVISION I-A BOWL APPEARANCE, *1999*. Times were tough in Boise for a few years after the Broncos moved to Division I-A in 1996 and joined the Big West Conference, but the 1999 season sees Boise State return to prominence. The Broncos win the Big West title and make their first major-college bowl appearance, a 34-31 win against Louisville in the Humanitarian Bowl.

BULLDOG STADIUM

SATURDAY SHRINES

FRESNO STATE

TOP 5 MOMENTS

1. CALIFORNIA BOWL COMEBACK, *December 18, 1982.* Fresno State completes a fourth-quarter comeback from a 28-7 deficit when quarterback Jeff Tedford finds receiver Vince Wesson in the end zone with 11 seconds left to give the Bulldogs a 29-28 win over Bowling Green. Tedford throws for 373 yards, and Stephone Paige has 15 receptions for 246 yards.

2. KEVIN SWEENEY'S STERLING CAREER, *1983-86.* Quarterback Kevin Sweeney passed for 10,808 yards in his career, an NCAA record that has since been broken. The son of Bulldogs coach Jim Sweeney, the man who put Fresno State football on the map, Sweeney was twice named MVP of the Pacific Coast Athletic Association and led the Bulldogs to a win in the 1985 California Bowl. Statistically, his best season was 1984, when he threw for 3,259 yards and 20 touchdowns.

3. BULLDOGS BLAST BEAVERS, *September 2, 2001.* Led by a breakout game from quarterback David Carr, who throws for 340 yards and four touchdowns, the Bulldogs wallop No. 10 Oregon State, 44-24. It is Fresno State's first win against a Top 10 team.

4. THE BOWL STREAK, *1999-2004.* The Bulldogs have gone to six straight bowls under coach Pat Hill, easily the longest streak in school history. Fresno State has won its last three bowl games.

5. THE FRESNO STATE QUARTERBACK TRADITION. Fresno State's list of quarterback products compares favorably to any college in the country; included in the roll call are Trent Dilfer, signal-caller for the Super Bowl XXXV champion Baltimore Ravens; David Carr, the No. 1 overall pick in the 2002 NFL draft; Kevin Sweeney, the former NCAA passing champion; and Billy Volek, currently with the Tennessee Titans.

SETTING Bulldog Stadium sits off the northwest corner of the Fresno State campus next to Beiden Field, the university's baseball diamond. Fans walking to the game from campus must cross Cedar Avenue to reach the stadium. Fans driving to the game have several parking options; there are two large parking lots within a few blocks of the stadium, and there is a large public lot on the east side of campus.

STRUCTURE Bulldog Stadium, finished in 1980, is one of the most beautiful stadiums in the Western Athletic Conference. It is lighted by a cantilevered system that extends down to concentrate light on the playing surface, and the stadium rests below ground level. The playing field is 37 feet below grade. The gently sloping seating gives the facility an open, airy feel. Construction of Bulldog Stadium was made possible by what at the time was the largest fundraising project in the San Joaquin Valley. Valley citizens raised in excess of $7 million for the project, making it unnecessary to use student fees or state tax dollars to build the stadium. The donors were rewarded with their own seating section—the university set aside 5,000 chairback seats on the west side of the stadium solely for the donors' use. Increasing fan support in the stadium's first

decade of operation led to an expansion in 1991 that increased the seating capacity to 41,031 and added 22 luxury suites. Each suite seats 20 people.

FANS Many schools have made efforts to regulate tailgating in recent years, and Fresno State is no exception. In 2003, the athletic department outlawed kegs, restricted imbibing to grass areas, controlled lots close to the stadium and began requiring tailgate party sponsors to register with the athletic department. Since the changes, the university's athletic complex has become the center of the tailgating environment. The Bulldog Marching Band and the Red Wave, as the school's fans are known, ensure that the atmosphere inside Bulldog Stadium is intimidating. The band has been cited on several occasions for being too loud.

FAST FACTS • Since Bulldog Stadium opened, Fresno State has completed 10 undefeated home seasons. • The school record for average attendance in a season is 42,802, set in 2001. • The California Bowl was played in Bulldog Stadium from 1981-91. Fresno State played in five of those games, going 4-1.

SATURDAY SHRINES

HAWAII

SETTING Aloha Stadium, which is 10 miles from the university campus, is located just east of Pearl Harbor. Access is easy because the stadium lies at the intersection of highways 1 and 78. Parking can be difficult, as there are only 8,000 spaces in the stadium's immediate vicinity.

STRUCTURE Aloha Stadium is one of the most versatile facilities in the world. It has four 7,000-seat mobile grandstands, allowing quick reconfiguration into an oval for football, a diamond for baseball or a triangle for concerts and plays. Aloha Stadium was built in 1975 as a replacement for Honolulu Stadium, which was known as the Termite Palace because of its deteriorating exterior. Frequently moving the grandstands would be rough on a grass field, but this stadium features a new FieldTurf playing surface, installed before the 2003 season.

FANS Food plays a prominent role in Hawaiian culture, and fans looking for a nice spread at a tailgate party will not be disappointed. Though tailgating is allowed only at the main parking sites around Aloha Stadium, the stadium received national acclaim from *USA Today* in 2000 for its tailgate menu, which includes poi (crushed taro-root paste), poke wraps (wrapped, cubed raw fish) and sashimi (sliced raw fish).

FAST FACTS
• In 2000, the Hawaii football team officially became the Warriors. The university's other sports teams were given the option to call themselves Rainbows, Rainbow Warriors, Warriors, Rainbow Wahine or Wahine.
• Each of Aloha Stadium's moving grandstands weighs 3.5 million pounds.

• The stadium hosts a variety of concerts, races and tractor pulls, but the biggest money-maker is the swap meet, held in the parking lot every Wednesday, Saturday and Sunday. Vendors sell virtually everything imaginable.
• The highest seat in Aloha Stadium is as high as a 10-story building.

Aloha Stadium is host to a variety of events, including the NFL's Pro Bowl. In 2003, the Hawaii Warriors mascot had some fun with MVP Ricky Williams.

TOP 5 MOMENTS

1. THE OTTO KLUM ERA. Otto Klum became the Hawaii coach in 1921 and began to establish the program. Under Klum, Hawaii began to play other colleges with some regularity (previously, it had taken on mostly local high school, club and military teams), scheduled its first game in the mainland United States and picked up the nickname "Rainbows." Klum presided over the defensively dominant 1924-25 "Wonder Years" teams, which went undefeated and scored impressive wins against Colorado, Colorado State and Washington State. Klum coached for 19 seasons.

2. JUNE JONES TURNS THINGS AROUND, *1999.* After Hawaii went 0-12 in 1998, June Jones, an experienced NFL coach, was brought in to resurrect the program with his high-scoring Run-and-Shoot offense. It takes Jones only one season to make a difference, as the Rainbows go 9-4 in '99, are WAC co-champions and beat Oregon State, 23-17, in the Oahu Bowl. The turnaround was the best in NCAA history. Jones remains at Hawaii and has taken the Rainbows to four bowl games in six seasons.

3. HAWAII ENDS BYU STRANGLEHOLD, *October 28, 1989.* The Rainbows, getting a strong performance from quarterback Garrett Gabriel, pound nationally ranked rival Brigham Young, 56-14, ending a 10-game losing streak against the Cougars. Hawaii makes it two wins in a row the next year, blowing out BYU, 59-28, on the day Cougars quarterback Ty Detmer is announced as the Heisman Trophy winner. In the two games, Gabriel passed for 799 yards and seven touchdowns.

4. TIMMY CHANG LEADS COMEBACK WIN IN THREE OTS, *December 25, 2003.* Playing in the hometown Hawaii Bowl, Hawaii falls behind Houston early but rebounds for a three-overtime, 54-48 victory as Timmy Chang comes off the bench and throws for 475 yards and five touchdowns. It is only the third bowl win in school history.

5. RAINBOWS SCORE BOWL BREAK-THROUGH, *1989 season.* After going 9-2-1 in the regular season, the Rainbows are selected to play in the Aloha Bowl, their first major bowl bid. Hawaii loses to Michigan State, 33-13, and has to wait until 1992 to make another postseason appearance.

MEMORIAL STADIUM

and also is one of the 10 oldest college football stadiums in the nation. The stadium has been substantially upgraded in the past eight years. In that time, permanent lights, a new lower concourse and concession area, a new home locker room, a new press box, a MegaVision video board and a new artificial surface were added.

FANS Kansas' most recognizable sports tradition is undoubtedly the Rock Chalk Chant, created by Kansas chemistry professor E.H.S. Bailey. The words are intoned in a low, monastic cadence: "Rock, Chalk, Jay-hawk, K-U." Those who have seen the Jayhawks score have seen another one of the fans' oldest football traditions: "Waving the Wheat." After each Kansas scoring drive, fans place their hands high in the air and wave their arms gently, imitating Kansas wheat bending in the breeze. Though Campanile Hill is the tailgating hub, a few parking lots also are designated for pregame cookouts. Nearby Potter Lake is the traditional depository for goalposts after big wins.

FAST FACTS • The Kansas Relays, a competition among high school, college and Olympic athletes, have been held for more than three-quarters of a century. • Memorial Stadium is built upon the remains of old McCook Field, the university's original football field. Students and faculty tore down the old field on May 21, 1921, known as "Stadium Day," to clear the way for the new structure. • The MegaVision video board, installed in the south end zone before the 1999 season, is 24 feet tall by 32 feet wide. During commencement, it provides live shots of graduating seniors as they walk from Campanile Hill to the stadium.

TOP 5 MOMENTS

1. GALE SAYERS' CAREER, *1962-64.* A two-time All-American, the Kansas Comet was a threat to score any time he touched the ball. He was the first player in recorded Division I-A history to make a 99-yard run, against Nebraska in 1963. Sayers was named to the All-Big Eight team each of his three years as a starter.

2. FINALLY, KANSAS TAKES MEASURE OF KANSAS STATE, *October 9, 2004.* After losing to the Wildcats by a combined score of 106-6 the previous two seasons, the Jayhawks beat their in-state rivals for the first time since 1992. Excited fans rush the field too soon and are forced to wait on the track until the 31-28 game was over.

3. ORANGE BOWL TEAM, *1968.* Kansas ties for the Big Eight title and makes its second Orange Bowl appearance. Kansas fans still are waiting for the Jayhawks' next league title.

4. TONY SANDS' BIG DAY, *November 23, 1991.* Kansas running back Tony Sands rips the Missouri defense for 396 yards on 58 carries (both NCAA records) as the Jayhawks thrash their archrival, 53-29. Though the yardage total has been surpassed, the record for carries still stands.

5. A LONG-DISTANCE JOURNEY VS. THE SOONERS, *October 4, 1997.* Eric Vann bolts 99 yards on a touchdown run against Oklahoma. KU wins, 20-17.

SETTING In the shadow of the campanile, Memorial Stadium is nestled in one of the most scenic parts of campus, tucked next to Potter Lake and the Spencer Museum of Art. It rests at the base of Mount Oread, whose chalky limestone is the inspiration for the "Rock Chalk Chant." An anchor at the base of Mount Oread, the highest point in Lawrence, the stadium is both part of a vibrant campus and adjacent to a bustling downtown area. Campanille Hill is a perfect setting for pregame picnicking—tailgating without the asphalt—and even for watching a game.

STRUCTURE The idea for a modern, concrete Kansas football stadium was born in 1920, when the Jayhawks tied Nebraska after trailing 20-0 at halftime. The Monday after the Nebraska game, fans, students and faculty gathered to celebrate the comeback and pledged more than $200,000 for the construction of a new facility. Kansas sports legend Phog Allen directed construction of the horseshoe-shaped stadium, which opened on October 29, 1921. Memorial Stadium was the first football stadium built on a college campus west of the Mississippi River

SATURDAY SHRINES

KANSAS STATE

SETTING Color KSU Stadium purple. "Purple Pride" purple. Nearby Aggieville, a historic shopping area and restaurant and bar district, is an essential part of game-day festivities—all campus tailgating areas are alcohol free. Known as The Little Apple, Manhattan offers both city living and recreational activity (at nearby Tuttle Creek Reservoir). Back on campus, Bramlage Coliseum and the 94,000-square-foot Indoor Football Facility, the nation's largest indoor workout plant, sit just south of the stadium.

STRUCTURE Many improvements have been made to KSU Stadium,

which was built in 1968. A $12.8 million expansion in 1998 added 8,000 seats and pushed capacity to 50,000. The playing surface was upgraded to FieldTurf in 2002, though Wagner Field is still named for Dave and Carol Wagner, fans from Dodge City who won the lottery in 1991 and gave the school $1 million to install AstroTurf.

FANS The Kansas State student section stands throughout the game and often leads the crowd in the "K-S-U Wildcats" cheer. "Wabash Cannonball" was first used as a fight song in 1969. That fall, the building that housed the music department burned, and all that

survived was the music in the band director's briefcase. The band needed something to play at the next game; "Wabash Cannonball," a song with no ties to the school, was one of the surviving pieces, and the band played it at the next game. Ever since, it has been a second fight song. When K-State plays Kansas, members of the Phi Gamma Delta fraternity of the visiting team must deliver the game ball to the home field. They run it there in a relay and raise money in the process for the Wichita-based Leukemia Foundation.

FAST FACT • K-State is 85-19-1 at KSU Stadium under Snyder.

TOP 5 MOMENTS

1. THE BILL SNYDER ERA, *1989-present.* In '89, coach Bill Snyder inherited a Kansas State team that was on a 0-21-1 streak and was referred to as the "Mildcats." He has built the program into a perennial Top 25 team, guiding it to 11 bowls, a Big 12 Conference crown and four Big 12 North titles.

2. KNOCKING OFF NEBRASKA, *November 14, 1998.* After losing to Nebraska for 29 consecutive years, the Wildcats finally upend the Cornhuskers, 40-30. Kansas State, ranked No. 2 at the time, goes on to its first No. 1 ranking in the ESPN/USA Today coaches poll. The Wildcats advance to the Big 12 championship game but fall to Texas A&M.

3. BOWL ELIGIBLE ONCE MORE, *October 30, 1993.* With a 21-7 win against then-No. 13 Oklahoma, the Wildcats become bowl eligible for the first time since 1982.

4. DARREN SPROLES' CAREER, *2001-04.* Sproles, a 5-7 running back, was equally dangerous as a runner, receiver and kick returner. He is the school record holder for all-purpose yards in a career (6,812) and in a single game (351).

5. DAVID ALLEN'S FEATS, *1997-2000.* Running back David Allen returned seven punts for touchdowns, tying the NCAA career record (since broken). Allen took four kicks to the house in 1998 alone.

BYRD STADIUM

SETTING Maryland's Byrd Stadium rests at the foot of the university's North Hill. The stadium saw significant renovations in the 1990s, but care was taken to ensure that the new structures and additions stayed consistent with the university's Georgian architecture. The stadium's proximity to the student union and several residence halls makes it easily accessible to students, but off-campus fans have a harder time getting to games. The parking areas close to Byrd Stadium are small and require a permit; free parking areas are fairly far away.

STRUCTURE Byrd Stadium, which opened in 1950, underwent three '90s additions that altered its appearance. The first was the Tyser Tower press box, completed after the 1990 season. This five-level structure, built on the stadium's south rim, has 300 exterior luxury suites, a photo deck, standard press booths and a large working press area. The next phase was the Gossett Football Team House behind the east end zone. This facility is home to all of the football program's needs and is guarded by a bronze Terrapin installed in 1992 to celebrate the school's 100th year of football. The final addition was a large upper deck, which added 12,000 seats on the north end of the stadium after the 1994 season.

FANS Before each home game, the band, mascot, spirit squad and fans line up on Terp Alley, on the north side of the stadium, to cheer the team as it walks past into the stadium. Ordinarily, when fans start jingling their keys at a sporting event, it is a signal to the opposing coach that the game is out of reach and they want to go home; at Maryland, fans jingle their keys instead of cheering to keep the noise level down for critical offensive plays. Most of the tailgating takes place in the parking lots near Byrd Stadium. There also are several university-organized tailgates, including one for former lettermen and their friends.

FAST FACT • Queen Elizabeth II and Prince Philip of England saw their first American football game at Byrd Stadium on October 19, 1957, as Maryland beat North Carolina 21-7.

TOP 5 MOMENTS

1. TERPS CLAIM 1953 NATIONAL TITLE. Maryland outscores its opponents, 298-31, in the regular season and rolls to a 10-0 record. The Terrapins are atop the Associated Press and United Press polls at the end of the regular season, thereby earning those wire services' designations as national champs. The Terps lose to Oklahoma, 7-0, in the Orange Bowl.

2. BEST OF THE EAST BETTER THAN BEST OF THE NATION, *September 24, 1955.* No. 5 Maryland defeats top-ranked UCLA, 7-0, at College Park in a clash of titans. The visitors have the ball at the Maryland 1-yard line and are primed to score the game's first touchdown in the second quarter, but Terrapins All-American Bob Pellegrini strips the ball from the UCLA ballcarrier and recovers the fumble. The Terps' offense drives 71 yards in the third quarter for the game's only TD. Historians call it one of the great games of the decade.

3. QUARTERBACK TRADITION. Maryland's quarterback legacy is one of the strongest in college football—13 Terrapins quarterbacks, including Boomer Esiason and Neil O'Donnell, have played in the NFL. Frank Reich, who led the Bills' miracle comeback against Houston in the 1992 playoffs, fueled Maryland's greatest rally. With the Terps behind, 31-0, at halftime of a 1984 game at Miami, Reich entered the fray and engineered a stunning 42-40 win.

4. SCOTT MILANOVICH'S CAREER, *1993-95.* Scott Milanovich was one of the most prolific passers in Maryland history, no small feat considering the pedigree of Terps quarterbacks. He still owns or shares 31 school passing records—including most yards in a game (498), single season (3,499) and career (7,301), and most career TDs (49).

5. LAMONT JORDAN RUNS OVER VIRGINIA, *November 20, 1999.* Lamont Jordan's 306-yard rushing performance against the Cavaliers sets a Maryland single-game record, but the Terrapins fall, 34-30.

MARYLAND

SPARTAN STADIUM

MICHIGAN STATE

SETTING Michigan State's Spartan Stadium, located in the center of campus, has been the team's home for more than three-quarters of a century. The scenery at the stadium is outstanding; the north end of the stadium is open, providing spectators an excellent view of the Red Cedar River and the Beal Botanical Garden across the river. The university steam plant, its smokestack rising high into the sky, borders the stadium to the south, as does the Ralph. H. Young outdoor track and field complex. The Duffy Daugherty Building, home of the football offices and indoor football facility, also is south across W. Shaw Lane. There are several large public parking lots near the stadium, making the facility easily accessible for off-campus fans.

STRUCTURE Spartan Stadium, built in 1923, is in the middle of a massive expansion project approved in 2003. The construction is adding 3,000 seats to the 72,027 capacity, a new press box and 24 luxury suites, and providing a new home for the MSU Alumni Association, University Development, the MSU Foundation and the 4-H Foundation. It also is creating an indoor home for The Spartan statue, or "Sparty" as it is popularly called, which currently is displayed at the entrance to the athletic complex. Experts have determined that the statue would suffer significant weather damage if it remained outside much longer.

FANS Open containers used to be allowed anywhere on campus, making tailgating a free-flowing, campus-wide event. However, the board of trustees put open-container restrictions into effect in February 2005, so tailgating at Michigan State will undergo change. This follows the midseason 2004 prohibition of drinking games and the accompanying paraphernalia, which was a response to 17 students being taken to the hospital because of high blood-alcohol levels. Tailgaters now will be limited to drinking in specified areas.

FAST FACTS • Spartan Stadium was the site of a hockey game between Michigan and Michigan State in 2001, drawing a world-record crowd of 74,554. • Spartan Stadium's field was brought back to its roots in 2002, when a field composed of nine types of grass replaced the artificial turf. • When The Spartan statue is placed in its new, indoor home, a bronze replica will take its place outside the athletic complex.

TOP 5 MOMENTS

1. "GAME OF THE CENTURY," *November 19, 1966.* No. 2 Michigan State has to settle for a 10-10 deadlock with No. 1 Notre Dame in the "Game of the Century." The Spartans lead, 10-0, early but can't hold off the Fighting Irish despite knocking starting Irish quarterback Terry Hanratty out of the game. The teams' rankings stay the same in the AP poll, but Michigan State slips into the top spot in the UPI vote. At season's end, though, Notre Dame is atop both polls and deemed the '66 national champion.

2. THE BIGGIE MUNN ERA, *1947-53.* Michigan State reached its peak under Munn, the Spartans winning the national championship in 1952, forging a 54-9-2 record and posting a 28-game winning streak from 1950-53.

3. THE DUFFY DAUGHERTY ERA, *1954-72.* Succeeding Munn was not easy, but Duffy Daugherty was up to the task. Daugherty's Spartans won a share of the national title in 1965 and went 109-69-5 over 19 seasons. Daugherty's often-hilarious quotes, known as "Duffyisms," are legendary.

4. LORENZO WHITE'S CAREER, *1984-87.* Lorenzo White is the most prolific running back in Michigan State history. He holds school career records for attempts (1,082), yards (4,887) and touchdowns (43). White also ranks No. 1 in single-season attempts (419) and yards (2,066) and has the highest single-game rushing output in Spartan Stadium history (292 yards against Indiana in 1987).

5. BLAKE EXOR FINDS A HOME IN THE END ZONE, *November 18, 1989.* In a 76-14 smashing of Northwestern, running back Blake Exor scores a Michigan State-record six touchdowns.

VAUGHT-HEMINGWAY STADIUM

MISSISSIPPI

SETTING Vaught-Hemingway Stadium sits off All-American Drive on the southeast side of the Mississippi campus. Most of the buildings around Vaught-Hemingway are academic halls, not other athletic facilities, which is unusual for a stadium setting. Those attending a game should be prepared to walk a fair distance. All-American Drive is shut

renovation. The field, named after Dr. Jerry Hollingsworth, one of the school's most generous boosters, also received an upgrade when AstroPlay synthetic turf was installed before the 2003 season. The facility is one of the oldest in the country, with students helping to build the first grandstand in 1915. The stadium was first named after judge William Hemingway, a

jostling for the best positions from which to cheer the passing players. In 1998, the Walk of Champions arch, donated by the unbeaten, untied 1962 team, was built on the east side of The Grove to create an official entrance for the players. The university's attitude toward tailgating shows respect for the tradition—at many schools, tailgating is limited to a few

down for each game, and the next closest street, University Avenue, is restricted to unloading purposes. After-game traffic also is notoriously bad because there is no exit to the north, and the south, east and west exits are limited to one-way traffic.

STRUCTURE Before the 2002 season, the south end zone at Vaught-Hemingway Stadium was enclosed and seating was added to bring the capacity to 60,580. Ole Miss has drawn its 10 largest crowds since that

law professor and longtime chairman of the university's athletic committee. Former coach John Vaught's name was added in 1982.

FANS Ole Miss has been called the best tailgating college in the nation. Its tailgating fame stems from The Grove, a 10-acre plot of oak trees in the center of campus. In 1985, coach Billy Brewer began walking his players through The Grove before each game. The Grove has become the prime tailgating spot, with fans

hours before kickoff, but at Ole Miss the green light is given at 6 a.m.

FAST FACTS • Before each game, a celebrity appears on the Sony JumboTron to lead the crowd in the "Hotty Totty" cheer. Participants have included Snoop Dogg, Dolly Parton and even astronauts in space. • In the 1960s, 1970s and 1980s, in particular, Mississippi Veterans Memorial Stadium in Jackson was the site of many Rebels (and Mississippi State) "home" games.

TOP 5 MOMENTS

1. OLE MISS JOINS THE ELITE, *1959-62.* In a great four-season run, Ole Miss fashioned a 39-3-1 record, won the Sugar Bowl three times, twice went undefeated and twice finished No. 2 in the final AP poll.

2. THE JOHN VAUGHT ERA, *1947-70, 1973.* Under coach John Vaught, Ole Miss became a power. During his tenure, the Rebels won six SEC championships and 10 bowl games. Ole Miss went to 18 bowls overall during the Vaught reign, including 14 straight beginning with the 1957 season. The Rebels posted a 190-61-12 record under Vaught, who came out of retirement early in the 1973 season and coached the Rebs for the remainder of the year.

3. THE LONGEST GAME, *November 3, 2001.* Arkansas and Ole Miss set a record (since tied) for the longest game in NCAA history, playing a seven-overtime thriller. The Rebels lose, 58-56, when they fail on a 2-point conversion attempt.

4. ARCHIE MANNING'S CAREER, *1968-70.* Long before Archie Manning became known as the father of two NFL quarterbacks, he was an exciting and dangerous passer and runner at Ole Miss (and in the NFL). He led the Rebels to three bowls and finished third in the 1970 Heisman balloting.

5. ELI MANNING'S CAREER, *2000-03.* Despite considerable pressure, Eli Manning had no problem carrying on the tradition that his father Archie and brother Peyton (Tennessee) started in the SEC. Eli broke almost every Mississippi passing record, and he helped the Rebels to a share of the SEC West championship in 2003. He threw for 10,119 career yards and 81 touchdowns (against only 35 interceptions) as a Rebel.

MISSOURI

SETTING The University of Missouri's Memorial Stadium—best known as Faurot Field—is located south of the campus, close enough to capture the excitement of the student atmosphere but far enough away to provide traveling fans easy access. Many fraternities have members park their cars on the shoulders of Stadium Boulevard so they can rent their parking lots to fans. At Homecoming, it is not uncommon for Stadium Boulevard to be lined by two to three miles of parked cars. Jesse Hall, the school's administration building, and Memorial Union, the university's meeting center and monument to Missouri's fallen soldiers, are visible over the northern bowl of the stadium.

STRUCTURE When entering the stadium, the most noticeable feature is the 90-foot-wide, 95-foot-tall white "M" on the stadium's north lawn. This landmark, which was carved from stone by the 1927 freshman class, links each class of Missouri students to that which came before it. Memorial Stadium was built in 1926. Peak attendance in the single-tiered facility was 30,832; after the latest renovations, the seating capacity is

68,349. The playing surface has been called Faurot Field since 1972, when it was named after legendary MU coach and athletic director Don Faurot.

FANS The "M-I-Z-Z-O-U" chant builds to a crescendo at Faurot, with "M-I-Z" resounding from the east side of the stadium, "Z-O-U" answering from the west side. Tailgating, once largely refined to Reactor Field west of the stadium, has become more scattered. The new hot spots are the Hearnes Center parking lot east of the stadium (for those fans willing to pay for their tailgating spots) and the roofs of nearby campus parking garages. When goalposts are torn down after a big win, they often are carried to a hangout called Harpo's and chopped up as souvenirs.

FAST FACTS • Missouri's Homecoming tradition began in 1911, when athletic director Chester L. Brewer invited Missouri alumni to "Come Home" for the Tigers' game against Kansas in an attempt to improve attendance. A record crowd showed up, and a tradition was born. • Don Faurot helped lay the original Memorial Stadium sod as a graduate student in 1926 and laid the final piece of turf when Faurot Field returned to grass in June 1995. • The most recent major stadium renovation occurred in 1995, when a new grass field (since replaced with artificial FieldTurf) was installed, the north lawn was reshaped to give the stadium a more consistent bowl shape and a brick wall was built around the grandstands.

TOP 5 MOMENTS

1. THE FIFTH-DOWN GAME, *October 6, 1990.* Colorado, trailing by a 31-27 score against a lightly regarded Missouri team with time about to run out, has the ball first-and-goal on the Missouri 3. Colorado quarterback Charles Johnson spikes the ball to stop the clock, and on the next play, Eric Bieniemy runs for 2 yards. Colorado then calls a timeout, but the chain crew fails to flip the down marker from second to third. After the teams return to the field, Bieniemy is stuffed on a run, and Johnson spikes the ball on the next play. The Buffaloes should have been done, but Colorado gets an extra down, and Johnson scores as time expires to give Colorado a 33-31 victory. The Buffs go on to win the Orange Bowl and a share of the national title.

2. THE KICKED-BALL GAME, *November 8, 1997.* Leading 38-31 with less than a minute remaining, it looks as if Missouri will beat the Cornhuskers for the first time since 1978. After driving his Huskers to the Missouri 12, Nebraska QB Scott Frost, on third down and with 7 seconds remaining, fires the ball to Shevin Wiggins in the end zone. Missouri's Julian Jones knocks the pass from Wiggins' hands, but Wiggins inadvertently kicks the ball into the air and into the hands of Matt Davison for a TD as time runs out. Nebraska prevails, 45-38, in overtime and goes on to a share of the national championship.

3. THE DECADE OF THE '60s. Under Dan Devine, the Tigers won four bowl games (including the Orange and Sugar) and posted a winning record every season.

4. THE DON FAUROT ERA, *1935-42, 1946-56.* Coach Don Faurot built the Tigers into a nationally respected program, leading MU to its first Big Six Conference title and first modern bowl game in 1939. Faurot created the split-T formation, instituting it at Missouri in 1941, and won 100 games in 19 seasons.

5. BRAD SMITH DAZZLES, *October 25, 2003.* Brad Smith shreds the Texas Tech defense for five rushing touchdowns, a school record, and 291 yards rushing, a Mizzou quarterback high, in a 62-31 pasting of the Red Raiders that makes the Tigers bowl eligible for the first time since 1998.

NAVY-MARINE CORPS MEMORIAL STADIUM

Association provides free rides to the game from the Harry S. Truman Park and Ride lot to reduce postgame traffic congestion. • Large groups attending the game often meet at the 1953 Pavilion, located in the northern end of the stadium. From there, fans can keep an eye on the pregame action while waiting for the rest of their party. • The stadium is dedicated to members of the Navy and the Marine Corps as a reminder of the service rendered to the country by members of those units.

TOP 5 MOMENTS

1. NAVY UPSETS SOUTH CAROLINA, *November 17, 1984.* The Midshipmen jolt the No. 2 Gamecocks, 38-21. Navy, which enters the game with a 3-5-1 record, intercepts four passes, recovers one fumble and blocks a field-goal attempt.

2. ROGER STAUBACH'S CAREER, *1962-64.* During his three years as a Navy starter, Roger Staubach won the Heisman Trophy, led Navy to the Cotton Bowl and established himself as one of the best scrambling quarterbacks ever. "Roger the Dodger" set the academy record for efficiency rating with a 196.3 mark in his 1963 Heisman season and at one time held 28 Navy records.

3. NAPOLEON McCALLUM'S CAREER, *1981-85.* A two-time All-American and one of the most versatile players in college football history, running back Napoleon McCallum amassed 7,172 all-purpose yards in his career, an NCAA record at the time, and set a bushelful of academy records. He rushed for 1,587 yards in one season and 4,179 in his career.

4. EDDIE MEYERS RUNS OVER SYRACUSE, *November 7, 1981.* Co-captain Eddie Meyers leads Navy to a 35-23 win against Syracuse, burning the Orange for an academy-record 298 yards on the ground and four touchdowns.

5. TDS ON THREE CONSECUTIVE CARRIES, *September 13, 1997.* In Navy's 36-7 triumph over Rutgers, Chris McCoy, one of the all-time-great rushing quarterbacks, runs for touchdowns on three consecutive carries.

SETTING Navy-Marine Corps Memorial Stadium in Annapolis, Md., is northwest of the U.S. Naval Academy campus and is appropriately flanked by water. Weems Creek is to the north and College Creek to the south, and the Severn River and Chesapeake Bay also are nearby. Pageantry is a huge part of the aura surrounding Navy football. The Brigade of Midshipmen—thousands of Naval Academy students—attends games in full dress uniform. And even the civilians adhere to a dress code: Fans on the stadium's east side wear gold, and fans on the west side wear blue. A clean, family-friendly atmosphere is treasured here, and pregame festivities are highlighted by the Billy the Kid Zone, where young fans can joust, run an obstacle course or pretend they're playing in the Army-Navy game.

STRUCTURE Memorial Stadium, completed in 1959, seats 34,000. The stadium was built with private donations—gifts totaling $3 million. The playing surface is named after Jackson T. Stephens, a 1947 graduate of the Naval Academy who donated $10 million to support ongoing field renovations and other projects. A three-phase, $40 million stadium renovation was finished in the summer of 2004. The project involved building a new press tower, constructing a

third level and banquet area, installing video boards and luxury suites and adding more seating in the south end zone and along the sidelines.

FANS The Naval Academy is a tradition-rich institution, and its football program is no different. One of the proudest moments on a Navy football Saturday is the march-on, in which the 4,000-strong Brigade of Midshipmen marches from the Naval Academy Yard to the stadium, where it is greeted with a standing ovation. Navy jets fly over the stadium before each game. Another Midshipmen tradition is rushing onto the field after a score and doing a pushup for each Navy point. The role of mascot has been filled by goats since 1904. Bill XXXI and Bill XXXII are the current mascots and are cared for by 15 handlers. Navy fans have many tailgating options around the stadium. NavyFest, sponsored by the school, is an easy way to organize parties for groups of 20 or 1,000. The Captain's BBQ is a good option for those who want to experience a Navy tailgate but have a smaller group; each game, a different caterer provides the food. There's also plenty of space for fans who want to tailgate out of their vehicles or under tents.

FAST FACTS • The Naval Academy Athletic

SATURDAY SHRINES

NORTH CAROLINA

SETTING Kenan Memorial Stadium is surrounded by Carolina pine trees, creating one of the most postcard-worthy settings in the country. The stadium rests in the middle of campus, south of the school's academic buildings and northeast of the residential and medical facilities, making student access to games easy. The Kenan Football Center, home of the football program's office and the North Carolina Hall of Honor, was built on the west end of the stadium. Also nearby is the 172-foot-tall Morehead-Patterson Bell Tower.

STRUCTURE Although the stadium has been upgraded many times since its construction in 1927, Kenan's classic look has been carefully maintained. A recent expansion project added luxury boxes and 8,000 seats to bring the capacity to 60,000. The scoreboard at the east end of the stadium and an improved public

basketball prowess—it won its fourth NCAA title in 2005—the Tar Heels have no problem filling Kenan Stadium. However, students wanting to tailgate have few options. The Rams Club, a members-only booster group, is the only body that tailgates on a regular basis. Tar Heel Town, an outdoor festival on the quad, attracts a lot of fans with its food, music and family-based activities and is only a short walk from the stadium. Current coach John Bunting has initiated the Old Well Walk. About 2½ hours before each home game, the Carolina players meet at the Old Well, one of the central campus landmarks, and fans cheer the players as they walk across campus to the stadium.

FAST FACTS • The world's largest sculpture of a ram guards the entrance to the Kenan Football Center.
• The Kenan Fieldhouse, located on the east end of

address system are the newest additions. The stadium originally was to be paid for through the alumni association's fundraising efforts, but when William Rand Kenan Jr. heard about the project, the Carolina alum offered to pay for the stadium if it were built as a memorial to his parents, William R. and Mary Kenan.

FANS Though North Carolina is known for its

the stadium, has its own Student Development Center complete with language lab, lecture hall, computer lab and reading rooms. • William Kenan's contributions to the stadium did not end with the initial cost of construction; he donated an additional $1 million in the 1950s to construct a second deck. And since Kenan's death in 1965, the trust established by his will has made numerous donations for stadium projects.

TOP 5 MOMENTS

1. THE 1990s SUCCESS. North Carolina went to seven bowl games in the '90s and won five of them. Strong defenses, led by Bracey Walker, Marcus Jones, Dre' Bly, Greg Ellis and Brian Simmons, were the backbone of those standout teams. The Tar Heels won 11 games in 1997, 10 in 1996 and 1993 and nine in 1992.

2. THE CHARLIE JUSTICE ERA, *1946-49.* Halfback Charlie "Choo Choo" Justice, considered one of the top players in the history of Southern football, was an All-American in 1948 and 1949—years in which he finished second in the Heisman Trophy voting. He led the Tar Heels to 32 victories over four seasons and to berths in two Sugar Bowls and one Cotton Bowl.

3. LAWRENCE TAYLOR WREAKS HAVOC. Linebacker Lawrence Taylor burst into college football prominence halfway through his junior year and capped his North Carolina career with a standout season in 1980. As a senior, he recorded 16 sacks and six other tackles for loss. He made game-saving plays against Texas Tech and Clemson in an 11-1 season and was named ACC Player of the Year.

4. DON McCAULEY RUNS OVER DUKE, *November 21, 1970.* Don McCauley saves his best for last in 1970, running 47 times for 279 yards and five touchdowns to lead the Tar Heels to a 59-34 victory against Duke in the regular-season finale. He sets still-standing ACC season records with 1,720 rushing yards and 21 touchdowns and is named ACC Player of the Year and an All-American.

5. DRE' BLY'S CAREER, *1996-98.* In 1996, cornerback Bly was a consensus All-American as a freshman—he intercepted 11 passes that season. Bly was a consensus pick again as a sophomore. And he finished his three seasons at Carolina with an ACC career record of 20 interceptions.

CARTER-FINLEY STADIUM

SETTING Carter-Finley Stadium is northeast of the North Carolina State campus, which sprawls across several miles of Raleigh. Though the stadium is a bit of a trek from the main section of campus, it is close enough for students to walk. Access by car is not too difficult, either, because the stadium is just a few miles from the intersection of I-40 and I-440. RBC Center, home to the Wolfpack basketball team and the NHL's Carolina Hurricanes, lies just north of the north end zone and is visible from inside the stadium. The North Carolina State Fairgrounds also is adjacent to the stadium, making parking close to the stadium easy except for the 10 days in October when the fair is being held. Fans attending a game during the fair had better be patient—with 150,000 people converging on a one-square-mile area, traffic gridlock is not unusual.

STRUCTURE The stadium is horseshoe shaped, with the Murphy Center closing the south end of the structure. Built in 1966, Carter-Finley Stadium is in the process of being upgraded. The first stage of construction was completed before the 2001 season and added 5,500 seats in the south end zone, bringing capacity to 51,500. A "Superscreen" scoreboard and a modern sound system also were installed. The projects in the second stage of renovation will cost $47 million and give the stadium another 5,000 seats in the north end zone and a new press box and suites above the west stands. The stadium was named after Harry and Nick Carter, school alumni and textile executives, and A.E. Finley, a local philanthropist. The playing surface is named after Wayne T. Day, an N.C. State graduate and CEO who donated $5 million to a school fundraising campaign.

FANS The fairgrounds area provides plenty of tailgating space, and Wolfpack fans take advantage. Yet tailgating at N.C .State games has become more restricted since two people were shot and killed at a tailgate party in 2004; fans may not enter lots more than three hours before games and people may not save spaces for their friends. A common sight in the Carter-Finley stands is the "Sign of the Wolf," which is made by touching the middle and ring fingers to your thumb to form the nose and holding the pinkie and index finger in the air to make the ears.

FAST FACTS • The Murphy Center, which covers 103,254 square feet, is the home of the football program's sports medicine department, strength training center and academic center. • The new press box, a three-tiered facility, was designed to provide television broadcasters, newspaper writers, scouts and coaches with their own areas.

TOP 5 MOMENTS

1. THE YEAR OF THE WHITE SHOES. The 1967 team upsets second-ranked Houston, posts an 8-2 regular-season record and defeats Georgia in the Liberty Bowl. Paced by its "White Shoes" defense—players polished their shoes white under the prompting of senior standout (and current Wolfpack coach) Chuck Amato—N.C. State holds opponents to 94 points over 11 games.

2. THE MOST NOTABLE SEASON, *2002.* An explosive offense powers N.C. State to 11 wins, the most in school history. The Wolfpack cap the season with a 28-6 triumph over Notre Dame in the Gator Bowl. N.C. State becomes the first ACC school to have a 3,000 yard passer (Philip Rivers), 1,000-yard rusher (T.A. McLendon) and 1,000-yard receiver (Jerricho Cotchery) in the same season.

3. TED BROWN'S CAREER, *1975-78.* Ted Brown remains the most prodigious rusher in school history with 4,602 career yards. Brown holds school records for rushing yards in a game (251, against Penn State in 1977) and a season (1,350 in 1978). During Brown's career, N.C. State went to three bowl games and won two.

4. BEATING NO. 2 FLORIDA STATE, *September 12, 1998.* After six years of frustration following the Seminoles' move into the ACC, the Wolfpack finally upend FSU, 24-7.

5. THE BROTHER ACT. In 1975, Dave and Don Buckey become the first brothers to be named first-team All-ACC in the same year. Dave, a quarterback, and Don, a wide receiver, help the Wolfpack to a 7-4-1 season.

NORTH CAROLINA STATE

SETTING The Carrier Dome is in the middle of campus, southwest of the university quadrangle. The dome stands out in the city skyline and is visible for several miles in all directions. Access to the stadium can be difficult, as the parking areas closest to the dome are restricted 24 hours a day, seven days a week. There are a few small lots southwest of the dome, but they don't provide nearly enough seats for a capacity crowd. There are several evening and weekend garages on the extreme southwest corner of the campus, but parking in one of those makes for a long walk to the game.

STRUCTURE The Carrier Dome seats 49,262. The cost for the facility, completed in 1980, was $26.85 million. The Carrier Corp. made a $2.75 million donation to have the dome named after it. The stadium is 570 feet long and 497 feet wide and covers 7.7 acres; the top of the dome is 160 feet above the playing surface. Two Daktronics LED video boards were installed before the 2003 season at a cost of more than $1 million, and FieldTurf was put down before the 2005 season. A portable maple court is set up for basketball games.

FANS Because there is little parking in the immediate vicinity of the Carrier Dome, tailgating is spread out and held mostly in private parking lots. After victories, Syracuse fans go to the Varsity, a local restaurant, and knock over the banner of the Orange's unsuccessful opponent. A popular student hangout is "44s," in the Marshall Street area, named after the great Orange players who have worn that number.

FAST FACTS • The roof of the dome, replaced in 1999, weighs 220 tons and is made of Teflon-coated Fiberglas. Sixteen fans, each five feet in diameter, hold the roof in place and, when necessary, circulate heated air to melt snow on the roof. • The AstroTurf field is made of 26 15-foot-wide rolls. A machine called a grasshopper installs the rolls on top of a ⅝-inch foam pad. Zippers hold the rolls together. • Each year, the facility plays host to a memorial in honor of the Rev. Dr. Martin Luther King Jr. • In 1979, while the Carrier Dome was being built, Syracuse played its entire schedule away from campus.

TOP 5 MOMENTS

1. THE MAGICAL 1987 SEASON. Syracuse goes 11-0 in the regular season and earns a berth in the Sugar Bowl, where it plays a 16-16 tie with Auburn. It is the Orange's first New Year's bowl appearance in 23 years. Quarterback Don McPherson finishes second in the Heisman voting and is named the Most Outstanding Offensive Player in the Sugar Bowl.

2. SYRACUSE UPSETS NEBRASKA, *September 29, 1984.* Just two years removed from a 2-9 season, the Syracuse program continues its upswing with a 17-9 upset of No. 1-ranked Nebraska. The Orange finish 6-5 and will return to bowl play the next season.

3. LET'S GO BOWLING, *1985-1992.* The Orange earned seven bowl bids in this eight-season stretch, winning five times and tying once. Top-notch quarterback play was a constant. Don McPherson and Marvin Graves were the most impressive signal-callers, with Graves winning three consecutive bowl awards (Most Outstanding Player, MVP, Offensive Player of the Game) from 1990-92.

4. THE TRADITION OF NO. 44. While USC may have its "Tailback U" tradition, Syracuse counters with the tradition of No. 44. Through the years, great running backs such as Jim Brown, Ernie Davis and Floyd Little have worn the number and led the Orange to victory. More recently, Rob Konrad became the first fullback to wear No. 44. Beginning in 1995, Konrad and quarterback Donovan McNabb helped power the Orange to four consecutive bowls.

5. THE ORANGE BLOWS PAST THE HURRICANES, *November 28, 1998.* Syracuse drops 45 points on Miami in the first half and buries the Hurricanes, 66-13. Donovan McNabb throws for a touchdown in the first quarter and runs for three scores in the second (one of those runs covering 51 yards). He adds a second TD pass in the third quarter.

SCOTT STADIUM

SETTING Scott Stadium sits on the east side of the campus and is one of the most conveniently accessed facilities in the nation because a good portion of Virginia's student housing is within just a few blocks. Access for off-campus visitors also is good because the campus is near the intersection of U.S. 250 and I-64. Though there is parking adjacent to the stadium, many fans park at University Hall (the basketball arena) and either make the walk to Scott from that lot or ride a shuttle. To the south of the stadium is Bryant Hall, home to the Virginia Football Hall of Fame. It was rebuilt and expanded in 1998.

STRUCTURE Scott Stadium, built in 1931, has undergone an $86 million renovation. After the expansion, the venue was renamed the Carl Smith Center, David A. Harrison III Field at Scott Stadium. The stadium's capacity, once in the lower third of the conference, now is in the upper third at 61,500. A $25 million grant from Smith, a Virginia alumnus, kick-started the project, and the expanded facility was named in his honor. As part of the three-year project, completed in 2000, an upper deck was installed at the south end of the field, turning Scott Stadium into a bowl. Other improvements include a new 600-space parking garage behind Bryant Hall, the construction of a second level for Bryant and new permanent seating on the north side of the field.

FANS Virginia's "Wah-hoo-wah" is one of the most unusual and mysterious chants in college football. Some accounts trace it to Natalie Floyd Otey's 1893 opera performance of "Where'er You Are, There Shall My Love Be," at a Charlottesville opera

house. Otey sang the first three words between each stanza, and the audience, composed largely of Virginia students, joined in. By the end of the night, "Where'er You Are" had become "Wah-hoo-wah," and the rest was history. Virginia's unofficial alma mater is "The Good Old Song," sung to the tune of "Auld Lang Syne." After each Cavaliers score and at the end of every game, Virginia fans

stand, link arms and sway as they sing the song.

FAST FACTS • Construction of Scott Stadium was a gift from Frederic William and Elisabeth Strother Scott, who dedicated the stadium to Frederic's grandparents. • The playing field is named after Virginia alumnus David A. Harrison III, who donated $5 million to the football program.

TOP 5 MOMENTS

1. VIRGINIA 33, NO. 2 FLORIDA STATE 28, *November 2, 1995.* Florida State had won its first 29 games as an ACC member, but the Cavaliers end that streak in exciting fashion, making a goal-line stop on the game's final play. The Seminoles become the highest-ranked team Virginia has ever beaten.

2. VIRGINIA 20, NO. 6 NORTH CAROLINA 17, *November 16, 1996.* Trailing the No. 6 Tar Heels, 17-3, after the third quarter, Virginia storms back. Freshman Antwan Harris' 95-yard interception return helps turn the tide, and Rafael Garcia drills a 32-yard field goal with 39 seconds left to win it.

3. THE BILL DUDLEY ERA, *1939-41.* Versatile Bill Dudley still holds the Virginia single-season scoring record with 134 points in 1941. After leading Virginia to an 8-1 record in '41, the backfield star became the top pick in the NFL draft and went on to a Hall of Fame career in the pros.

4. THE MOORE CONNECTION. A potent combination from 1988 through 1990, quarterback Shawn Moore and receiver Herman Moore (not related) led the Cavaliers to two bowl appearances and a share of an ACC title. The co-title came in 1989, a year in which Virginia set a school high with 10 victories. In '90, the duo fueled an attack that set three ACC offensive records.

5. SEEING DOUBLE, *1994-96.* Tiki and Ronde Barber may rank as the best set of twins in college football history. Running back Tiki was the first Virginia player to record back-to-back 1,000-yard seasons. Cornerback Ronde led the ACC in interceptions in 1994 with eight.

VIRGINIA

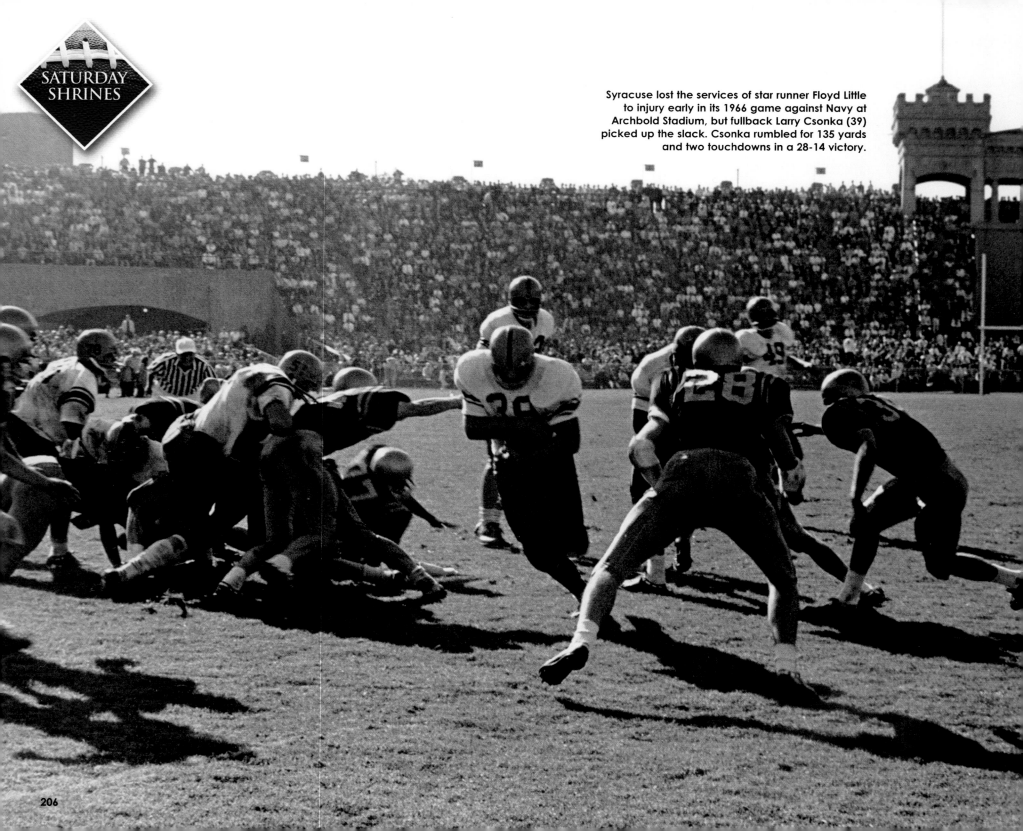

Syracuse lost the services of star runner Floyd Little to injury early in its 1966 game against Navy at Archbold Stadium, but fullback Larry Csonka (39) picked up the slack. Csonka rumbled for 135 yards and two touchdowns in a 28-14 victory.

DEAD STADIUMS

By Michael Bradley

They have put luxury boxes in Ohio Stadium. Fans at Michigan Stadium are paying fees to buy better tickets. College football is changing, right down to the athletic palaces that play host to the games. Call it progress or just good business. But things are different—and necessary. That's why we don't see some of the old places anymore. They weren't comfortable, or they had poor access to the hot dog stand. They didn't look nice. The press boxes were decrepit. But those stadiums symbolized college football's past. And though they are no longer around, they are still remembered.

ARCHBOLD STADIUM, SYRACUSE

At the end, Syracuse's home field wasn't very appealing. Seating capacity had been reduced, and the Orange still couldn't fill it. Then-coach Frank Maloney wouldn't even let recruits see the place.

"It was a disaster," said Jake Crouthamel, Syracuse athletic director from 1978-2004. "It was old and crumbling, and it had seen its day."

That it had. Archbold Stadium, home of the Orange from 1907 through '78, had been the site of the school's football glory days. All-time greats like Jim Brown, Ernie Davis, Larry Csonka, Floyd Little, John Mackey and Joe Morris played there. Ben Schwartzwalder coached there. And in 1959, the Orange won a national championship there. "Some truly great players from Syracuse and other teams played in Archbold in its heyday," Crouthamel said.

When Archbold opened its gates, it was deemed the "Greatest Athletic Arena in America." It was built to resemble the Colosseum in Rome and was made of concrete. The huge oval sat high above campus and gave spectators a view of Lake Onondaga

Now consigned to history's scrapheap, Archbold was a heap of trouble for the opposition—particularly from 1958-68.

MIAMI FIELD, MIAMI (OHIO)

Miami is known as the "Cradle of Coaches." Accordingly, Miami Field served as its nursery. There, sideline legends such as Paul Brown, Earl "Red" Blaik, Ara Parseghian, Bo Schembechler, Weeb Ewbank, John Pont, Paul Dietzel and Carmen Cozza learned the game as players before taking their insight to schools and professional teams with tremendous success.

Those who remember Miami Field know it was a modest start for such esteemed names in college football history. It held just 15,000 people and was never the home of any nationally prominent teams, although Miami was a power on its own level, fashioning a 32-1-1 record from 1973-75. The stadium was a quaint, regional facility that had more than its share of good times and history.

"People here at Miami consider it a magical place, because we're the Cradle of Coaches," said Dave Young, a longtime sports information director at Miami.

Miami Field began as Athletic Park, an unassuming patch of land that was dedicated in May 1896 and played host to its first football game on October 17 of that year, a 26-0 win over Earlham College. The field was located just on the outskirts of the campus, although the site later became a prime location of an expanded university, a situation that hastened the call for its demise by those who wished to replace it with an academic

and the Onondaga Valley. Its west gate featured a signature 40-foot arch and two castle towers, while the south side was dominated by a large gothic grandstand. "It really was a great facility when it was built," said Maury Youmans, who grew up in Syracuse and played tackle on the '59 title team.

The stadium was used primarily for football, but in 1920 the Syracuse Stars of baseball's International League played there. Babe Ruth participated in several baseball exhibitions at Archbold, and in '78, the first Empire State Games were staged at the venerable structure.

But Archbold was about football, first and foremost. And Syracuse accomplished plenty there. From 1915-27, the Orange was 61-10-6 at Archbold; teams from 1958-68 were even better, racking up 47 wins and losing just six times. The 1959 squad was the most memorable, of course. It featured Davis, a brilliant sophomore back who would win the 1961 Heisman Trophy. The '59 SU defense may have been even more impressive than Davis, allowing a total of 193 rushing yards in 10 regular-season games.

"We didn't have any inkling at the beginning of the season that we were going to be that good," Youmans said. "By midseason, we didn't think anybody could beat us. We had that attitude."

Archbold was home to many impressive performances.

Perhaps the most memorable came in 1956, when Jim Brown, playing his final home game, scored six touchdowns and kicked seven extra points in a 61-7 drubbing of Colgate. The Syracuse defense rose to the occasion in 1911, holding back Jim Thorpe and his Carlisle teammates in a 12-11 victory. In 1962, Navy and quarterback Roger Staubach traveled to Archbold but were stymied, 34-6.

By the mid-1970s, it was clear that Archbold was ready for history's scrapheap. Its once robust 42,000-seat capacity had been diminished by more than 15,000, a condition that left Syracuse in danger of being ineligible for certification by the College Football Association, which oversaw big-time football in those days. What was left was uncomfortable. The players had it almost as bad, particularly the visitors. They dressed in an auxiliary gymnasium next to Archbold and then had to reach the field via a treacherous spiral staircase.

So, plans were made for a new stadium—the state-of-the-art Carrier Dome, which would be built on the same site. On November 11, 1978, coach Frank Maloney's Orange played host to 18th-ranked Navy in the final game at Archbold. Syracuse upset the Midshipmen, 20-17, behind Morris' 203 yards rushing. It was a fitting conclusion to a once-proud relic and a reminder that great things had happened at Archbold.

structure. (A science building stands there today.)

In 1915, the Miami Board of Trustees renamed the stadium Miami Field, a name that took a few years to catch hold. The facility remained simple in premise: a pair of long bleachers on each side and smaller stands behind the end zones. It offered a picturesque view of the tree-filled Miami campus and its Georgian architecture. It also offered a home to Redskins (now RedHawks) teams coached by the likes of Sid Gillman, Woody Haves, Parseghian and Schembechler, and to teams that never had a losing season from 1943-75.

On November 6, 1982, Miami defeated Central Michigan, 23-0, in the final game at Miami Field. Afterward, the student section was uprooted and incorporated into new Yager Stadium, which holds more than 30,000 fans. And a few of the "Miami Gates," which served as entrances to the field, also were moved. "We took the best of Miami Field with us to the new stadium," Young said.

But they couldn't take those coaching legends.

TULANE STADIUM, TULANE

Bill Curl reported for duty at Tulane Stadium at 8 a.m. that Sunday morning, December 2, 1973, looking to clean up a few odds and ends from the previous day—a day on which Tulane had defeated LSU for the first time in 25 years with a 14-0 win over the eighth-ranked Tigers. Since he had been up most of the night celebrating, Curl could only imagine what Green Wave fans were doing. When he arrived at the stadium, he found out.

Scattered throughout the stadium were small pockets of fans, about 300 all together, just sitting and looking out at the empty field. Curl was puzzled and asked a security guard what was going on.

"He told me they wanted to come back and sit in their seats just to think about the game," said Curl, who was Tulane's sports information director from 1966-73.

Almost a year to the day later, the Green Wave said farewell to Tulane Stadium, losing a desultory 26-10 decision to Mississippi in the cold and gloom of a damp New Orleans afternoon. The facility closed for good after two more games—Nebraska's win over Florida in the Sugar Bowl and the Pittsburgh Steelers' triumph over the Minnesota Vikings in Super Bowl IX. The Steelers' victory on January 12, 1975, ended a nearly half-century ride that had begun in 1926, when a 35,000-seat stadium was built on what had been the Etienne

Tulane Stadium was home to the Green Wave, the NFL's Saints, the Sugar Bowl and three Super Bowls.

de Bore plantation, thought to be the first place in the U.S. where sugar was granulated. That's how the Sugar Bowl got its name.

Tulane Stadium was nine years old before the Sugar Bowl football classic made its debut. Prior to that, coaches Clark Shaughnessy and Bernie Bierman, each of whom would develop sterling reputations at other schools, had led Tulane to prominence. Though the Wave had some success in the 1940s and again in the early 1970s (after the school had de-emphasized football for a period), Tulane Stadium was known mostly as the site of the Sugar Bowl game, the venue for three Super Bowls and the original home of the expansion New Orleans Saints of the National Football League.

Tulane Stadium's capacity eventually swelled to just over 80,000, although that '73 game against LSU attracted 86,598 fans. "We sold seats on the photo decks and put bleachers in behind the hedges in the end zones for that game," Curl said.

The stadium was bowl-shaped, with four pie slices cut out of the corners, and had an upper deck that ran around three-quarters of the facility. It was largely made of steel, so that when fans banged their feet, the sound of rolling thunder cascaded down to the field. It sat near the heart of the Tulane campus (a dorm, recreation center and intramural field now occupy the area) and had about 80 parking spaces. Really. For big games, some fans had to walk 20-30 blocks from their cars to the stadium.

The walk often was worth it, prime examples being the Sugar Bowl of December 31, 1973, when Notre Dame defeated Alabama, 24-23, to win the national title, and Super Bowl IV, in which Hank Stram's Kansas City Chiefs surprised Joe Kapp and the Minnesota Vikings. Still, no one came back to Tulane Stadium the next day just to sit. That was reserved for beating LSU.

The "Cradle of Coaches" rocked in the heyday of Miami Field (below), a facility whose signature entrance gates (left)—a few of them, anyway—were included in the move to a new stadium.

MEMORIAL STADIUM, MINNESOTA

Of all the places in the world it would seem logical to have a domed stadium, Minneapolis ranks just behind Anchorage, Vladivostok and Reykjavik on the list. But for 58 seasons, the Minnesota Golden Gophers took on all comers at Memorial Stadium, a brick campus horseshoe that died an untimely death in 1981. And perhaps due to global warming—not to mention a decided lack of home-field advantage at the Metrodome—the Gophers want back outside and have been discussing building a new on-campus home, even if it means playing in wintry conditions.

"We traditionally played against Wisconsin in the last game of the season, and very often it was a snow-filled stadium that needed to be shoveled and plowed," said Bill Peterson, who served as the Gophers' sports information director for two decades.

Built in 1924 and named in honor of university graduates and workers who served in World War I, Memorial Stadium featured 1,000,000 bricks (give or take) and was described by an edition of the *Minnesota Alumni Weekly* as "a great horseshoe magnet," thanks to its ability to draw a crowd of 43,000 for a '24 visit by Michigan. Memorial was home of the Bernie Bierman teams that stormed to national titles in 1934, 1935, 1936, 1940 and 1941. Bruce Smith, the 1941 Heisman winner, played for the Gophers, and so did Pug Lund, Paul Giel and Sandy Stephens.

The stadium was pretty basic, with a few flaws. Because the facility had a track around it, the seats in the curved end of the horseshoe were rather distant from the action. Although the field was moved toward the closed end, it didn't make much of a difference. Then there was the press box. Though it was serviceable, it lacked an elevator. "You had to walk up about 50 rows to the top," Peterson said. And there was one other problem: A design flaw gave the stadium a roundish, bowl-like shape that forced thousands of spectators in the corners to crane their necks around those in front of them to catch parts of the on-field activities.

By the 1970s, it became clear that Memorial Stadium was in need of a facelift. But the university didn't have the money. "And we weren't about to get any state funding," Peterson said. With the Metrodome going up relatively close to the UM campus, and no one willing to step up with the $10-15 million estimated to fix the decaying structure, Minnesota decided to move out of Memorial and into the domed stadium. On November 21, 1981, the Gophers dropped a 26-21 decision to Wisconsin in the traditional season-ender for both teams. The Gophers went inside the following fall—alumni, aquatic and rec centers now grace the old football grounds—but they just might head back outdoors one of these years.

No matter how cold it gets.

Before the Gophers came in from the cold, their "great horseshoe magnet" attracted plenty of fans.

PITT STADIUM, PITTSBURGH

Parking. A lot of it was about parking. OK, so Pitt Stadium had a track around its field, pushing fans farther from the action than was deemed ideal. The restrooms and concession stands were somewhat inaccessible and certainly not up-to-date. The metal bleachers weren't comfortable. And making that trek up "Cardiac Hill" to the stadium wasn't all that enticing.

But perhaps the biggest reason Pitt Stadium became expendable, after years of dwindling crowds (brought on in no small part by the Pittsburgh Panthers' flagging football fortunes), was a dearth of available, convenient parking.

"When the stadium was built in 1925, people didn't have cars, and a lot of people lived in the city," said Beano Cook, Pitt alumnus, longtime Steel City resident, former Panthers sports information director, college football historian and general bon vivant. "It was easy to get to the game then. But as people started to move to the suburbs, it became harder, because there was no parking."

The old bowl was home to some truly great Pitt outfits, beginning with Jock Sutherland's juggernauts of the '20s and '30s and including the 1970s and early-1980s titans of

PALMER STADIUM, PRINCETON

Cosmo Iacavazzi is a purist. As a Princeton freshman and later as a former Tigers backfield star, he loved to sit in Palmer Stadium's cavernous end zone, protected from the cold, hard concrete seats by a blanket, and watch a game unfold. "Anybody who really wants to know football has to sit there," he said.

And anyone who wants to know football history had better take a look at Palmer Stadium, which played host to Princeton football from 1914 through 1997. (The Tigers play at the same location nowadays, but in a modern facility). The old horseshoe certainly had no creature comforts when it was christened, nor many in the next eight decades as well.

Still, Palmer Stadium was one of the shrines of football's early history. Long the second-oldest football stadium in the country (behind Harvard's), it needed only eight years for some true magic to unfold. In 1922, coach Bill Roper's "Tiger Team of Destiny" ran up an 8-0 record to become the second unbeaten team to play in Palmer. (The other was the '20 Tigers squad, which won six games and tied one.) Though the '22 team's most famous victory—a 21-18 triumph over Chicago—was accomplished away from home, Roper's bunch brought glory to Princeton's young home.

Five other unbeaten teams played in Palmer, with Iacavazzi's 1964 Tigers the final perfect squad. Not that there weren't other highlights, from Ivy League championships (the last came in '95) to the 1935 win over Dartmouth in near-blizzard conditions to a '50 triumph over the Big Green in a game played in torrential rain and 80-mph winds. And then there was Kaz. Dick Kazmaier and his teammates, running the single wing, compiled an 18-1 mark at Palmer during Kazmaier's years (1949-51) with the Tigers. Princeton was perfect in both '50 and '51, and Kazmaier won the Heisman Trophy in his senior season

You can bet Iacavazzi would have loved watching Kazmaier from the end zone.

Johnny Majors and Jackie Sherrill. Most especially, there was Majors' 1976 national championship team that featured Heisman Trophy winner Tony Dorsett. Also, from 1964-69, the stadium served as home to the Pittsburgh Steelers, who were awful in their new digs after moving from Forbes Field.

Pitt Stadium had an impressive concrete exterior, complete with a majestic archway as its main entrance. In 1969, the field was converted to an artificial surface, and a few years later the stadium's wooden bleachers were replaced with metal seats. But as the win totals started to drop in the 1980s and '90s, so did attendance. And interest in the program.

Soon, Pitt chancellor Mark Nordenberg was decrying the stadium's inability to provide adequate hospitality for fans or sufficiently impress recruits. On November 13, 1999, with more than 60,000 fans on hand, the Panthers played their final game in the stadium and defeated Notre Dame, 37-27. After playing at Three Rivers Stadium in 2000, Pitt moved into Heinz Field, sharing the space with the Steelers. Pitt Stadium was razed and replaced by the Peterson Events Center, which houses the Panthers' basketball programs and other Pitt teams, while providing students with myriad recreational opportunities.

But still not a lot of parking.

Pitt Stadium (above) lacked many amenities—adequate parking being high on the list—and Palmer Stadium was short on creature comforts, too. Yet each structure rates a prominent place in the history of college football.

DIVISION I-A STADIUM CHART

School (location)	Stadium Capacity	Story Behind the Name	First Game in Stadium	One to Remember	Stadium Record	Fast Fact
Air Force (Colorado Springs, Colo.)	Falcon (52,480)	The falcon was chosen as the school's mascot in the fall of 1955. The falcon's flight pattern represents the combat techniques used by the Air Force.	Sept. 22, 1962 (Air Force 34, Colorado State 0)	Sept. 24, 1988 (Wyoming 48, Air Force 45) The Cowboys answered a late Falcons touchdown with a game-winning field goal with one second left.	155-98-4	Each game features fly-bys, mostly by F-16s.
Akron (Ohio)	Rubber Bowl (34,000)	Akron is known as the Rubber City. The university has a College of Polymer Science and Polymer Engineering.	Oct. 4, 1940 (Western Reserve 6, Akron 0)	Nov. 5, 2004 (Akron 31, Marshall 28) The game appeared headed to overtime before Marshall's punter muffed a snap, setting up the Zips' game-winning 43-yard field goal as time expired.	180-114-10	The stadium's site originally was a recreation area carved out of a dirt hill at the nearby airport.
Alabama (Tuscaloosa)	Bryant-Denny (83,818)	Named for Coach Paul "Bear" Bryant, who coached the Crimson Tide from 1958-1982. George Denny was the school's first president.	Sept. 28, 1929 (Alabama 55, Mississippi College 0)	Oct. 1, 1994 (Alabama 29, Georgia 28) A duel between Crimson Tide quarterback Jay Barker and Bulldogs QB Eric Zeier is decided by a last-minute field goal by Michael Proctor.	193-43-3	The 2004 season was the 76th at Bryant-Denny Stadium.
Arizona (Tucson)	Arizona (56,002)	Named for the school.	Oct. 12, 1929 (Arizona 35, California Tech 0)	Nov. 7, 1992 (Arizona 16, Washington 3) This win over the No. 1 Huskies marked the birth of the "Desert Swarm" defense that would lead the Wildcats to a 10-2 mark the next year.	267-157	The "Ring of Fame" surrounds the stadium and honors Arizona's All-American players and those who hold national statistical records.
Arizona State (Tempe)	Sun Devil/Frank Kush Field (73,379)	Sparky the Sun Devil became Arizona State's mascot on Aug. 20, 1946. He was designed by late Disney artist Bert Anthony. Frank Kush was ASU's winningest coach. The Sun Devils captured eight conference titles in his 21 seasons.	Oct. 4, 1958 (Arizona State 16, West Texas State 13)	Sept. 21, 1996 (Arizona State 19, Nebraska 0) The Sun Devils ended two-time defending national champion and No. 1-ranked Nebraska's 26-game winning streak en route to the Rose Bowl.	227-80-3	Parts of the movie *Jerry Maguire* were filmed here. Also, Super Bowl 30 was played at Sun Devil, with the Cowboys defeating the Steelers, 27-17.
Arkansas (Fayetteville)	Reynolds Razorback (72,000)	A gift from the Donald W. Reynolds Foundation helped increase seating from 51,000 to 72,000.	Sept. 24, 1938 (Arkansas 27, Oklahoma A&M 7)	Oct. 17, 1981 (Arkansas 42, Texas 11) The unranked Razorbacks routed No. 1 Texas, forcing seven turnovers along the way.	143-65-4	The Razorbacks also play games at War Memorial Stadium in Little Rock.
Arkansas State (Jonesboro)	Indian (30,458)	Named for the mascot.	Sept. 28, 1974 (Louisiana Tech 20, Arkansas State 7)	Sept. 18, 2004 (Memphis 47, Arkansas State 35) Arkansas State was ahead with four minutes to play, but the Tigers roared back.	90-62-1	The "Ring of Honor," located on the west side of the stadium, recognizes Indians greats like Bill Bergey and Maurice Carthon.
Army (West Point, N.Y.)	Michie/Blaik Field (40,000)	Named for Dennis Mahan Michie, the first coach, organizer and manager of football at West Point. Earl "Red" Blaik coached Army to two national championships.	Oct. 4, 1924 (Army 17, Saint Louis University 0)	Oct. 7, 1999 (Army 59, Louisville 52, 2OT) Michael Wallace ran for a school-record 269 yards and four scores.	303-128-7	Army has had three Heisman Trophy winners: Felix "Doc" Blanchard (1945), Glenn Davis (1946) and Pete Dawkins (1958). Only four other schools—Notre Dame (7), Ohio State (6), USC (6) and Oklahoma (4)—have had more winners.
Auburn (Ala.)	Jordan-Hare (86,063)	Ralph "Shug" Jordan is the all-time winningest coach at Auburn. Clifford Leroy Hare was a member of Auburn's first team, president of the old Southern Conference and longtime chairman of Auburn's Faculty Athletic Committee.	Nov. 30, 1939 (Auburn 7, Florida 7)	Nov. 20, 1993 (Auburn 22, Alabama 14) Behind RB James Bostic and QB Patrick Nix, the Tigers capped a perfect season in the Iron Bowl.	244-61-7	When the facility was renamed Jordan-Hare Stadium in 1973, it became the first stadium in the country to be named for an active coach. ... Auburn is the only school at which John Heisman coached that produced a Heisman Trophy winner.
Ball State (Muncie, Ind.)	Ball State (22,500)	The Ball brothers, two Muncie industrialists, bought the campus and buildings and gave them to the state of Indiana in 1918.	Oct. 21, 1967 (Ball State 65, Butler 7)	Oct. 9, 1993 (Ball State 31, Toledo 30) The Cardinals scored 20 unanswered points in the fourth quarter.	117-64-4	The first night game in Muncie was played on Aug. 28, 2003, against Indiana State. Temporary lights were used. Ball State won, 31-7.
Baylor (Waco, Texas)	Floyd Casey (50,000)	The late Carl B. Casey and his wife, Thelma, donated $5 million to renovate the stadium in honor of Carl's father, Floyd Casey.	Sept. 30, 1950 (Baylor 34, Houston 7)	Nov. 9, 1974 (Baylor 34, Texas 24) Entering the game, Baylor was 4-3. But the Bears upset the No. 12 Longhorns en route to winning the Southwest Conference title and making their first Cotton Bowl appearance.	155-125-6	Floyd Casey Stadium is the fourth football facility the Bears have used since 1902.

School (location)	Stadium Capacity	Story Behind the Name	First Game in Stadium	One to Remember	Stadium Record	Fast Fact
Boise State (Idaho)	Bronco (30,000)	Named for the mascot.	Sept. 11, 1970 (Boise State 49, Chico State 14)	Dec. 30, 1999 (Boise State 34, Louisville 31) The Broncos finished 10-3, capping their fourth I-A season with a win in the Humanitarian Bowl on their own turf. The game featured 10 lead changes.	184-48	Bronco Stadium has the only blue playing surface in the nation.
Boston College (Chestnut Hill, Mass.)	Alumni (44,500)	It was named by the Rev. Charles W. Lyons, S.J., in 1915, in honor of school alumni.	Sept. 21, 1957 (Navy 46, Boston College 6). Then a U.S. senator, John F. Kennedy arranged the stadium's opening game.	Sept. 11, 1976 (Boston College 14, Texas 13) The unranked Eagles knocked off the No. 7 Longhorns.	169-89-2	Boston College uses a structure called "The Bubble" for practices. The inflatable dome streches across the football field and forms a dome-shaped roof.
Bowling Green (Ohio)	Doyt Perry (30,599)	Doyt Perry was Bowling Green's coach from 1955-1964. In 1965, he became the school's athletic director.	Sept. 24, 1966 (Bowling Green 13, Dayton 0)	Oct. 25, 2003 (Bowling Green 34, Northern Illinois 18) Both teams were nationally ranked and it was the first nationally televised game in Falcons history.	133-58-6	Until 2004, Bowling Green had the oldest scoreboard in Division I. Installed in 1966, it was replaced for the '04 season.
Buffalo (N.Y.)	University (31,000)	Named for the school.	Sept. 4, 1993 (Maine 30, Buffalo 27)	Sept. 23, 2000 (Buffalo 20, Bowling Green 17) It was the Bulls' first Mid-American Conference game and first win as a I-A program.	18-48	The venue was the site of the 1993 World University Games track and field competition.
BYU (Provo, Utah)	LaVell Edwards (64,045)	LaVell Edwards was BYU's coach from 1972-2000 and compiled a record of 257-101-3.	Oct. 2, 1964 (New Mexico 26, BYU 14)	Sept. 8, 1990 (BYU 28, Miami 21) The Cougars held the Hurricanes scoreless in the final 26:48.	245-124-6	LaVell Edwards Stadium is the largest sports venue in the state of Utah.
California (Berkeley)	Memorial (73,347)	The stadium honors military personnel who lost their lives in World War I.	Nov. 24, 1923 (Cal 9, Stanford 0)	Nov. 20, 1982 (California 25, Stanford 20) The Big Game featured "The Play," during which Cal lateraled the ball five times on a kickoff return and ran through the Stanford band on the way to a winning TD as time expired.	287-202-16	The stadium is modeled after the Colosseum in Rome and located in Strawberry Canyon.
Central Florida (Orlando)	Citrus Bowl (70,188)	In 1983, the Florida Department of Citrus began giving an annual sponsorship of $250,000 to the stadium, which is city-owned.	Sept. 29, 1979 (Central Florida 7, Fort Benning 6)	Dec. 1, 1990 (Central Florida 52, William & Mary 38) The victory sent UCF to the semifinals of the Division I-AA playoffs.	104-53-1	The stadium was a Depression-era (1936) project that came about as a result of President Franklin Roosevelt's jobs-creating Works Progress Administration.
Central Michigan (Mount Pleasant)	Kelly/Shorts (30,199)	Named in honor of R. Perry Shorts, an alumnus and donor, and for Kenneth "Bill" Kelly, Chippewas coach from 1951-1966.	Nov. 4, 1972 (Central Michigan 28, Illinois State 21)	Nov. 11, 2000 (Central Michigan 21, Western Michigan 17) Entering the game, Central was 1-8 and Western was 8-1.	122-46-4	The site also is used for women's field hockey.
Cincinnati (Ohio)	Nippert (35,000)	Football player Jimmy Nippert suffered a spike injury in a 1923 game and later died of blood poisoning. His grandfather, James N. Gamble of Procter & Gamble, donated the money needed to build the stadium.	The facility was dedicated on Nov. 8, 1924 (Oberlin College 13, Cincinnati 0). UC first played at the site in 1902, and the stadium went up in 1916.	Nov. 23, 1968 (Cincinnati 23, Miami of Ohio 21) Cincinnati won the game with a field goal as time expired.	273-162-13	In 1968, the Cincinnati Bengals played their first games at Nippert while Riverfront Stadium was being built.
Clemson (S.C.)	Memorial/Frank Howard Field (81,473)	The stadium commemorates Clemson students who lost their lives in World Wars I and II. Frank Howard was a legendary coach.	Sept. 19, 1942 (Clemson 32, Presbyterian 13)	Nov. 8, 2003 (Clemson 26, Florida State 10) It was Tommy Bowden's first victory over father Bobby, and No. 3 FSU was the highest-ranked opponent ever beaten by Clemson.	226-88-7	It was nicknamed "Death Valley" by Presbyterian coach Lonnie McMillian after his teams lost several lopsided games there.
Colorado (Boulder)	Folsom Field (53,750)	Fred G. Folsom was the first coach of the Buffaloes. He was 77-23-2 over 15 seasons.	Oct. 11, 1924 (Colorado 39, Regis College 0)	Nov. 23, 2001 (Colorado 62, Nebraska 36) To that point in Huskers history, no team had ever scored that many points against Nebraska.	275-131-10	Mascot Ralphie leads the Buffs onto the field in thunderous style.
Colorado State (Fort Collins)	Hughes/Sonny Lubick Field (30,000)	Sonny Lubick is the Rams' current and most successful coach. He has been named confer-ence coach of the year four times. Harry Hughes was CSU's coach from 1911-1941.	Sept. 28, 1968 (North Texas 17, Colorado State 12)	Oct. 22, 1994 (Utah 45, Colorado State 31) The Rams ranked No. 10 nationally and the Utes were No. 15. The largest crowd in school histo-ry was on hand.	105-82-2	An "A" that measures 300 by 250 feet sits at the edge of the foothills representing CSU's old nickname, the Aggies. Every year, a fraternity and the freshman football players repaint the letter.
Connecticut (Storrs)	Rentschler Field (40,000)	Pratt and Whitney founder Frederick Rentschler donated money to the state.	Aug. 30, 2003 (UConn 34, Indiana 10)	Sept. 30, 2004 (UConn 29, Pittsburgh 17) Led by QB Dan Orlovsky, the Huskies rolled in the first Big East game in the stadium.	11-2	The facility is managed by Madison Square Garden.
Duke (Durham, N.C.)	Wallace Wade (33,941)	Wallace Wade coached the Blue Devils for 16 seasons and won 110 games.	Oct. 5, 1929 (Pittsburgh 52, Duke 7)	Jan. 1, 1942 (Oregon State 20, Duke 16) The Rose Bowl moved east—to Duke's stadium— as the West Coast was deemed unsafe follow-ing the bombing of Pearl Harbor.	204-145-5	Wallace Wade is the only facility to play host to the Rose Bowl besides the home city of Pasadena, Calif. To recall the event, rose bushes line the stadium entrance.

School (location)	Stadium Capacity	Story Behind the Name	First Game in Stadium	One to Remember	Stadium Record	Fast Fact
East Carolina (Greenville, N.C.)	Dowdy-Ficklen (43,000)	James Skinner Ficklen was a tobacco dealer who gave money for student aid. Ron and Mary Ellen Dowdy contributed $1 million to the university.	Sept. 21, 1963 (East Carolina 20, Wake Forest 10)	Nov. 20, 1999 (East Carolina 23, N.C. State 6) QB David Garrard scored three touchdowns and helped ECU clinch a bowl invitation.	135-72-1	The team runs onto the field through purple smoke while Jimi Hendrix's "Purple Haze" blares over the P.A.
Eastern Michigan (Ypsilanti)	Rynearson (30,200)	Elton J. Rynearson Sr. coached at Eastern Michigan for 26 seasons.	Sept. 27, 1969 (Eastern Michigan 10, Akron 3)	Oct. 17, 1987 (Eastern Michigan 35, Ball State 28) EMU trailed, 28-27, before RB Gary Patton ripped off a 72-yard TD run with 3:55 left.	90-90-5	The Detroit Wheels of the World Football League played in Rynearson Stadium in 1974.
Florida (Gainesville)	Ben Hill Griffin/Florida Field (88,548)	Ben Hill Griffin was a lifelong Gators fan and benefactor to the university. Florida Field is dedicated to servicemen who fought and died in World War I.	Nov. 8, 1930 (Alabama 20, Florida 0)	Nov. 16, 1991 (Florida 35, Kentucky 26) Steve Spurrier coached the Gators to their first SEC crown.	263-82-13	At the end of the 1991 season, Spurrier dubbed the venue "The Swamp," saying, "The swamp is where Gators live. We feel comfortable there, but we hope our opponents feel tentative. ..."
Florida Atlantic (Boca Raton)	Lockhart (20,000)	The facility is named for a civic leader who donated the land for the project.	Sept. 6, 2003 (Valdosta State 45, Florida Atlantic 17)	Dec. 13, 2003 (Colgate 36, Florida Atlantic 24) The Owls couldn't contain the Red Raiders' ground game and finished one victory short of the I-AA championship game.	7-4	The stadium was once home to the Florida Fusion of the MLS.
Florida International (Miami)	FIU Stadium (17,000)	Named after the school.	Aug. 29, 2002 (Florida International 27, St. Peter's 3)	Aug. 29, 2002 (Florida International 27, St. Peter's 3) Before the largest crowd in school history, FIU prevailed in the first game played in the stadium.	8-12	The stadium site served as host to Pope John Paul II in 1987.
Florida State (Tallahassee)	Doak Campbell (82,300)	Doak S. Campbell was an FSU president.	Oct. 7, 1950 (Florida State 40, Randolph-Macon 7)	Nov. 26, 1994 (Florida State 31, Florida 31) Trailing 31-3, the Seminoles equaled an NCAA-record for fourth-quarter comebacks by scoring 28 points to forge a tie.	235-73-4	Bobby Bowden has been honored with a stained glass window and statue at the stadium.
Fresno State (Calif.)	Bulldog (41,031)	Named after the mascot.	Nov. 25, 1980 (Fresno State 21, Montana State 14)	Sept. 2, 2001 (Fresno State 44, Oregon State 24) The triumph over the No. 10 Beavers is the Bulldogs' first against a Top 10 team.	121-27-2	Bulldog Stadium was home to the California Bowl from 1981-1991. Fresno State played in the bowl five times and notched four victories.
Georgia (Athens)	Sanford (92,746)	Named for Dr. Steadman Vincent Sanford, former president and chancellor of the university.	Oct. 12, 1929 (Georgia 15, Yale 0)	Nov. 1, 1980 (Georgia 13, South Carolina 10) This classic matchup pitted 1980 Heisman winner George Rogers (Gamecocks) against the Bulldogs' Herschel Walker, who would win the honor in 1982.	279-90-9	Sanford Stadium played host to the medal round of the men's and women's soccer competition during the 1996 Atlanta Olympics.
Georgia Tech (Atlanta)	Bobby Dodd/Grant Field (55,000)	Bobby Dodd was Georgia Tech's coach from 1945-66, posting a 165-64-8 record, and served as the school's athletic director from 1950-1976.	Oct. 7, 1905 (Georgia Tech 54, Dahlonega 0)	Oct. 7, 1916 (Georgia Tech 222, Cumberland 0) This was the most lopsided game in college history.	443-189-24	This is the oldest on-campus Division I-A college stadium.
Hawaii (Honolulu)	Aloha (50,000)	Named after a native word, which means hello and goodbye.	Sept. 13, 1975 (Texas A&M-Kingsville 43, Hawaii 9)	Dec. 25, 2003 (Hawaii 54, Houston 48, 3 OTs) QB Timmy Chang came off the bench and threw for 475 yards and five TDs in the Hawaii Bowl, which was marred by a postgame brawl.	145-97-4	Site of the NFL's Pro Bowl, the facility can convert from a baseball field to a football field to a triangular setting for concerts in 30 minutes.
Houston	Robertson/John O'Quinn Field (30,757)	The John and Julie O'Quinn Foundation donated $6 million to the renovation of Robertson Stadium in 1998.	Sept. 21, 1946 (Southwestern Louisiana 13, Houston 7)	Nov. 9, 1996 (Houston 56, Southern Miss 49, OT) The Cougars clinched their first and only Conference USA title as RB Antowain Smith scored six touchdowns.	34-36-1 (since Sept. 12, 1998)	The stadium, formerly called Public School, was renamed Jeppesen in 1970 before being renamed Robertson in 1980. Houston began playing a full schedule at Robertson in 1998, the first time the school played its games on campus since 1949.
Idaho (Moscow)	Kibbie Dome (16,000)	The Kibbie Dome honors alum William H. Kibbie, president of the industrial contracting firm JELCO, and donor of $300,000 to begin the facility's construction.	Sept. 27, 1975 (Idaho State 29, Idaho 14)	Oct. 21, 1995 (Idaho 55, Montana 43). The Vandals, then a I-AA team, built a 49-16 lead and withstood a rally by the Grizzlies—thanks to six TD passes by Eric Hisaw.	101-40-1	The Kibbie Dome was awarded America's Outstanding Structural Engineering Achievement of 1976 because of its barrel-arched roof, an engineering feat at the time.
Illinois (Champaign)	Memorial (69,249)	Memorial Stadium was built in 1923 and dedicated to Illinois men and women who gave their lives in World War I.	Nov. 3, 1923 (Illinois 7, Chicago 0)	Oct. 18, 1924 (Illinois 39, Michigan 14) On stadium dedication day, Red Grange scored five TDs and passed for a sixth.	230-190-12	The names of the war dead are on the 200 columns on the east and west sides of the stadium.

School (location)	Stadium Capacity	Story Behind the Name	First Game in Stadium	One to Remember	Stadium Record	Fast Fact
Indiana (Bloomington)	Memorial (52,180)	Memorial Stadium commemorates war veterans.	Oct. 8, 1960 (Oregon State 20, Indiana 6)	Oct. 24, 1987 (Indiana 14, Michigan 10) The comeback win in a rainstorm was the Hoosiers' first since 1967 vs. the Wolverines and moved IU into first place in the Big Ten.	114-131-3	On Oct. 22, 1960, Memorial Stadium was dedicated. Homecoming queen Judy Curtis broke a bottle filled with Jordan River water on the goalpost.
Iowa (Iowa City)	Kinnick (70,397)	Named in honor of 1939 Heisman Trophy winner Nile Kinnick, who died serving his country.	Oct. 5, 1929 (Iowa 46, Monmouth 0)	Oct. 19, 1985 (Iowa 12, Michigan 10) Rob Houghtlin kicked a last-second field goal to lift No. 1 Iowa over No. 2 Michigan. The Hawkeyes marched on to the Rose Bowl.	130-85-3	The stadium was called Iowa Stadium before being renamed Kinnick in 1972.
Iowa State (Ames)	Jack Trice (45,814)	Jack Trice Stadium is named in honor of Iowa State's first African-American football player. Trice died of injuries suffered during a game in 1923.	Sept. 20, 1975 (Iowa State 17, Air Force 12)	Nov. 13, 1976 (Iowa State 37, Nebraska 28) It was the Cyclones' first win over the Huskers, ranked No. 9, since 1960 and their first over an AP Top 10 team.	88-91-3	Iowa State had two previous homes before Jack Trice: State Field (1892-1913) and Clyde Williams Field (1914-1974).
Kansas (Lawrence)	Memorial (50,250)	Memorial Stadium is dedicated to Kansas students and alumni who fought and died in World War I.	Oct. 29, 1921(Kansas 21, Kansas State 7)	Oct. 27, 1984 (Kansas 28, Oklahoma 11) Before a Homecoming crowd, the Jayhawks stunned the No. 2-ranked Sooners.	213-202-16	The Jayhawks' longest winning streak in the stadium has been eight games, achieved over 1951-52 and 1967-68.
Kansas State (Manhattan)	KSU (50,000)	Named for the school.	Sept. 21, 1968 (Kansas State 21, Colorado State 0)	Nov. 14, 1998 (Kansas State 40, Nebraska 30) The Wildcats had lost 29 consecutive games to the Cornhuskers entering this clash in Manhattan.	130-85-3	On Nov. 11, 2000, 53,811 fans witnessed Kansas State's 29-28 win over Nebraska, the largest crowd to witness a sporting event in the state.
Kent State (Kent, Ohio)	Dix (29,287)	Robert C. Dix was on the Board of Trustees for three decades.	Sept. 13, 1969 (Kent State 24, Dayton 14)	Nov. 18, 1972 (Kent State 27, Toledo 9) The victory gave Kent State its only MAC championship.	79-105	This was the venue for the 2001 NCAA Division I field hockey championship.
Kentucky (Lexington)	Commonwealth (67,530)	"Commonwealth" was another name for state when Kentucky entered the Union in 1792.	Sept. 15, 1973 (Kentucky 31, Virginia Tech 26)	Oct. 4, 1997 (Kentucky 40, Alabama 34, OT) Led by QB Tim Couch, the Wildcats defeated the Crimson Tide for the first time in 75 years.	105-91-4	On game day, Commonwealth Stadium becomes the third largest "city" in Kentucky, with crowds exceeding 70,000.
Louisiana-Lafayette	Cajun Field (31,000)	Named for the mascot.	Sept. 25, 1971 (Louisiana-Lafayette 21, Santa Clara 0)	Sept. 14, 1996 (Louisiana-Lafayette 29, Texas A&M 22) The win over the No. 25 Aggies was the Cajuns' first against a ranked team.	96-82-2	Nicknamed "The Swamp," Cajun Field sits two feet below sea level. Cypress Swamp sits on top of the school's original field, which was used in the early 1900s.
Louisiana-Monroe	Malone (30,427)	James L. Malone was the school's football coach when it became a four-year institution in 1951.	Sept. 16, 1978 (Louisiana-Monroe 21, Arkansas State 13)	Dec. 12, 1987 (Louisiana-Monroe 44, Northern Iowa 41, OT) The victory propelled the Indians to the I-AA title game (which they won).	87-47-1	Malone Stadium never has had a sellout.
Louisiana Tech (Ruston)	Joe Aillet (30,600)	Joe Aillet was a coach and athletic director at Louisiana Tech.	Sept. 28, 1968 (Louisiana Tech 35, East Carolina 7)	Oct. 2, 2004 (Louisiana Tech 28, Fresno State 21) Tech toppled No. 17 Fresno State behind Ryan Moats' 236 yards rushing and four TDs.	131-53-3	Louisiana Tech has had 10 perfect seasons in the facility.
Louisville (Ky.)	Papa John's Cardinal (42,000)	John Schnatter runs Papa John's, which is headquartered in Louisville.	Sept. 5, 1998 (Kentucky 68, Louisville 34)	Sept. 26, 2002 (Louisville 26, Florida State 20, OT) In a rainstorm, the Cardinals stunned the No. 4 Seminoles.	34-9	Papa John's Cardinal Stadium was one of three facilities to play host to the 1999 Women's World Cup.
LSU (Baton Rouge)	Tiger (91,600)	Named for the mascot.	Nov. 25, 1924 (Tulane 13, LSU 0)	Oct. 31, 1959 (LSU 7, Ole Miss 3) A stunning 89-yard punt return by Billy Cannon enabled the No. 1 Tigers to beat the No. 3 Rebels. Cannon went on to win the Heisman Trophy.	348-138-18	The team lived in Tiger Stadium in 1986 when players' dormitories were being built.
Marshall (Huntington, W.Va.)	Joan C. Edwards (38,019)	Named in honor of Joan C. Edwards, who has given more than $50 million to Marshall athletics, academics, arts and sciences.	Sept. 7, 1991 (Marshall 24, New Hampshire 23)	Dec. 21, 1996 (Marshall 49, Montana 29) The Herd, led by Randy Moss' four touchdown receptions, capped a 15-0 season and won its second I-AA title.	79-5	This is one of two Division I-A stadiums named for a woman. (The other is South Carolina.)
Maryland (College Park)	Byrd (48,055)	Named in honor of H.C. Byrd, a multi-sport athlete, football coach and university president at Maryland.	Sept. 30, 1950 (Maryland 35, Navy 21)	Sept. 24, 1955 (Maryland 7, UCLA 0) The No. 1 Bruins turned the ball over on the Terrapins' 1 in the second quarter. The switch in momentum was crucial as the fifth-ranked Terps went on to win.	185-111-3	Queen Elizabeth II and Prince Philip visited Byrd Stadium on Oct. 19, 1957. The queen saw her first football game as the Terrapins defeated North Carolina, 21-7.
Memphis (Tenn.)	Liberty Bowl/Rex Dockery Field (62,380)	It is a memorial to veterans of World Wars I and II and the Korean War.	Sept. 18, 1965 (Ole Miss 34, Memphis 14)	Nov. 9, 1996 (Memphis 21, Tennessee 17) The Tigers used great defense and a late score to stun the Peyton Manning-led Vols. It was the Tigers' first win in 15 tries against Tennessee.	116-105-6	The stadium is the site of the Southern Heritage Classic, which annually pits Jackson State vs. Tennessee State.

School (location)	Stadium Capacity	Story Behind the Name	First Game in Stadium	One to Remember	Stadium Record	Fast Fact
Miami	Orange Bowl (72,319)	The Orange Bowl, owned by the city of Miami, originally was called Roddy Burdine Stadium before being named in homage to the state's citrus industry.	Dec. 10, 1937 (Georgia 26, Miami 0)	Jan. 2, 1984 (Miami 31, Nebraska 30) A failed two-point conversion cost the Huskers the Orange Bowl, giving the Hurricanes their first national championship.	300-137-6	The Hurricanes enter the playing field by running through a wave of smoke. The tradition began in the 1950s when Bob Nalette, a transportation director, built pipes that blew out the smoke. The same pipes are used today.
Miami (Oxford, Ohio)	Yager (30,012)	The stadium is named for Fred C. Yager, a 1914 Miami graduate who helped finance the facility's construction.	Oct. 1, 1983 (Western Michigan 20, Miami of Ohio 18)	Oct. 13, 2001 (Miami of Ohio 30, Akron 27) Ben Roethlisberger threw a 70-yard touchdown pass to Eddie Tillitz as time expired.	68-35-4	Yager Stadium contains the "Cradle of Coaches" room. More than 100 Miami (Ohio) graduates have become coaches at the collegiate and professional levels.
Michigan (Ann Arbor)	Michigan (107,501)	Named for the school.	Oct. 1, 1927 (Michigan 33, Ohio Wesleyan 0)	Nov. 22, 1997 (Michigan 20, Ohio State 14) Charles Woodson ran back a punt 78 yards for a TD, caught a pass for 37 yards and played great defense. He won the Heisman in '97 and Michigan took a share of the national title.	357-103-15	Michigan Stadium was built on land that previously was an underground spring. During construction, the moist soil engulfed a crane that remains under the field to this day.
Michigan State (East Lansing)	Spartan (72,027)	Named for the mascot.	Oct. 6, 1923 (Michigan State 21, Lake Forest 6)	Nov. 19, 1966 (Notre Dame 10, Michigan State 10) Referred to by some as the "Game of the Century," many grumbled when the Fighting Irish played for a tie.	300-126-12	On Oct. 6, 2001, Spartan Stadium was the site of a hockey game between Michigan and Michigan State that drew 74,554 fans.
Middle Tennessee (Murfreesboro)	Floyd/Horace Jones Field (30,788)	Named for Johnny "Red" Floyd, former coach. Horace Jones was head of the math department and a one-man athletic committee until faculty representatives were used.	Oct. 14, 1933 (Middle Tenn 0, Jacksonville State 0)	Oct. 27, 2001 (Middle Tennessee 39, New Mexico State 35) The Blue Raiders entered the fourth quarter down 24 points but scored on every possession the rest of the game to claim victory.	241-101-13	When major renovations were done on the original stadium in 1998, the construction workers left a small area of original concrete seating.
Minnesota (Minneapolis)	H.H.H. Metrodome (64,172)	Hubert H. Humphrey was mayor of Minneapolis, a U.S. senator and vice president of the United States.	Sept. 11, 1982 (Minnesota 57, Ohio 3)	Oct. 10, 2003 (Michigan 38, Minnesota 35) The Wolverines dug themselves out of a 28-7 third-quarter hole with a 31-point fourth-quarter explosion.	74-66-2	Fans enter the Metrodome through revolving doors to ensure that air stays inside the facility. The dome requires 250,000 cubic feet of air pressure to stay inflated.
Mississippi (Oxford)	Vaught-Hemingway/ Hollingsworth Field (60,580)	Judge William Hemingway was a professor of law and chairman of the university's athletic committee. John Vaught coached the Rebels to a 190-61-12 record and 18 bowl games. Dr. Jerry Hollingsworth has been a generous booster to the athletic department.	Oct. 2, 1915 (Arkansas A&M 10, Mississippi 0)	Nov. 28, 1992 (Mississippi 17, Mississippi State 10) The Rebels halted the Bulldogs on 11 plays inside the 4 with less than two minutes to play.	221-62-8	Ole Miss is home to some of the nation's best tailgating at The Grove.
Mississippi State (Starkville)	Davis Wade Stadium at Scott Field (55,082)	In 1914, the student body called a fledgling facility the "New Athletic Field." In 1920, the field was renamed Scott Field in honor of Don Scott, an Olympian in the half-mile and a football player at Mississippi State.	Oct. 3, 1914 (Mississippi State 54, Marion (Ala.) Military Institute 0)	Nov. 16, 1996 (Mississippi State 17 Alabama 16) The Bulldogs top the No. 8 Tide for the first time at Scott Field.	207-109-13	The field is surrounded by holly bush fences and landscaped end zones.
Missouri (Columbia)	Memorial/Faurot Field (68,349)	Faurot Field is named for Don Faurot, Tigers coach from 1935-1956 (with a three-year interruption because of military duty). Memorial Stadium is named for the 112 students who fought and died in World War I.	Oct. 2, 1926 (Missouri 0, Tulane 0)	1997 (Nebraska 45, Missouri 38, OT) The Huskers forced overtime on a miraculous play that saw a pass to wingback Shevin Wiggins bound off his hands, then his foot and into the hands of a diving Matt Davison as time expired.	230-164-19	In the north end of the stadium lies a block "M" carved from the same rock from which the stadium was built.
Navy (Annapolis, Md.)	Jack Stephens Field at Navy-Marine Corps Memorial Stadium (30,000)	The stadium is "dedicated to those who have served and will serve as upholders of the traditions and renown of the Navy and Marine Corps of the United States." Jackson T. Stephens is a 1947 graduate and a donor.	Sept. 26, 1959 (Navy 29, William & Mary 2)	Nov. 17, 1984 (Navy 38, South Carolina 21) The Gamecocks came in 9-0 and ranked No. 2.	107-84-1	When the Midshipmen score, uniformed students run across the field to the north end zone and do pushups that match the point total.
Nebraska (Lincoln)	Memorial/Tom Osborne Field (73,918)	The stadium is named to honor Nebraskans who served in the Civil and Spanish-American Wars and the Nebraskans who died in World Wars I and II, Korea and Vietnam. Tom Osborne compiled a 255-49-3 record as coach.	Oct. 13, 1923 (Nebraska 24, Oklahoma 0)	Oct. 31, 1959 (Nebraska 25, Oklahoma 21) Oklahoma boasted a 74-game conference unbeaten streak entering the game.	347-104-13	Fans are known to applaud the opposing players as they leave the field following games.

School (location)	Stadium Capacity	Story Behind the Name	First Game in Stadium	One to Remember	Stadium Record	Fast Fact
Nevada (Reno)	Mackay (31,900)	Named after university benefactor Clarence Mackay.	Oct. 1, 1966 (Nevada 33, UC Santa Barbara 17)	Nov. 14, 1992 (Nevada 48, Utah State 47) The victory gave the Big West title to Nevada in its first year as a I-A team. The Wolfpack went to the Las Vegas Bowl, the school's first bowl in 44 years.	165-66-2	The quarterback in the first game at new Mackay Stadium was current coach Chris Ault.
New Mexico (Albuquerque)	University (37,370)	Named for the university.	Sept. 17, 1960 (New Mexico 77, National University of Mexico 6)	Nov. 5, 1994 (New Mexico 23, Utah 21) The 3-7 Lobos were down 21-3 in the second quarter but rallied against the 8-0 Utes, ranked No. 9. A 22-yard field goal with 32 seconds left won it.	130-119-3	Before New Mexico played at University Stadium, the Lobos called Zimmerman Field (1938-59) and University Field (1892-1937) home.
New Mexico State (Las Cruces)	Aggie Memorial (30,343)	Named for the mascot.	Sept. 16, 1978 (New Mexico State 35, UTEP 32)	Sept. 19, 1998 (New Mexico State 28, New Mexico 27) It's called the "Miracle on Aggie Alley." Ryan Shaw caught a 50-yard TD pass from Ty Houghtaling with 50 seconds remaining to give the Aggies the victory.	52-83	The Eagles, Paul McCartney and Guns 'n' Roses, among others, have played Aggie Memorial.
North Carolina (Chapel Hill)	Fouts Field (30,500)	The stadium is named in honor of benefactor William Kenan Jr.'s parents.	Nov. 12, 1927 (North Carolina 27, Davidson 0)	Sept. 25, 1948 (North Carolina 34, Texas 7) Behind RB Charlie "Choo-Choo" Justice, the Tar Heels used the win as a launching pad toward a bid to the Sugar Bowl, where they suffered their only loss of the season.	242-153-16	The first night games at Kenan Stadium were in 1991 against Cincinnati and Clemson.
North Carolina State (Raleigh)	Kenan (60,000)	Named for Harry and Nick Carter, N.C. State alumni, and philanthropist A.E. Finley. Wayne T. Day Field is named for a Wolfpack alumnus and donor.	Oct. 8, 1966 (South Carolina 31, N.C. State 21)	Sept. 12, 1998 (N.C. State 24, Florida State 7) Torry Holt led the Wolfpack with a touchdown catch and a punt return for a score to stun the No. 2 Seminoles.	148-79-6	Carter-Finley is located on the North Carolina State Fairgrounds.
North Texas (Denton)	Carter-Finley/Wayne T. Day Field (51,500)	Theron J. Fouts came to the university in 1920, started track and field as the first varsity sport, coached multiple sports and eventually became athletic director.	Sept. 27, 1952 (North Texas 55, North Dakota 0)	Nov. 13, 1976 (Florida State 21, North Texas 20) It was North Texas' Hayden Fry vs. Bobby Bowden, who was in his first season at FSU. The Seminoles scored late to escape with a victory in a game played in a snowstorm.	154-78-7	In 1992, an increase in student fees was approved to fund stadium renovations that were completed in 1994.
Northern Illinois (DeKalb)	Brigham Field at Huskie Stadium (28,000)	Robert J. Brigham was a student-athlete, assistant coach, head coach, director of athletics and special assistant to the president. The facility also is named for the mascot.	Nov. 6, 1965 (Northern Illinois 48, Illinois State 6)	Oct. 6, 1990 (Northern Illinois 73, Fresno State 18) The Huskies total a school-record 806 yards of offense. Fresno State allowed the most points ever by a Top 25 team.	117-87-2	The stadium is nicknamed "The Doghouse" and "The House That George Bork Built." Bork was a star Huskies quarterback in the early 1960s.
Northwestern (Evanston, Ill.)	Ryan Field (47,130)	Named in honor of the Patrick G. Ryan family. Mr. Ryan is an alumnus of Northwestern and the chair of Northwestern's Board of Trustees.	Oct. 2, 1926 (Northwestern 34, South Dakota 0)	Nov. 4, 2000 (Northwestern 54, Michigan 51) After forcing a fumble, the Wildcats scored the winning touchdown with 20 seconds remaining. Northwestern had 654 yards of offense.	190-225-8	The stadium once was known as Dyche Stadium/Ryan Field. In 1997, the newly renovated stadium opened and its official name became Ryan Field.
Notre Dame (South Bend, Ind.)	Notre Dame (80,795)	Named for the school.	Oct. 4, 1930 (Notre Dame 20, Southern Methodist 14)	Oct. 15, 1988 (Notre Dame 31, Miami, Fla. 30) Pat Terrell knocked down Steve Walsh's two-point conversion pass to beat No. 1 Miami, ending the Hurricanes' 36-game regular-season winning streak.	287-87-5	Touchdown Jesus, the Grotto, Fair Catch Corby, "We're No. 1" Moses … what more could you want?
Ohio (Athens)	Peden (24,000)	Named for former head coach Bob Peden. He coached Ohio from 1924-1942 and 1945-1946, compiling a 121-46-11 record.	The stadium was dedicated in a 14-0 triumph over Miami (Ohio) in 1929.	Oct. 19, 1968 (Ohio 24, Miami of Ohio 7) The triumph sent Ohio to the Tangerine Bowl.	137-119-5 (since 1947; unavailable for previous years)	The stadium contains Victory Hill, a grassy area at the south end that is used for overflow seating.
Ohio State (Columbus)	Ohio (101,568)	Named for the school.	Oct. 7, 1922 (Ohio State 5, Ohio Wesleyan 0)	Nov. 23, 1968 (Ohio State 50, Michigan 14) The No. 2 Buckeyes pounded the No. 4 Wolverines and rolled on to the national championship.	380-117-20	The rotunda entrance contains three stained glass windows, and its architecture is modeled after the Pantheon in Rome.
Oklahoma (Norman)	Gaylord Family-Oklahoma Memorial Stadium (81,207)	Named in honor of university personnel who served in World War I.	Oct. 20, 1923 (Oklahoma 62, Washington, Mo. 7)	Nov. 25, 1971 (Nebraska 35, Oklahoma 31) Billed as the "Game of the Century," a battle of unbeatens saw No. 1 Nebraska score a late touchdown to edge past No. 2 Oklahoma.	315-76-15	As part of stadium renovations, a war memorial was constructed to honor OU faculty, staff and students who had given their lives in military service.
Oklahoma State (Stillwater)	Boone Pickens (48,000)	Boone Pickens donated $75 million to his alma mater, the largest contribution ever to Oklahoma State, to support OSU athletics.	Oct. 3, 1914 (Oklahoma State 134, Phillips 0)	Nov. 30, 2002 (Oklahoma State 38, Oklahoma 28) The unranked Cowboys toppled the No. 3 Sooners.	256-161-20	During renovation, a workman placed bricks in the shape of the letters "OU" on the side of the stadium to represent cross-state rival Oklahoma. The "mistake" was fixed.

School (location)	Stadium Capacity	Story Behind the Name	First Game in Stadium	One to Remember	Stadium Record	Fast Fact
Oregon (Eugene)	Autzen (54,000)	Named for Thomas J. Autzen, a Portland lumberman, sportsman and philanthropist.	Sept. 23, 1967 (Colorado 17, Oregon 13)	Oct. 22, 1994 (Oregon 31, Washington 20) Kenny Wheaton's interception return for a TD helped seal the win that propelled the Ducks to their first Rose Bowl since the 1957 season.	108-106-4	The expansion of the stadium, completed in 2002, cost $90 million; the original stadium cost only $2.5 million.
Oregon State (Corvallis)	Reser (35,362)	Formerly known as Parker Stadium, the venue's name was changed to Reser Stadium after Al and Pat Reser made a seven-figure gift on June 14, 1999.	Nov. 14, 1953 (Oregon State 7, Washington State 0)	Nov. 11, 1967 (Oregon State 3, USC 0) The "Giant Killers" stymied O.J. Simpson and beat the No. 1 team in the nation.	126-86-5	The facility also is used for field hockey and soccer.
Penn State (State College, Pa.)	Beaver (107,282)	Named for James A. Beaver, a former superior court judge, governor of Pennsylvania and president of the Penn State Board of Trustees.	September 17, 1960 (Penn State 20, Boston University 0)	Sept. 25, 1982 (Penn State 27, Nebraska 24) The Nittany Lions scored a last-second TD to defeat No. 2 Nebraska. It was a crucial early step on the way to the national championship.	211-55-0	Beaver Stadium becomes Pennsylvania's third-largest "city" on game day.
Pittsburgh	Heinz Field (65,000)	On June 15, 2001, the H.J. Heinz Co. won the naming rights of the stadium, which is home of the Pittsburgh Panthers and the Pittsburgh Steelers.	Sept. 1, 2001 (Pittsburgh 31, East Tennessee State 0)	Nov. 8, 2003 (Pittsburgh 31, Virginia Tech 28) The Panthers scored the winning TD with 47 seconds to play to top the No. 5 Hokies.	17-8	Heinz is a grass field with an underground heating system. Approximately 35 miles of tubing run underneath the field.
Purdue (West Lafayette, Ind.)	Ross-Ade (62,500)	David E. Ross, late president of the Board of Trustees, and George Ade, alumnus, writer and humorist, purchased the 65-acre spot where the stadium lies and donated it to the school.	Nov. 22, 1924 (Purdue 26, Indiana 7)	Sept. 25, 1965 (Purdue 25, Notre Dame 21) Behind the right arm of Bob Griese, the No. 6 Boilermakers upset No. 1 Notre Dame.	239-137-13	The 65-acre lot that was purchased for the stadium site was once a dairy farm.
Rice (Houston)	Rice (70,000)	Named for the school.	Sept. 30, 1950 (Rice 27, Santa Clara 7)	Nov. 16, 1957 (Rice 7, Texas A&M 6) The victory sent Rice to the Cotton Bowl. The Owls have not been back.	137-154-7	Rice Stadium's capacity is 70,000, even though the school has only 2,900 undergraduate students.
Rutgers (New Brunswick, N.J.)	Rutgers (41,500)	Named for the school.	Sept. 24, 1938 (Rutgers 20, Marietta 0); Sept. 3, 1994, stadium renovated and reopened (Rutgers 28, Kent 6)	Nov. 25, 1961 (Rutgers 32, Columbia 19) The win gave Rutgers its first undefeated season in 93 years.	196-92-4	On Nov. 6, 1869, Rutgers and Princeton played the first intercollegiate football game. … When Rutgers Stadium was built, a blended turf (Kentucky bluegrass, Bermuda and Princeton 104) was installed.
San Diego State (Calif.)	Qualcomm (54,000)	In 1997, a renovation project totaling $66.4 million took place at San Diego Jack Murphy Stadium. The wireless technology company Qualcomm paid $18 million for the naming rights for the next 20 years.	Sept. 15, 1967 (San Diego State 16, Tennessee State 8)	Nov. 19, 1977 (San Diego State 41, Florida State 16) The Aztecs trounced No. 13 FSU and went on to finish No. 16 in the AP poll with a 10-1 record.	157-73-6	One World Series, a major league All-Star Game and three Super Bowls have been played at Qualcomm Stadium.
San Jose State (Calif.)	Spartan (31,218)	Named for the mascot.	Oct. 7, 1933 (San Jose State 44, San Francisco State 6)	Oct. 4, 1986 (San Jose State 45, Fresno State 41). The outcome knocked No. 19 Fresno State out of the rankings.	204-109-17	The 1999 Women's World Cup and 1999 NCAA Women's College Cup were played at Spartan Stadium.
SMU (Dallas)	Gerald J. Ford (32,000)	Gerald J. Ford is an alumnus who donated money toward construction.	Sept. 2, 2000 (SMU 31, Kansas 17)	Sept. 2, 2000 (SMU 31, Kansas 17) In the inaugural game at Gerald J. Ford Stadium, the Mustangs scored on their first four possessions.	10-19	The stadium's Collegiate-Gregorian architecture is consient with the rest of the campus.
South Carolina (Columbia)	Williams-Brice (80,250)	Nephews of Martha Williams Brice gave a donation from her estate to expand the stadium from 43,000 to 54,000 seats in 1972.	Sept. 29, 1934 (South Carolina 25, Erskine 0)	Sept. 29, 2001 (South Carolina 37, Alabama 36) The Gamecocks, previously 0-9 against the Crimson Tide, won in the last minute.	227-160-14	The stadium is located off campus on the state fairgrounds.
South Florida (Tampa)	Raymond James (65,000)	The stadium is named for the Raymond James investment firm in St. Petersburg, Fla.	Oct. 3, 1998 (South Floriida 45, The Citadel 6)	Oct. 4, 2003 (South Floriida 31, Louisville 28 2OT) The Bulls scored a TD with 10 seconds left to force overtime en route to extending a 21-game home winning streak.	35-8	The stadium is the home of the Tampa Bay Buccaneers. It is known to fans as "The Ray Jay."
Southern Miss (Hattiesburg)	Carlisle-Faulkner Field at M.M. Roberts Stadium (33,000)	Gene Carlisle has been a generous contributor to USM athletics. L.E. Faulkner bought the materials and equipment for the original facility. M.M. Roberts was on the Board of Trustees of State Institutions of Higher Learning.	Sept. 25, 1976 (Mississippi 28, Southern Miss 0)	Nov. 20, 2003 (Southern Miss 40, TCU 28) The Golden Eagles knocked off the No. 9 Horned Frogs, the first ranked team to fall at USM, to claim at least a share of the Conference USA title.	99-34	The stadium is known to Golden Eagles fans as "The Rock at Southern Miss." In 1938, several Southern Miss players worked with the contractors. Athletes hauled the cement used to build additions to the structure.

School (location)	Stadium Capacity	Story Behind the Name	First Game in Stadium	One to Remember	Stadium Record	Fast Fact
Stanford (Palo Alto, Calif.)	Stanford/Louis W. Foster Family Field (85,500)	Named for the school and for Louis W. Foster of 21st Century Insurance Co. Foster, a 1935 graduate, donated money.	Nov. 19, 1921 (California 42, Stanford 7). The stadium opened on the last day of the season.	Oct. 10, 1970 (Stanford 24, USC 14) Led by Heisman Trophy-bound QB Jim Plunkett, Stanford captured its first victory over USC since 1957 on the way to winning the Pac-8 championship.	283-178-15	The stadium is the nation's largest privately owned college football facility. It has been the site of Olympic soccer, World Cup soccer, a Super Bowl and Herbert Hoover's presidential nomination acceptance speech.
Syracuse (N.Y.)	Carrier Dome (49,262)	The Carrier Corp. provided a $2.75 million gift to name the facility.	Sept. 20, 1980 (Syracuse 36, Miami of Ohio 24)	Sept. 29, 1984 (Syracuse 17, Nebraska 9) The Orange limited the high-scoring and top-ranked Huskers to 214 total yards.	103-43-2	The Dome's roof weighs 220 tons. Air pressure from 16 fans keeps the roof inflated, and the fans can heat air to melt any snow that has accumulated.
TCU (Fort Worth, Texas)	Amon G. Carter /W.A. Moncrief Field (44,008)	Amon G. Carter, publisher of the *Fort Worth Star-Telegram*, was a driving force behind construction of the stadium.	Oct. 11, 1930 (TCU 40, Arkansas 0)	Nov. 30, 1935 (SMU 20, TCU 14) Billed as the "Game of the First Half Century," the Mustangs won on a fake punt in a game between two 10-0 teams.	200-154-15	The Horned Frogs run onto the field and celebrate touchdowns to the sound of a 120-decibel "Frog Horn."
Temple (Philadelphia)	Lincoln Financial Field (68,532)	Named after a financial services company.	Sept. 6, 2003 (Villanova 23, Temple 20)	Nov. 15, 2003 Virginia Tech 24, Temple 23) The Owls scored 17 unanswered fourth-quarter points to force OT vs. the No. 12 Hokies.	2-9	Temple used to play home games at Veterans Stadium and Franklin Field.
Tennessee (Knoxville)	Neyland/Shields-Watkins Field (104,079)	Colonel W.S. Shields was president of Knoxville's City National Bank and a UT trustee. Alice Watkins was Shields' wife. General Robert R. Neyland was Tennessee coach for 21 seasons and compiled a 173-31-12 record.	Sept. 24, 1921 (Tennessee 27, Emory & Henry 0)	Sept. 19, 1998 (Tennessee 20, Florida 17, OT) The Gators missed a game-tying field goal in OT. The Volunteers used the win as a stepping-stone to the national crown.	404-89-17	The checkerboard end zone design was introduced when Doug Dickey became coach in 1964. It fell by the wayside for a time before making a comeback in 1989.
Texas (Austin)	Royal-Texas Memorial/Joe Jamail Field (80,082)	The stadium honors Texans who fought in World War I. Darrell K. Royal coached the Longhorns to three national championships and 11 Southwest Conference titles. Joe Jamail is a Houston attorney who has given millions to Texas higher education.	Nov. 8, 1924 (Baylor 28, Texas 10)	Nov. 27, 1998 (Texas 26, No. 6 Texas A&M 24) Ricky Williams surpassed the NCAA career rushing record on a 60-yard scoring run. The jaunt sealed the Heisman for Williams.	314-87-9	In 1999, a running track around the field was removed, the field lowered and seats added to bring the stadium to its current capacity.
Texas A&M (College Station)	Kyle Field (82,600)	E.J. Kyle, president of General Athletic Association, took an area used for his horticulture experiments and transformed it into a fenced-off area with small wooden bleachers used for football.	Oct. 7, 1905 (Texas A&M 29, Houston YMCA 0)	Nov. 9, 2002 (Texas A&M 30, Oklahoma 26) QB Reggie McNeal tossed four TD passes and ran for 89 yards as the Aggies earned their first win over a No. 1 team.	252-121-12	The stadium is an unofficial memorial to the Aggies who died in World War I.
Texas Tech (Lubbock)	Jones SBC (53,000)	A former president of the university, Clifford Jones contributed $100,000 to the building of the stadium. SBC also has partial naming rights.	Nov. 29, 1947 (Texas Tech 14, Hardin-Simmons 6)	Nov. 20, 1976 (Houston 27, Texas Tech 19) The No. 4 Red Raiders needed to win to cop their first Southwest Conference title.	202-116-6	The stadium follows the Spanish Renaissance architecture that is found throughout campus.
Toledo (Ohio)	Glass Bowl (26,248)	In 1946, glass was used to rebuild the stadium; glass blocks were installed, as well as a glass electric scoreboard. Also, the city of Toledo is a leader in glass production.	Sept. 27, 1937 (Toledo 26, Bluffton 0)	Oct. 11, 1969 (Toledo 27, Bowling Green 26) Toledo won on a game-ending field goal, giving the Rockets their fourth victory in a row in what would become a 35-game winning streak.	238-105-9	The Glass Bowl was built as a Works Progress Administration project. It was paid for with a $272,000 grant from the federal government and $41,558 from the city of Toledo and the university.
Troy (Ala.)	Movie Gallery Veterans (30,000)	It honors university and Pike County citizens who died in World War II. Troy also has a corporate partnership with the Movie Gallery company.	Sept. 16, 1950 (Southeastern Louisiana 18, Troy 7)	Sept. 9, 2004 (Troy 24, Missouri 14) The Trojans' win over the No. 19 Tigers was highlighted by offensive lineman Junior Louissaint's 63-yard fumble return for a TD.	164-74-3	When the stadium was renovated in 2002, the Jesse H. Colley Track was relocated to another location to make Movie Gallery Veterans a football-only venue.
Tulane (New Orleans)	Louisiana Superdome (72,675)	At the time it was built, the Superdome was the biggest facility of its kind and the world's largest steel-constructed facility unobstructed by posts.	Sept. 20, 1975 (Tulane 14, Mississippi 3)	Nov. 24, 1979 (Tulane 24, LSU 13) The Green Wave upset the No. 20 Tigers to earn a trip to the Liberty Bowl.	81-91	The Louisiana Superdome has been the site of six Super Bowls, a visit by Pope John Paul II and a Republican National Convention.
Tulsa (Okla.)	Skelly (40,385)	William Skelly gave $125,000 to the university, and another $150,000 was raised to build a stadium.	Oct. 4, 1930 (Tulsa 26, Arkansas 6)	Oct. 31, 1964 (Tulsa 61, Oklahoma State 14) QB Jerry Rhome threw for 488 yards and four TDs, and Howard Twilley caught 15 passes for 217 yards.	280-141-14	Skelly Stadium was known as Skelly Field until north end zone seats were added.
UAB (Birmingham, Ala.)	Legion Field (83,091)	Named for the American Legion, in memory of Americans who gave their lives in battle.	Nov. 19, 1927 (Howard 9, Birmingham-Southern 0). Howard is now Samford; Birmingham Southern is now UAB.	Nov. 6, 1999 (UAB 36, East Carolina 17) The win over the No. 17 Pirates was the Blazers' first vs. a ranked I-A opponent.	52-23-1	Legion Field was host to first-round soccer games in the 1996 Summer Olympics.

School (location)	Stadium Capacity	Story Behind the Name	First Game in Stadium	One to Remember	Stadium Record	Fast Fact
UCLA (Los Angeles)	Rose Bowl (91,136)	The Rose Bowl was given its name by Harlan W. Hall, a police reporter. Hall had another bowl in mind, the Yale Bowl, when he envisioned the Pasadena stadium.	Sept. 11, 1982 (UCLA 41, Long Beach State 10)	Jan. 2, 1984 (UCLA 45, Illinois 9) The unranked Bruins walloped No. 4 Illinois behind QB Rick Neuheisel in the "Grand Daddy" of all bowl games, played on their home field.	99-45-2	The Rose Bowl has been the site of five Super Bowls.
UNLV (Las Vegas)	Sam Boyd (36,800)	Sam Boyd, a casino owner, donated money to the school.	Oct. 23, 1971 (Weber State 30, UNLV 17)	Nov. 24, 1984 (UNLV 27, Fresno State 13) Led by QB Randall Cunningham, the Rebels downed the Bulldogs to clinch their first league (Pacific Coast Athletic Association) title.	121-84-3	The stadium is home of the Las Vegas Bowl.
USC (Los Angeles)	Los Angeles Memorial Coliseum (92,000)	The "memorial" designation was in tribute to those who gave their lives in World War I.	Oct. 6, 1923 (USC 23, Pomona 7)	1974 (USC 55, Notre Dame 24) The Trojans came back from a 24-0 deficit to crush the Fighting Irish. USC scored all of its points in just 17 minutes.	380-122-27	The L.A. Coliseum has served as home to many teams over the years, including the L.A. Rams, L.A. Raiders and UCLA—and even baseball's Dodgers.
Utah (Salt Lake City)	Rice-Eccles (45,017)	Robert. L. Rice gave $1 million to renovate Ute Stadium in 1972. The George S. and Dolores Dore Eccles Foundation contributed $10 million to the construction of the new stadium.	Sept. 12, 1998 (Utah 45, Louisville 22)	Nov. 20, 2004 (Utah 52, BYU 21). The win capped an 11-0 regular season and assured Utah of becoming the first non-BCS school to receive a BCS bid.	28-11	The Olympic cauldron from the 2002 Salt Lake City Games still stands in the stadium.
Utah State (Logan)	Romney (30,257)	E.L. "Dick" Romney was Utah State's win-ningest coach (128 victories in 29 seasons) and a former USU athletic director.	Sept. 14, 1968 (Utah State 28, New Mexico State 12)	Oct. 30, 1993 (Utah State 58, BYU 56) Aggies QB Anthony Calvillo threw for 472 yards and five TDs.	98-74	The 1998 expansion was financed by the student body.
UTEP (El Paso, Texas)	Sun Bowl (51,500)	The Sun Bowl game was played at the facility, then called Kidd Field, and the site was renamed for the postseason game.	Sept. 21, 1963 (UTEP 34, North Texas State 7)	Oct. 26, 1985 (UTEP 23, BYU 16) The Miners upended the defending national champs, notching their lone win of the year.	97-137-3	Coach Mike Price has introduced what he hopes will become a tradition: The players and coaches enter the field through a mine shaft that connects the locker rooms to the playing field.
Vanderbilt (Nashville)	Vanderbilt (39,773)	Named for the school.	Sept. 12, 1981 (Vanderbilt 23, Maryland 17)	Nov. 27, 1982 (Vanderbilt 28, Tennessee 21) The victory guaranteed the Commodores a bowl appearance. They haven't been to the postseason since.	49-88-1	In 1963, President John F. Kennedy spoke to 33,000 people.
Virginia (Charlottesville)	Carl Smith Center, David A. Harrison III Field at Scott (61,500)	Carl W. Smith made an alumnus grant to reno-vate Scott Stadium. David A. Harrison III gave $5 million to the football program. And Frederic William and Elisabeth Strother Scott donated funds for the stadium and dedicated the facility to his grandparents.	Sept. 19, 1931 (Virginia 18, Roanoke 0)	Nov. 2, 1995 (Virginia 33, Florida State 28). The Cavaliers used a late goal-line stand to top the No. 2 Seminoles, dealing FSU its first ACC defeat after 29 victories.	215-152-12	According to a student thesis by Reid A. Dunn at Virginia, "The major axis of the sta-dium has a bearing of N 36 degrees W. This was arrived at as the bearing which would place the sun above the center of the field at 4 p.m. in late November, thus giving nei-ther team the disadvantage of having the sun in their eyes."
Virginia Tech (Blacksburg)	Lane/Worsham Field (65,115)	It is named for Edward H. Lane, alumnus and member of the Board of Visitors, and dedicated in honor of Wes and Janet Worsham, longtime Virginia Tech fans.	Oct. 2, 1965 (Virginia Tech 9, William & Mary 7)	Nov. 26, 1999 (Virginia Tech 38, Boston College 14) The victory earned the Hokies a bid to the Sugar Bowl and a chance to play for the national title.	151-63-6	Worsham Field is the first to use GreenTech ITM natural grass sports field turf. The grass can handle up to 16 inches of rain per hour.
Wake Forest (Winston-Salem, N.C.)	Groves (31,500)	Brothers Henry and Earl Groves were stadium benefactors.	Sep. 14, 1968 (N.C. State 10, Wake Forest 6)	Oct. 27, 1979 (Wake Forest 42, Auburn 38) The Demon Deacons rallied from a 38-20 halftime deficit.	84-121-4	In 1987, N.C. State faced Wake Forest in the 100th game at Groves Stadium. These teams played in the first game at Groves, too.
Washington (Seattle)	Husky (72,500)	Named for the mascot.	Nov. 27, 1920 (Dartmouth 28, Washington 7)	Nov. 22, 1975 Washington 28, Washington State, 27) The Huskies overcame the Cougars' 13-point lead with three minutes left.	344-142-19	It rained for 46 days during construction of the stadium, and the facility wasn't ready for use until just 12 hours before the kickoff of the 1920 season finale.
Washington State (Pullman)	Martin (35,117)	Rogers Stadium was renamed Martin Stadium in 1970 in honor of Clarence D. Martin. Martin and John R. Rogers were governors of Washington. The Martin family donated $250,000 to name the facility.	Sept. 26, 1936 (Washington State 19, Montana 0)	Nov. 19, 1988 (Washington State 32, Washington 31) The Cougars win an invitation to the Aloha Bowl (only the fourth bowl game in school history to that point) by rallying from a 28-16 halftime deficit on a snowy night.	135-95-9	In April 1970, a fire destroyed the south stands of the stadium and $1 million was raised to rebuild the stands.
West Virginia (Morgantown)	Mountaineer Field at Milan Puskar Stadium (63,500)	The stadium is named for Milan "Mike" Puskar, a Morgantown philanthropist and businessman.	Sept. 6, 1980 (West Virginia 41, Cincinnati 27)	Oct. 20, 1984 (West Virginia 21, Boston College 20) WVU was down, 20-6, at the half but came back to win against the Doug Flutie-led Eagles.	107-45-4	The stadium is built on what used to be a university golf course.

School (location)	Stadium Capacity	Story Behind the Name	First Game in Stadium	One to Remember	Stadium Record	Fast Fact
Western Michigan (Kalamazoo)	Waldo (30,200)	Dwight B. Waldo was the school's first president.	Oct. 7, 1939 (Western Michigan 6, Miami of Ohio 0)	Nov. 13, 1999 (Marshall 31, Western Michigan 17) The Herd, led by QB Byron Leftwich, were ranked 11th. Both teams were unbeaten in MAC play.	202-132-4	The Broncos began playing night games at Waldo in 1993.
Wisconsin (Madison)	Camp Randall (80,000)	The stadium site was formerly a training ground for military troops.	Oct. 6, 1917 (Wisconsin 34, Beloit 0)	Oct. 30, 1993 (Wisconsin 13, Michigan 10) The win helped propel the Badgers to their first Rose Bowl since the 1962 season. Many fans were hurt when a fence collapsed as they rushed the field after the game.	276-200-23	Camp Randall is the fourth-oldest university-owned stadium in Division I-A.
Wyoming (Laramie)	War Memorial (33,500)	War Memorial Stadium honors veterans from the state who fought in World War II. Veterans Memorial Plaza (in the north end zone) honors Wyoming veterans who served in other wars.	Sept. 16, 1950 (Wyoming 61, Montana State 13)	Sept. 30, 1972 (Wyoming 45, Arizona State 43) The Cowboys forged a 30-7 third-quarter lead but needed to recover a late onside kick to hang on vs. the No. 6 Sun Devils.	194-85-7	War Memorial Stadium is the country's highest stadium, reaching 7,220 feet.

A LETTER FROM
TIM BRANDO

Greetings, college football fans ...

You picked up this book because you are like me—you love college football. Sure, the games are great, but what goes on in and around the stadiums, before and after the games, is what makes the sport special.

The next time you're standing in your favorite college football stadium, take a moment to pause. If you're at Texas A&M's Kyle Field, you'll notice the

towering grandstands that reach for the sky. At Oregon, it's impossible not to marvel at the swoop that defines the unique shape of Autzen Stadium.

What transforms these stadiums into places of worship—*Saturday Shrines*—begins with early-morning parades of RVs that inch down two-lane roads toward Penn State's Beaver Stadium. And then there are the plumes of smoke that billow from grills that dot the landscape around Clemson's Memorial Stadium.

Soon, the marching band at Alabama announces its arrival amid a cacophony of pomp, circumstance and pageantry. Fans balloon with pride at seeing their school colors on display. And that's the thing I've often said: College fans view their schools as defining who they are as humans. That's what sets this great sport apart.

If the entire pregame preamble isn't enough, there are the traditions. Florida State's Chief Osceola plunging his flaming spear into the Doak Campbell Stadium turf, Uga standing sentinel over the hedges of Sanford Stadium and Ralphie taking charge of Folsom Field. Get out of the way and enjoy. It's all a part of the heartbeat of the fall. And it's a heartbeat that I've been lucky enough to feel pulsate.

I remember game time at the Cotton Bowl, Texas-Oklahoma, the Red River Shootout. My father took me the first time. Boy, did I get an education about how much passion those people shoehorned into the

Sure, the games are great, but what goes on in and around the stadiums, before and after the games, is what makes the sport special.

Cotton Bowl had for their Longhorns and their Sooners. It was a great atmosphere that was cocooned by the sights, sounds and smells of the Texas State Fair.

I remember Saturday night in Baton Rouge. In 1979, I covered my first game as a professional journalist. LSU vs. No. 1 USC. And let me tell you: The noise was earthshaking. I've had Trojan players since that have come up to me and said, "So that's what they mean when they talk about football in the South."

I remember West Point and Michie Stadium, home of the Black Knights of the Hudson. That's holy, hollowed ground, brother. You think of the All-Americans—and great Americans—who have played there. The patriotic display reminds you that it's great to be able to watch a game on our soil.

I remember the third Saturday in October. That's when the boys become men, the leaves begin to turn and the rivalry of Alabama-Tennessee is reborn. You definitely want to see that game in Knoxville. There's the sea of orange, the checkerboard end zones and the Vol Navy cruising toward Neyland Stadium on the Tennessee River. As legendary broadcaster Chris Schenkel used to say, "What a way to spend an autumn afternoon."

And this book is a great way to relive and enjoy moments like those.

Tim Brando